edexcel
advancing learning, changing lives

Edexcel AS Psychology

D0537468

Christine Brain   Karren Smith   Susan Harty   Anna Major
Examzone by Dawn Collis

STUDENT BOOK

This book also includes

Active Book

A PEARSON COMPANY

Pearson Education Limited
Edinburgh Gate
Harlow
Essex
CM20 2JE
England
www.longman.co.uk

First published 2008
10 9 8 7

ISBN 978 1 846 902611

Printed in Malaysia (CTP-VVP)
Edited by Sue Chapple
Designed by Ian Foulis
Indexed by Helen Gough
Picture research by Sarah Purtill

Dedications
Christine Brain: For Alex, Jenny, Douglas, and Sarah. And for Paul, Kevin and Lee – my 'absent friends'. But mainly for Jonathan, from Grandma!
Karren Smith: For my wonderful husband Nick and beautiful children Emily, James and Olivia.
Susan Harty: Thanks to my colleagues at John Leggott College.
Anna Major: To Russ

The publisher would like to thank the following for their kind permission to reproduce their photographs:

Alamy Images: pg 35 (Dennis MacDonald), pg 51 (Geoffrey Kidd), pg 61 (Adrian Sherratt), pg 86 (The Print Collector), pg 99 (Big Cheese Photo LLC), pg 102 (Medical-on-Line (b). PunchStock: Brand X Pictures (t)). **Albert Bandura:** pg 142 (Albert Bandura, D. Ross & S.A. Ross, Imitation of film-mediated aggressive models. "Journal of Abnormal and Social Psychology", 1963, 66. P.8). **Alexandra Milgram:** pg 14 (From the film Obedience © 1968 by Stanley Milgram, © renewed 1993 by Alexandra Milgram, and distibuted by Penn State Media Sales). **Bridgeman Art Library Ltd:** pg 90 (The Nightmare, 1781 (oil on canvas) , Fuseli, Henry (Fussli, Johann Heinrich, 1741-1825) / The Detroit Institute of Arts, USA, Founders Society purchase with Mr and Mrs Bert L Smokler / The Bridgeman Art Library). **Corbis:** pg 12 (Bettmann), pg 22 (Alinari Archives, © ADAGP, Paris and DACS, London 2008 © DACS (b); Francis G. Mayer, © DACS 2008 (t)), pg 54 (Phil Schermeister), pg 146 (Reuters / Charles Platiau). **Education Photos:** pg 9 (John Walmsley). **Getty Images:** pg 20 (Time & Life Pictures / Donald Uhrbrock), pg 26 (AFP / Wathiq Khuzaie), pg 101 (Ed Freeman), pg 117 (Time & Life Pictures / Stan Wayman). **ITN Source / Fox Movietone:** pg 127. **Melinda Podor:** 129 (Photographers Direct). **MRC Cognition and Brain Sciences Unit:** pg 49 © Copyright UK Medical Research Council 1951 used by kind permission. **PA Photos:** pg 7 (PA Archive / John Giles). **PunchStock:** pg 18 (Johner Images) ,pg 72 (UpperCut RF), pg 83 (BananaStock), PunchStock: pg 89 (zefa). **Rex Features:** pg 16 (Peter Lawson), pg 29 (Sipa Press), pg 70 (Denis Cameron), pg 111 (Sipa Press), pg 114 (Phanie / Burger), pg 137 (Simon Runting). **Richard B. Levine:** pg 93 (Photographers Direct). **Science Photo Library Ltd:** pg 38 (Sovereign, Ism), pg 96 (AJ Photo).

All other images © Pearson Education

Contents

About this book   **4**

Chapter 1: Social Approach   6
Defining the approach
Methodology
Content
Studies
Key issues
Evidence of practice
Summary

Chapter 2: Cognitive Approach   38
Defining the approach
Methodology
Content
Studies
Key Issues
Evidence of Practice
Summary

Chapter 3: Psychodynamic Approach   70
Defining the approach
Methodology
Content
Studies
Key issues
Evidence of practice
Summary

Chapter 4: Biological Approach   98
Defining the approach
Methodology
Content
Studies
Key issues
Evidence of practice
Summary

Chapter 5: Learning Approach   126
Defining the approach
Methodology
Content
Studies
Key issues
Evidence of practice
Summary

Exam advice   **154**

Exam guidance   **156**

Revsion advice   **158**

Glossary   **160**

Index   **166**

AS Psychology 'About This Book'

This AS Psychology Student Book and ActiveBook CDROM provides all the content and assessment practice you need to study Edexcel's Advanced Subsidary GCE in Psychology.

Written by a team of experts including experienced examiners and teachers, you can be sure that you have everything you need to succeed!

An exciting mix of Student Book and Active Book CD-ROM brings the specification content to life by contextualising the study of Psychology in the real world.

Important psychological **key terms**. Each is clearly explained in a comprehensive glossary at the end of the book.

What you will learn about provides a clear overview of the chapter content.

What you need to know gives an overview of the content and skills required for the assessment.

Key Features of the Student book

Psychodynamic Approach: Freud

3. Psychodynamic Approach: Freud

Key terms

- id, ego, superego
- oral, anal, phallic, latency and genital stages
- repression
- Oedipus complex
- defence mechanisms
- conscious, preconscious, unconscious

What you will learn about in this chapter

- Sigmund Freud – his research, theories, practices and influence on society in the 20th century and today.
- The conscious and unconscious mind (the 'iceberg' model) and theories of its working, including neuroses, dreams, repression and memory, and the role of psychoanalysis.
- Psychosexual development, including the role of the id, ego and superego (Freud's explanation of personality), five stages of development and the Oedipus complex.

What you need to know

- You must be able to describe and evaluate Freud's theory of psychosexual development.
- You must be able to describe two defence mechanisms, including repression, and one other such as denial, regression and projection.
- You must be able to evaluate Freud's theory as an explanation of gender development and behaviour.
- You must be able to describe and evaluate research methods, including psychodynamic ones.

Defining the Psychodynamic Approach

The Psychodynamic Approach is about the mind (*psyche*) and about energy (*dynamic*). The idea is that people have a certain amount of energy, and if much of that energy is needed to deal with the past then there might not be enough left to move forward in life. It is about developing in a mentally healthy way and about curing neuroses. The way to do this is by releasing energy by exposing unconscious wishes and desires and making them conscious. Neuroses are mental problems that can be understood by the individual, as opposed to psychoses, where there is no insight. Insight is important in understanding unconscious thoughts in order to release them, so neuroses are treated, not psychoses.

Sigmund Freud, born in Austria in 1856, is the main person involved in the approach, with some of his followers breaking away to develop their own theories, such as Jung and Adler. There are also more modern versions of the approach but for this year of the course you will only consider Freud's ideas.

◆ **Who was Freud?**

Freud lived in Vienna, in 'high' society in Austria, and treated people who were often quite wealthy. He trained as a doctor and as a young man was horrified at the lack of knowledge and treatment for mentally ill people. He was an ambitious man with a high opinion of his own ability.

▲ The couch Freud's patients used for psychoanalysis

70 AS Psychology

Psychology is brought to life through **photos and diagrams** that contextualise core content.

At the end of each approach you can consolidate your knowledge with exam-style questions in the Examzone section.

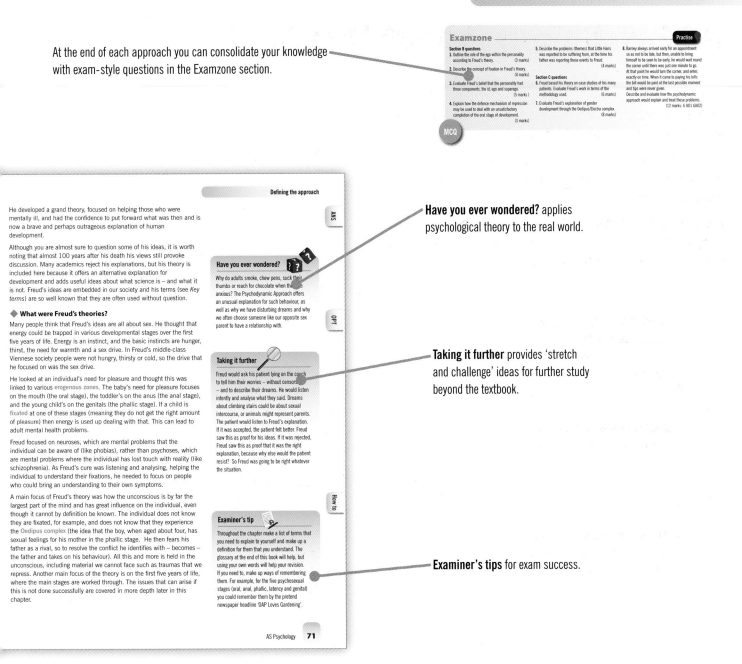

Examzone — Practise

Section B questions
1. Outline the role of the ego within the personality according to Freud's theory. (3 marks)
2. Describe the concept of fixation in Freud's theory. (4 marks)
3. Evaluate Freud's belief that the personality had three components, the id, ego and superego. (5 marks)
4. Explain how the defence mechanism of repression may be used to deal with an unsatisfactory completion of the oral stage of development. (3 marks)

5. Describe the problems (themes) that Little Hans was reported to be suffering from, at the time his father was reporting these events to Freud. (4 marks)

Section C questions
6. Freud based his theory on case studies of his many patients. Evaluate Freud's work in terms of the methodology used. (6 marks)
7. Evaluate Freud's explanation of gender development through the Oedipus/Electra complex. (8 marks)

8. Barney always arrived early for an appointment so as not to be late, but then, unable to bring himself to be seen to be early, he would wait round the corner until there was just one minute to go. At that point he would turn the corner, and enter, exactly on time. When it came to paying his bills the bill would be paid at the last possible moment and tips were never given.
Describe and evaluate how the psychodynamic approach would explain and treat these problems. (12 marks: 6 AO1 6AO2)

MCQ

Defining the approach

He developed a grand theory, focused on helping those who were mentally ill, and had the confidence to put forward what was then and is now a brave and perhaps outrageous explanation of human development.

Although you are almost sure to question some of his ideas, it is worth noting that almost 100 years after his death his views still provoke discussion. Many academics reject his explanations, but his theory is included here because it offers an alternative explanation for development and adds useful ideas about what science is – and what it is not. Freud's ideas are embedded in our society and his terms (see *Key terms*) are so well known that they are often used without question.

◆ **What were Freud's theories?**

Many people think that Freud's ideas are all about sex. He thought that energy could be trapped in various developmental stages over the first five years of life. Energy is an instinct, and the basic instincts are hunger, thirst, the need for warmth and a sex drive. In Freud's middle-class Viennese society people were not hungry, thirsty or cold, so the drive that he focused on was the sex drive.

He looked at an individual's need for pleasure and thought this was linked to various erogenous zones. The baby's need for pleasure focuses on the mouth (the oral stage), the toddler's on the anus (the anal stage), and the young child's on the genitals (the phallic stage). If a child is fixated at one of these stages (meaning they do not get the right amount of pleasure) then energy is used up dealing with that. This can lead to adult mental health problems.

Freud focused on neuroses, which are mental problems that the individual can be aware of (like phobias), rather than psychoses, which are mental problems where the individual has lost touch with reality (like schizophrenia). As Freud's cure was listening and analysing, helping the individual to understand their fixations, he needed to focus on people who could bring an understanding to their own symptoms.

A main focus of Freud's theory was how the unconscious is by far the largest part of the mind and has great influence on the individual, even though it cannot by definition be known. The individual does not know they are fixated, for example, and does not know that they experience the Oedipus complex (the idea that the boy, when aged about four, has sexual feelings for his mother in the phallic stage. He then fears his father as a rival, so to resolve the conflict he identifies with – becomes – the father and takes on his behaviour). All this and more is held in the unconscious, including material we cannot face such as traumas that we repress. Another main focus of the theory is on the first five years of life, where the main stages are worked through. The issues that can arise if this is not done successfully are covered in more depth later in this chapter.

ANS

Have you ever wondered? ?

Why do adults smoke, chew pens, suck their thumbs or reach for chocolate when they are anxious? The Psychodynamic Approach offers an unusual explanation for such behaviour, as well as why we have disturbing dreams and why we often choose someone like our opposite sex parent to have a relationship with.

OPT

Taking it further 🔍

Freud would ask his patient lying on the couch to tell him their worries – without censorship – and to describe their dreams. He would listen intently and analyse what they said. Dreams about climbing stairs could be about sexual intercourse, or animals might represent parents. The patient would listen to Freud's explanation. If it was accepted, the patient felt better. Freud saw this as proof for his ideas. If it was rejected, Freud saw this as proof that it was the right explanation, because why else would the patient resist? So Freud was going to be right whatever the situation.

How to

Examiner's tip ✎

Throughout the chapter make a list of terms that you need to explain to yourself and make up a definition for them that you understand. The glossary at the end of this book will help, but using your own words will help your revision. If you need to, make up ways of remembering them. For example, for the five psychosexual stages (oral, anal, phallic, latency and genital) you could remember them by the pretend newspaper headline 'OAP Loves Gardening'.

AS Psychology **71**

Have you ever wondered? applies psychological theory to the real world.

Taking it further provides 'stretch and challenge' ideas for further study beyond the textbook.

Examiner's tips for exam success.

Key features of the ActiveBook

The ActiveBook allows you to open your student book on screen and have access to a wide range of additional material including:

SUM — Content **summaries** that revise key facts.

EG — Extra **examples** further contextualise key terms and content.

ANS — Full **answers** to all Student Book questions that enable you to self-check your work and track your progress.

Opt — **Option** material providing extension work on core content, case studies, etc.

How to — **How to** skills sheets providing a step by step guide to the key methods you need to be able to carry out.

MCQ — Interactive **multiple-choice questions** that allow you to track your progress.

1. Social Approach

Key terms

- agentic state
- autonomous state
- moral strain
- in-group/out-group
- social categorisation
- social identification
- social comparison

What you will learn about in this chapter

- The work of Stanley Milgram – his research into and his theory about the reasons for blind obedience.
- Social Identity Theory (Tajfel) and research that categorisation, identification and comparison lead to prejudice.
- How to sample from a target population and what ethical issues you need to consider before conducting research.
- How social psychology can be used to explain key issues in today's society, such as prisoner abuse during war.

What you need to know

- Theories about obedience that are used to explain why seemingly good people sometimes do bad things.
- Agency theory, an explanation of obedience that suggests we operate in either an agentic state or an autonomous state.
- Prejudice - what it is and one theory of how it works.
- Ethics and sampling methods relevant to psychological research to enable you to carry out your own survey.

Defining the Social Approach

Social psychology is the study of how our behaviour is influenced by the presence, attitudes and actions of other people. Using psychological research methods, social psychologists investigate such things as: the effect of our culture on our behaviour; what happens when we join groups; why we help others (and why we sometimes don't!); as well as big topics such as the origins and mechanics of prejudice and obedience. In common with other psychologists, social psychologists develop theories to explain observed behaviour, then gather data to test those theories.

◆ The history of social psychology

Social psychology came to prominence towards the middle of the 20th century, although one of the earliest studies credited to social psychology was carried out by Norman Triplett in 1898. Triplett did not classify his research as social psychology, as it was not seen as a separate discipline at the time, but it certainly fits our definition as he was interested in the effect on performance of having another person present, doing the same task. He had his participants wind up fishing reels under timed conditions and measured their performance first on their own and then again when another person performed the same task alongside them. He found that some went faster, some went slower and just a few were apparently unaffected, suggesting that the presence of other people does change how we behave.

Social psychology looks at the way people interact and behave.

From Triplett's experiments we can see how social psychology can be applied to the real world. In sport, for example, the inclusion of a pace maker in a race can increase the performance of a runner. Further applications arise from other research, and you will learn about some of the most important ones in this chapter. This includes how social psychologists explain blind obedience that leads to harm of other people, and how prejudice forms between groups in society, which can result in violence between them. An example of this is violence between supporters of rival football teams.

◆ Ethics in social psychology

Perhaps one of the most important contributions of social psychology to psychology in general is the development of the **ethical guidelines** that now are an integral part of all psychological research (these will be covered in detail later in the chapter). They arose out of concern for participants in some of the most famous experiments, which were conducted primarily to test theories of social psychology. (Note that people who take part in research studies used to be known as subjects but this changed because of increased appreciation for the part they play in research and the development of these strong ethical guidelines to protect their rights and dignity.)

Critics were concerned about the levels of stress that participants seemed to suffer and the fact that they could have gone from the study feeling bad about themselves. This is because the researchers were manipulating the social situations that people were in so that they could see what effect it had on their behaviour. For example, Asch's 1951 study aimed to test conformity to group norms. Participants were asked to give a judgement about which line matched a target line when several other people were giving an obviously wrong answer. The participant was put under pressure either to go against the group and give a non-conformist but right answer or to conform with the group. Would people go along with the group or would they ignore the group and give an individual answer?

Have you ever wondered?

Why might you shout abuse at a person wearing the colours of a rival football team – and would you be just as likely to do this when you are on your own or with a group of like-minded friends? Why might you pick up litter when told to by a teacher or a police officer but probably not when told to by a child? If you are male, why don't you routinely wear a skirt? Social psychology helps answer such questions by examining human behaviour.

Examiner's tip

It is a good idea to develop a concepts map. This is simply a mind map or spider diagram that allows you to situate the concepts you are learning about here in the context of the whole chapter. Your central concept might be social psychology and this would link to obedience, with a definition, which would then link to Milgram's study, then his theory and then on to a key issue. Links coming from Milgram could include ethical guidelines. Use the glossary of terms to ensure you have covered all the concepts.

Taking it further

Find out what happened by researching Asch's study

Methodology

What you need to know

- In this section you will learn about how psychologists do research. You need to be able to describe and evaluate the survey as a research method in psychology, including the questionnaire and interview.
- You must be able to describe and compare qualitative and quantitative data.
- You need to be able to describe, assess and apply guidelines about the use of humans in psychological research.
- You need to be able to identify, describe and apply different sampling techniques.

A method commonly used in social psychology is the survey. This is an umbrella term for a number of different research designs, including questionnaires and interviews, which are used to investigate specific research questions by gathering self-report data. At the core of this method is **questioning**. Before you can undertake a survey, it is essential to identify clearly what you want to find out by setting up a hypothesis.

◆ Hypotheses

ANS

Question 1

What is an alternative hypothesis?

Hypotheses are specific testable predictions about what you expect to find after analysing the data from your participants. For example, you may predict that young people would be less likely to think they would obey a man in uniform than older people would. This is known as an alternative hypothesis, as it is an alternative to the null hypothesis, which states that there is no such effect except that found by chance. In this example, the null hypothesis would state that age would have no effect on willingness to obey a man in uniform.

In research, you test the null hypothesis. If this is rejected, it means that your data does indicate a real effect and you have found support for your alternative hypothesis.

◆ Types of questions and types of data

ANS

Question 2

Decide what type of question this is:
Why did you start to study psychology?

The key to getting useful results in a survey is asking the right questions.
- An open question is one that can be answered in any way the participant chooses. It yields qualitative data. This is data that consists of words that describe the participant's views.
- A closed question limits the responses that can be made. It yields quantitative data – data that can reduce to numbers and quantities.

Examiners' tip

Notice how the strength of one type of data is a weakness of the other, and vice versa.

Each type of data has its own strengths and weaknesses:

	Strength	Weakness
Qualitative	Descriptive nature allows for more depth of analysis leading to more meaningful conclusions about the participant's views. This could increase validity.	It is difficult to draw comparisons between groups or to arrive at a reliable conclusion about a specific thing.
Quantitative	It is possible to analyse data in order to draw comparisons between groups and to draw conclusions about the thing in question.	The reduction of thoughts and feelings to numbers gives a very superficial view of the behaviour being researched, which may lack validity in other contexts.

Gathering data

How you ask the questions is also important:

- You could interview your participants, which involves meeting them face to face (or possibly on the phone), asking the questions and recording their answers.
- You could send them a questionnaire, which is a written set of questions, asking them to write their answers and return it to you.

Either method allows you to ask open or closed questions.

Types of interview

It is possible to ask closed questions during an interview but this may be regarded as a wasted opportunity, when you could probe the participant and find out what lies behind superficial attitudes.

- The interview method most likely to give qualitative data is the **unstructured interview**, where the questions are open and the structure of the interview is flexible. There will be a research question around which the interview is based but otherwise things are left unspecified to see what emerges.
- The **structured interview** has a pre-set order of questions, leaving little room for the researcher to follow up on answers of interest.
- In between the two is the **semi-structured interview**, in which there will be a schedule of questions that should be answered but the researcher will have freedom to follow up on some responses.

Questionnaires

The written format of a standard questionnaire means that there is no flexibility about the questions. There may be space for the participant to write comments but otherwise they have to answer the questions set. The questions are most likely to be closed and may make use of a Likert-type scale.

Designing surveys

Some issues that need to be considered when designing surveys include:

- Wording the questions so that the participant can understand what you mean. The response to a question can only be treated as valid if the participant and the researcher have a shared understanding of it. You can check this using a pilot study, testing it with a few people first.
- How are you going to ask the questions – face to face or on a written questionnaire? Consider the amount of time it will take to answer all the questions and to analyse the data. Participants could give up if there are too many questions. Also, if you have a lot of open questions the amount of data generated is potentially huge and therefore very time-consuming to analyse.
- Consider your sample, in terms of its size and representativeness. With a questionnaire the response rate is typically low, so to get a decent-sized sample many people will need to be targeted. With an interview you still need to consider representativeness – you may select an unusual person to participate and then have a problem generalising your findings beyond the sample.

▲ Surveys are an effective method of obtaining data.

Have you ever wondered?

How are people's attitudes turned into headline figures? The answer comes through survey research, where people from the population are asked their opinions and the researcher analyses this to produce conclusions – which political party is currently the most popular, for example.

Taking it further

Here is an example of a Likert-type scale question:
Please indicate your level of agreement with this statement where 5 equates to strong agreement, 3 to no real opinion and 1 to strong disagreement.
1   2   3   4   5
See if you can find other examples.

Question 3

Identify one advantage of using a Likert-type scale.

ANS

◆ Sampling methods

Unless your **target population** is very small, it is unlikely that you can test every person. This means you have to select a sample to represent the population. Here is a summary of the sampling methods you need to know:

Method	Procedure	Strength	Weakness
Random sampling	Every member of the target population has an equal chance of being selected, e.g. by numbering and listing them all and using a random number generator.	Likely to be unbiased as the researcher does not control who is chosen.	Very hard to do unless you only have a small population.
Stratified sampling	The sample is a proportional representation of the target population. You break down the population into its constituent groups and recreate a smaller version, e.g. males/females or by age group.	Likely to be very representative of the population if done properly.	Likely to be very time-consuming and difficult.
Opportunity sampling	Participants are selected from whoever is available at the time of the study, for example whoever happens to be in your class when you want to gather data.	Really easy and quick. Likely to be ethical.	Probably not very representative, as drawn from a small section of the community.
Volunteer or self-selecting	Participants select themselves. For example, you advertise for participants to take part and whoever comes forward is chosen.	Will probably access a variety of people you would not normally have access to – and they are likely to be motivated.	Motivation may make them behave differently. Volunteers may have special qualities.

◆ Ethical issues

In the UK all psychological research is monitored by the British Psychological Society (BPS). Their guidelines aim to protect the rights and dignity of participants and must be followed when conducting research. Here are the key principles:

- Participants should give their **fully-informed consent** to taking part. This means that, wherever possible, they should be told the aims of the study and what the procedure will entail. Sometimes this is not possible, as it would affect the behaviour of the participants and not allow a true picture of their responses to emerge. In such cases the participants must be **debriefed** thoroughly (see below).
- **Deception** should not be used unless it is vital to preserve the experimental validity. Even then it should only be used where there is significant scientific justification and/or there would be limited consequences. If it is used there must be a full and frank debriefing.
- Participants should be made aware at the outset of their **right to withdraw**. They should feel free to leave at any point and have the right to take their data with them or have it destroyed. If they have been paid to take part they keep the money even if they withdraw.
- Researchers should not make judgements about participants unless they are **competent** to do so (qualified). They do have a responsibility to let the participant know if they find physical or psychological problems **but** only if not telling would put them in danger.
- Participants must be **debriefed** at the end of the study, reminded of their right to withdraw and offered the chance to ask any questions.

The debriefing should explain the true aim and nature of the study. It also gives the researcher the chance to find out about the participant's experience. The participant should leave feeling good about themselves by being reassured that their behaviour is normal.

- Participants should be **protected** from psychological and physical harm and not be put through anything that they would not normally experience unless there is serious scientific justification.

◆ Evaluation of survey methods

Reliability
This concerns the consistency of the data – if we have a reliable test, we could expect that, if we did it over and over again with people possessing similar characteristics, we would get very similar data.

Validity
This concerns the genuineness of the results. Did we actually test and measure what we said we did? In psychology we can seldom access the things we are testing as they tend to be abstract concepts like obedience. It is assumed that such things are demonstrated by behaviour which is observable, so it is behaviour change we measure, on the basis that this is motivated by the psychological concept we are testing. However, we may be wrong in this assumption – something else may cause the behaviour and our data and conclusions are then not valid.

Subjectivity
This concerns the interpretation of the data. Is our view of the results likely to be shared by others, or is it coloured by our own expectations and experiences? The goal of scientific research is to gain an objective view of something that can be established as value-free and factual. This table summarises the issues for each data-gathering technique:

Method	Strengths	Weaknesses
Unstructured interview	High validity Flexible In-depth data	Cannot be replicated Subjective May be unreliable Likely to be small scale
Closed question questionnaire	Replicable Reliable Objective Can be large scale	Low validity Can be superficial Rigid

So, in an unstructured interview analysis can be in-depth and detailed, yielding a valid conclusion about that person's views, but there is likely to be a lack of reliability and conclusions drawn may be subjective. The highly-structured questionnaire is reliable as there can be many participants and the data gathered is more objective, but validity may be lost as participants don't give real thought to their answers and there is no way of exploring issues in depth.

Taking it further

Log on to the BPS website (www.bps.org.uk) and look at the ethical guidelines. You might consider becoming a student member of the BPS.

SUM

Examiner's tip

You can evaluate research by looking at the sampling method used and the type of people sampled, in order to ascertain **population validity** – the sample should represent the target population (i.e. the wider population that the research will be applied to).

Examiner's tip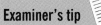

When evaluating, try using the PEE method to ensure that you convince the examiner you really understand what you are saying:

- Make a **Point** (for example, you say that the unstructured interview lacks reliability).
- **Explain** what this means (for example, that you are unlikely to get the same results from others asked the same question but in a different setting).
- Give an **Example** (for example, the participant may answer differently depending on whether they like the researcher). Or you could provide **Evidence**, or **Elaborate**.

Content

What you need to know

- You need to be able to describe and evaluate research related to the Social Approach, including Milgram's (1963) study of obedience, variation studies and the Agency Theory of Obedience (Milgram, 1973).
- You need to know about one study of obedience from a country other than Milgram's (USA) and be able to compare this study with Milgram's (1963) obedience study, drawing cross-cultural conclusions.
- You need to be aware of the ethical issues arising from obedience research.
- You need to know what is meant by prejudice and discrimination and know about Tajfel's (1970) Social Identity Theory as an explanation of prejudice.

Obedience

Obedience is following an order given by a person with recognised authority over you. Most of the time this is a sensible thing to do, for example when told by a police officer to evacuate a building during a security alert, and many jobs rely on people following orders. However, obedience has sometimes been blamed for ordinary people committing horrible acts.

Observations from war crimes trials, (such as for those committed in Nazi Germany during World War II) reveal that the excuse of 'following orders' was often given as an explanation for committing atrocious acts: 'From 1939 to 1945 millions of innocent persons were slaughtered on command' (Milgram, 1963). One case that is often cited is that of Adolph Eichmann, a Nazi administrator who organised and supervised the transport of millions of Jews to concentration camps, where they were then murdered.

This case encapsulates the debate about the causes of such behaviour, whether it lies in the person (an abnormally immoral person and therefore not explainable by social psychology) or the situation they find themselves in. This situationist view is consistent with the social explanation because it takes account of how other people in the social setting influence what you do at that time. Eichmann's defence was that he was simply obeying orders, and that if he did not do it someone else put in that situation would.

◆ Behavioural study of obedience to malevolent authority (Milgram, 1963)

Remember that, although the participant believed the situation was real, it was a complete set-up and no-one was physically harmed.

Aim

The aim was to establish a baseline measure of how obedient naïve participants would be when ordered to administer increasingly intense electric shocks to an innocent victim.

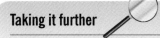

Taking it further

Research into Eichmann's trial and find out what happened to him.

▲ Lieutenant Colonel Adolph Eichmann standing trial.

Method

A sample of 40 volunteers (referred to as subjects) was selected by advertising in a newspaper for participants in a study on human memory. The advert offered $4.00 plus car fare to any adult local man (not in high school or college) prepared to come to Yale University for the study.

Participants were told individually that they and another man (actually a confederate) would take part in a study on the effect of punishment on memory. In a rigged draw, the true participant (naïve participant) was always given the role of teacher and the confederate the role of learner. They were shown the equipment – a shock generator with switches and lights going from 15v to 450v with various descriptions about the shock levels, and a chair with straps on wired to the generator. The chair was in the next room.

They separated and the experiment began with the teacher (naïve participant) reading the word list and testing the learner (confederate), with the researcher telling the teacher to give a shock to the learner and increase the shock every time an answer was wrong.

In fact, the learner response was scripted and no shocks were given. At various points he complained of pain, said his heart was starting to bother him and refused to continue, before going silent at 315v. The researcher consistently encouraged the teacher to continue, despite his protestations.

Obedience was measured by how far up the generator the teacher went before refusing to obey any more.

Results

These were surprising. Milgram surveyed groups of people (including psychology professionals) before the research. When asked what level of shock they thought the participants would go up to, most thought they would stop at the point that the victim asked to be released (140v), and believed that few, if any, would go beyond very strong shock. But what people say and what they actually do were proved to be very different.

In fact, every participant went to at least 300v, 14 stopped between 300 and 375. The remaining 26 (65%) went all the way to 450v.

Conclusions

Milgram concluded that the social setting is a powerful determinant of behaviour – we are socialised to recognise authority and to react with obedience. When the participants entered the experiment they felt that they were part of the situation and as such found it very difficult to break away. Having started to obey it became harder and harder to say no.

Examiner's tip

If asked to define a concept, ensure that you don't just reuse the word ('Obedience means to obey', for example!) You must change it so that you demonstrate understanding. If there are 2 marks available, always try to make two distinct points. For example: 'Obedience is to follow orders (1 point as it does not simply restate the obey word) given by a person whose authority you recognise (2nd point). You can also demonstrate your understanding by giving a relevant example.

Many participants showed signs of stress and questioned the researcher, threatening to drop out of the study. One sign of tension exhibited was laughter; they also 'sweated, trembled, stuttered, bit their lips, groaned, dug fingernails into their flesh' (Milgram, 1963). Yet 65% of them continued to obey.

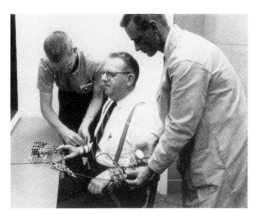

▲ The confederate being strapped into the chair to receive the 'shocks'.

Variations on the baseline

Milgram went on to conduct several variations to see which changes to the situation would affect obedience.

- In the baseline experiment the learner could be heard but not seen.
- When the learner could not be heard **or** seen, **all** participants went up to the end.
- When the learner was in the same room as the teacher so could be both seen **and** heard, only 40% of the participants shocked to the end.
- When the teacher had to physically hold the learner's hand onto the electrode to receive a 'shock' it dropped further to 30% (which is still a big proportion of the population).

◆ Evaluation of Milgram's study

Critics argue about whether this was a **valid** test of obedience to authority. The argument centres on whether the participants truly believed they were shocking someone, or were simply going along with the researcher, comfortable in the knowledge that you don't generally inflict painful shocks on someone else in an experiment (especially at Yale).

Experimental validity

Did the participants believe? The description of Milgram's procedure shows he took care to ensure the **experimental validity** of his method, for example through the initial meeting of the true participant with Mr Wallace (the actor-confederate) and the rigged draw to see who was going to be teacher. He also staged a sample 45v shock, used convincing equipment, and organised cries of pain and wall pounding. These made the situation entirely believable. In a post-experimental interview – before the debriefing – he asked the participants how painful they thought the last few shocks were. Most said extremely painful. With the obvious stress and tension the participants suffered, all the evidence strongly suggests that they believed what was happening was real.

Ecological validity

Do the results tell us anything about real-world behaviour? Perhaps the participants felt protected from the consequences of their actions and would not normally behave this way. Here are some points to consider:

- In the real world, people recognise authority and comply with its demands and there are usually serious repercussions for disobedience.
- Milgram tested whether the laboratory setting had a major impact on obedience levels. Using the same paradigm, but a more realistic setting of an inner-city office, he found that obedience dropped but was still a very high 48%.
- Hofling's (1966) study offers further support, as it was conducted in a hospital setting and the participants were unaware that they were being tested (giving high **ecological validity**). Hofling found even higher rates of obedience in the real world – 95% of nurses broke the rules and gave an 'overdose' of a drug to a patient on the orders of a doctor.

Population validity

Milgram's sample consisted of adult males of varied backgrounds so you could argue that he had population validity only for American males. Would the results apply to females? Put simply, yes! Milgram tested females in exactly the same way and found identical levels of obedience.

A major criticism is that the result cannot be generalised to people from other cultures, who might behave differently. However, studies testing obedience across the world have yielded similar results, many showing even higher levels of obedience. (One exception to this is Kilham and Mann's (1974) study in Australia. They found that male students were only 40% obedient and female students only 16%; however, the victim in this study varied – being a fellow student and, in the case of the female study, also female. See Smith and Bond, 1993, for a full discussion.)

Reliability

Milgram's study was reliable. He ran his participants one at a time and followed a standardised procedure which meant that every participant got exactly the same experience. This is demonstrated in the similarity of the behaviour the participants displayed. It is possible to replicate Milgram's study – indeed this has been done in other cultures and in the variations done by Milgram himself.

Ethics

The most common criticism of Milgram's research concerns the welfare of the participants:
1. They did not know the true aim of the study.
2. They were continually deceived.
3. They were put under extreme stress.
4. They were prompted to continue even when they wanted to stop.
5. However, he did ensure there was a thorough debriefing.

However, if Milgram had given the true aim of the study and not deceived the participants into thinking the situation was real, his study would have been pointless.

Participants were put under stress but in a follow-up questionnaire 84% said they were glad or very glad to have participated. Fewer than 2% said they were sorry to have taken part and 74% claimed to have learned something of personal importance. None of the participants when examined later showed any signs of having been harmed psychologically.

Two final points:
- Participants could and did withdraw when they defied the experimenter.
- Milgram believed his work would have wider benefits to society, in that knowledge of how easy it is to follow the route to destructive obedience may lead to avoidance of such incidents in future.

Taking it further

Find out more about Meeus and Raaijmakers' study. Research what happened when they introduced a rebel participant who defied the researcher, or what happened when the researcher gave the orders by phone.

▲ Studies indicate we are more likely to obey those with authority.

We are brought up to recognise legitimate authority and to respond accordingly, so we usually do as we are told. This recognition is triggered by years of experience when we do as we are told by our parents and teachers, etc. So, when the naive participant obeyed the researcher and shocked the learner, they were acting as an agent for a recognised higher authority. Only when they became defiant did they act autonomously.

◆ Administrative Obedience: Carrying Out Orders to use Psychological-Administrative Violence (Meeus and Raaijmakers, 1985)

Aim

This study was carried out in the Netherlands some 20 years after Milgram's study. Dutch culture is somewhat more liberal than 1960s US culture. The aim of the study was to test obedience where harm would be done but in a more up-to-date way – 'violence typical of our times', which is less physical but more psychological in nature.

Method

The method used was experimental and was based on Milgram's paradigm of having a researcher order a naïve participant do something that would be harmful to another person. The participants were ordered to harass an apparent job applicant (this was a confederate) to make him nervous while sitting a test to determine whether he would get the job. They were told that this was in the context of a research project.

Results

The results showed that 92% of the participants obeyed and disturbed and criticised the applicant when told to do so by the researcher, even though they thought it was unfair and did not want to do it. Variations on the baseline included removing the presence of the researcher and introducing two rebellious peers for the participant (they refused to follow the orders). Obedience dropped substantially in both cases.

Conclusions

The conclusions that can be drawn from this study are that, even in a more liberal culture than that of Milgram's studies, people obeyed an authority figure and went against their better nature to do something designed to harm another person.

◆ Evaluation and comparison with Milgram

Validity

The researchers felt the task was ecologically valid, arguing that this kind of psychological violence was more in tune with the times than the physical violence Milgram ordered. However, it was still an unlikely scenario so the task may have lacked experimental validity. The sample comprised Dutch adults from the general population and is therefore representative, and the results are consistent with other tests of in Europe, so we could argue that the study has population validity.

The results support Milgram's findings and in turn are supported by Milgram, suggesting this is a genuine and robust effect of recognising authority. Although the level of obedience is higher than Milgram found, this could be explained by the non-physical punishment the participants had to give.

◆ Agency Theory

Milgram's research led to the development of Agency Theory as a way of explaining obedience. Milgram proposed that human behaviour evolved to include the tendency to obey because rule-based behaviour enables stability in a complex human society.

Behaviour consists of two opposing states, the **autonomous** and the **agentic state**. We switch between the two. An autonomous state is where we use our free will and take responsibility for our actions. An agentic state is where we act on behalf of another – we are merely the means to an end that was determined by someone else. Milgram believed that when we respond to legitimate authority we tend to operate in the agentic state.

Evaluation of Agency Theory

One key aspect of this theory is that it helps to explain **moral strain**, where we do something that goes against our principles but seems to be for the greater good. None of the participants in Milgram's experiment would choose to shock the learner on their own. However, when continually told you must do something by someone whose authority you recognise, you do as you are told, even if it makes you feel bad.

Agency Theory does have a great deal of empirical support:
- Milgram's own research supports the theory.
- Hofling's research and cross-cultural research provides similar support.
- Further support comes from Bushman (1988), who varied the authoritativeness of the authority figure. When a request was made to give a motorist change for a parking meter, it was much more likely to be obeyed when the person requesting had the trappings of authority (a uniform).

On the other hand, not everyone obeys, so there are individual differences. One third of Milgram's participants refused to go all the way to the end, so there must be more happening than a simple switch to agency. Some people may simply not obey orders, which cannot easily be explained by the evolution of an agentic state.

Looking at the real world, it seems that Agency Theory does successfully explain some phenomena. Eichmann's testimony, for example, seems to reflect the theory very well:
- He was following orders.
- He was part of the ruling organisation.
- He did not choose to do what he did.
- If he did not do it, someone else would.

If we accept Agency Theory, it can successfully explain abhorrent acts by ordinary people under certain conditions – but it could also be offered as an excuse for bad behaviour. On the positive side, knowledge of Agency Theory could help to inoculate against being destructively obedient, and safeguards could be built in to basic training of those most at risk (police, armed forces, etc.) to avoid blind obedience in every situation.

Taking it further

Look up the case of Lieutenant William Calley, who was court-martialled following the massacre of the inhabitants of the village of Mi Lai during the Vietnam War. (See also page 28.) His defence was one of acting on orders.

Examiner's tip

To evaluate a **theory**, look at the research evidence gathered from studies that aim to test the theory's claims. You could also look for real-world behaviour that the theory can explain and see whether the theory has any useful applications. Could it be used to make the world a better place?

Prejudice and discrimination

Prejudice is an attitude towards another person based on little or no actual knowledge of them. For example, your friend wants to introduce you to Eustace telling you that he regularly competes in cat shows (or at least his cats do!). At this point you develop an attitude towards Eustace – it may be positive (yippee, a really interesting person with a deep love of cats) or it may be negative (oh no, a deeply inadequate wimp who can only relate to cats). Either way, you have developed an attitude based on only one fact and this attitude is coloured by how you feel about this one fact.

Discrimination is behaviour towards another person based on prejudice. So, having been briefed on Eustace, you are given the opportunity to meet. If you have a positive attitude you are likely to agree to meet him but if you have a negative attitude you may refuse, despite having very little information to go on.

Prejudice and discrimination are extremely commonplace in society. We all have prejudices but they do not always lead to discrimination; indeed, there are laws to stop groups of people being discriminated against, such as The Equal Opportunities Act. However, this does not stop it from occurring – racism, sexism, ageism, homophobia are all forms of prejudice that could and do lead to discrimination.

◆ Social Identity Theory (Tajfel, 1970)

Social Identity Theory states that the simple act of being grouped will inevitably lead to prejudice against another group. This happens in three stages:

1. Social categorisation: This is an automatic act of putting self and others into groups. It triggers stereotypical beliefs you may have about groups, such as that Heavy Metal fans are all headbangers. A group that you belong to is called your in-group, and a related group that you do not belong to is an out-group.

2. Social identification: As a member of an in-group, you absorb the culture of your group, you associate your self with the group's values and norms and notice differences between yourself and people in the out-group. You may emphasise group membership by wearing particular clothes. The group becomes an important part of how you view yourself – it becomes part of your social identity. If the group is doing well then you feel good about yourself, but if it is not you may feel bad.

◀ Teenagers often join groups they identify with.

3. **Social comparison:** In order to boost your own self-esteem, you need your group to appear better than a chosen out-group, so you try to engineer this by making the out-group look bad in comparison. If given a chance to make your group look good, you take it. Conversely, you might try and make a member of the out-group look bad. This is in-group favouritism; the out-group denigration is discrimination stemming from prejudice caused by grouping.

Evaluation of Social Identity Theory

The theory successfully explains real-world behaviour, such as football fan behaviour. Club fans often feel negatively about the fans of specific other clubs, particularly if they are based in the same town. This is easily explained if they are in direct competition with each other but quite often they are not and could even be in different leagues. If your team is not doing too well, your social identity suffers; if the other team is doing worse then you feel better because at least you are not one of them! This might explain fighting between rival fan groups – they are merely seeking to improve their social identity by proving themselves to be better than another group of fans.

The theory has **evidence** to support it. Tajfel's Minimal Group Study (see pages 22-23) show that the act of putting people into groups will lead to them discriminating in favour of the group they are in, at the expense of a very similar out-group. Sherif's study (1961) also shows support – boys at a summer camp, when put into groups, became hostile to the out-group as soon as they were informed of their existence and before any competition was introduced.

The theory has **useful applications**. If we accept that prejudice stems from grouping, we could tackle prejudice between groups by changing the group boundaries and creating one big in-group. This is the Common In-group Identity Model suggested by Gaertner (1993). For example, if you support United and dislike City, then when England play your identity changes to England fan, you may actually get on with City fans who also support England (although you might just transfer hostilities to Scotland fans!). So we could make a UK team and all get together to hate France, etc. Eventually we would need an alien invasion to unite the whole world.

The downside to this theory is that it simplifies complex human relations. Groups of people have shared histories involving conflict, often for scarce resources, and it may be that this history influences how we feel about each other and that grouping is just one aspect of it. Our social identities are bound up in our cultural history and a range of factors affect how we feel about other groups, not just a basic drive to improve our social standing.

Have you ever wondered?

Why can rival football fans show such hostility to each other, based only on knowledge of which team they support? Why can this can evaporate when they come together to watch the national team play?

Taking it further

Look at other theories, such as the Frustration Aggression Hypothesis put forward by Dollard et al. (1939) or Adorno's (1950) Authoritarian Personality. These also explain prejudice but without the strong emphasis on group membership.
You could also research the Realistic Conflict Theory (Sherif, 1966).

Studies

Remember at the time of the study nearly all nurses were female!

Experimental Study in Nurse-Physician Relationships (Hofling et al., 1966)

◆ Aim

To investigate aspects of the nurse-physician relationship, specifically what happens when a nurse is ordered to carry out a procedure which goes against her professional standards.

◆ Procedure

This was a field study involving three hospitals in the Midwest of the USA, with one hospital acting as a control. Twelve graduate nurses and 21 student nurses were asked to fill out a questionnaire about what they would do if confronted by the experimental situation. Twenty-two nurses from the other two hospitals doing normal duties were targeted for the actual field experiment and put in the following position: While alone on the ward, they receive a phone call from an unknown doctor.

1. The nurse is asked to give an overdose of a drug to a patient (in reality it was a placebo).
2. The medication order is given over the phone by the doctor (yet hospital policy requires that such orders are given in person).
3. The drug is unauthorised for use on the ward where she is working.
4. The order is given by an unfamiliar voice.

The researchers placed fake pills in bottles labelled 'Astroten 5 mg capsules' amongst the ward's drugs. Dosage instructions were clearly marked. A written script was used by the 'doctor' to standardise the conversation and all conversations were recorded. The experiment ended when: the nurse complied and went to issue the medicine; refused consistently to give the medicine; went to get advice; became emotionally upset; or if the call went on for more than 10 minutes.

A researcher was on hand to debrief the nurse within half an hour.

◆ Results

Questionnaire

Ten of the 12 graduate nurses, and all 21 students, said they would not have given the medication. Most believed other nurses would behave in the same way.

▲ Hofling (1966) found that nurses were unlikely to question a doctor's instructions.

Experimental situation

Twenty-one of the 22 nurses tested started to give the medication. The calls were generally brief without any resistance from the nurses. During the debriefing only 11 nurses were aware of the dosage limits for Astroten, none became hostile to the caller and nearly all admitted that they knew they should not have followed these orders as it is against hospital policy – but stated that it was a fairly common occurrence.

◆ Conclusion

Nurses will knowingly break hospital rules in a situation where a doctor tells them to, even if it could endanger a patient's life.

◆ Evaluation

This study has high ecological validity. The nurses were unaware of the test so their behaviour was natural. It demonstrates the difference between what people think they would do and what they actually do.

However, because of the reality of the situation, we can question the ethics. Informed consent was not gained but, as in Milgram's case, it would have made a nonsense of the study! In the debriefing interviews the nurses commonly admitted to feeing shame, guilt and embarrassment. They had their professionalism undermined and were undoubtedly affected by what happened.

However, as with Milgram, the participants received a thorough debriefing. The nurses were reassured that they had acted normally and that there was no chance patient care had suffered. They were not criticised.

Population validity was high as the nurses were simply those on duty at the time. However, it could be argued that people in the USA at the time were more likely to obey authority than people from other cultures.

The study had high experimental validity because none of the nurses was aware that it was a set-up. This means that the experiment did test what it set out to test, the nature of the nurse/doctor relationship.

The study was reliable. It was run 22 times and the procedure and conditions were the same throughout. The results were very similar, indicating that each nurse experienced the same situation. However, in a field study it is impossible to control all extraneous variables, and it may be that some of the nurses had demands on their time which caused them to react without thinking – though Hofling had an observer on each ward who signalled when the circumstances for the study were right.

The research supports Agency Theory and backs up Milgram's findings. The nurses' actions were consistent with being in an agentic state – they automatically recognised the doctor's authority and responded in most cases without question. The level of obedience was even higher than in Milgram's experiments.

The major criticism of this study lies in the ethical issues as they relate to the participants but perhaps the ends justify the means.

Examiner's tip

When asked to describe a study make sure you can summarise it without giving too much detail on any one aspect. Include information about the aim, the method, the results or findings and a conclusion to give a well-rounded account.

Taking it further

Try and get hold of the original write-up of the research by Hofling et al. He gives an interesting interpretation of the nurses' behaviour based on psychodynamic principles.

▲ Artwork by Klee and Kandinsky was used in Tajfel's 1971 study into prejudice.

Social Categorisation and Intergroup Behaviour (Tajfel et al., 1971)

◆ Aim

To test whether the simple act of grouping was enough to produce prejudice between groups of very similar people. The study is also known as the Minimal Groups Study.

◆ Procedure

A sample of schoolboys was given a fake art task to do and allocated into one of two groups on the basis of this (Klee group and Kandinsky group). In fact, the grouping was purely random. They were then given a rewards allocation task where they were asked to award points to two other boys (one from each group) at a time. The only information they were given was which group they were in. The point scores for each boy were tied together, so that when a participant chose a particular score for one boy, the other boy automatically got the score tied to it.

For example, if the participant was asked to allocate points from the grid below and chose to give 14 points to Klee group member 25, then Kandinsky group member 2 got 1 point.

Klee group member number 25	1	3	5	7	8	10	12	14
Kandinsky group member number 2	14	12	10	8	7	5	3	1

Would they discriminate in favour of boys in their in-group and award them more points than boys in their out-group?

◆ Results

It was found that the boys typically awarded more points to members of their in-group, showing strong in-group favouritism. This was clearly in their best interest, as they had been told that points earned prizes for the group!

Tajfel varied the grid to test this further and see whether the boys would still show this favouritism when it was not in their best interest to do so. He manipulated the grids so that the maximum points they could give to their in-group meant that the out-group member automatically got more points.

Klee group member 13	7	9	11	13	15	17	19
Kandinsky member 8	1	5	9	13	17	25	21

A Klee group member could then follow one of four strategies:

- He could choose 19 for the Klee group, as this would earn the most points, a strategy known as maximising the in-group profit.
- He could choose 13, so that each group does equally well, a strategy known as maximum fairness. This makes sense, as he may well have friends in the other group.
- He could opt for getting as many points as possible for all the boys (17 for the Klee member, giving 25 to the Kandinsky group member), regardless of the grouping, a strategy known as maximum joint profit.
- He could choose to maximise the difference in favour of the in-group, by choosing 7 – giving the group a 6-point advantage.

In practice, the majority opted to maximise the difference in favour of the in-group. This may not seem rational, as it meant the group ended up with fewer overall points but it can be explained in terms of social identity; the boys made themselves superior by boosting their group's status.

◆ Conclusion

Categorising boys into meaningless groups caused them to identify with their in-group and engineer a positive social identity by giving their group more points. They did this even if it meant ending up with fewer points, as long as their group came out on top.

◆ Evaluation

The groups were made deliberately meaningless in order to test the effect of grouping without any element of historical competition. However, it could be argued that the forced choice nature of the task implied competition and this caused the boys to discriminate. In support of its **validity**, this type of study has been replicated with tests on different samples. For example, Locksley, Ortiz and Hepburn (1980) created explicitly random groups (where the members knew they had been randomly assigned), removed the forced choice task and got them to divide poker chips between anonymous members of the groups. They also found strong in-group favouritism.

The study itself was very **reliable**. With strict controls over the information the boys were given and the experience they had, the study was replicable. On the down side, validity is questionable – perhaps the boys only behaved this way because they were very aware of the experiment, they were in a university setting which was not natural to them and they may have been more prone to try and behave in a way they believed the researchers wanted.

You could also argue that the study lacked **population validity** because of the limited nature of the sample used. Further studies have tested other groups, for example adults in Cardiff (Branthwaite and Jones, 1975), female adults in California (Brewer and Rothbart, 1980) and soldiers in the German army (Dann and Doise, 1974). All showed the same minimal group effect of Tajfel's original research.

Ethically, the study does not provide any special concerns. The boys were not put under stress, but they were in a school-type situation and they may have found it hard to withhold their consent.

The study provides a useful insight into the mechanics of prejudice, showing that simply being put into a group is enough to start the process. The findings are consistent with Social Identity Theory and there is supporting evidence from studies with similar aims/methods.

Examiner's tip

Random assignation to groups is good experimental technique as it avoids the possibility of the experimental group consisting of participants that are somehow different from the control group. It is easy to do once you have your sample; at its most simple you could draw lots from a hat, or throw a dice. It is important that every participant has an equal chance of being in either group.

Summaries of two other studies

◆ Intergroup conflict and co-operation: The Robber's Cave experiment (Sherif et al., 1961)

Aim

To see whether it is possible to instil prejudice between two very similar groups by putting them in competition with each other.

Procedure

In this field study, 22 boys took part at a summer camp. They were all from a similar background, were well-adjusted and normal. On arrival they were allocated to one of two groups. The researchers acted as camp counsellors.

Each group was initially unaware of the other's existence. They soon had a distinctive set of rules and ideas about how to behave, had chosen a name and flag. After a week, the groups were made aware of each other. Researchers observed that in-group/out-group terms started to be used.

The next stage was the introduction of competition, a tournament with prizes. The researchers manipulated the points so that they could control the competition. Even before the tournament began the groups were fighting with each other and one group burnt the other's flag. The prizes, when awarded, were stolen by the losing group.

Results

A strong in-group preference was shown by the boys in each group.

Conclusion

Competition increased prejudice and discrimination, leading to clear inter-group conflict.

Evaluation

- Ecological validity is high as the boys were in a natural environment.
- The study had experimental validity – the boys were unaware they were being observed.
- The sample did not represent the wider population, so the study possibly lacked population validity.

◆ Rethinking the psychology of tyranny: The BBC prison study (Reicher and Haslam, 2006)

Aim

To investigate the effects on behaviour of putting participants into two groups unequal in terms of power.

Procedure

This field study was conducted in conjunction with the BBC who later broadcast it. Fifteen men took part in a study in a simulated prison-style environment. Participants were all well-adjusted and there was a range of age, social class and ethnicity. They were put into five groups of three on the basis of being most similar to each other and one was randomly selected from each group to join the guards, group. Participants were psychometrically tested every day and a physical measure of stress taken.

The guards were told their job was to ensure the prison ran smoothly and were asked to draw up a series of rules and punishments that complied with basic human rights and could not include violence. They had access to surveillance of the cells, trappings of authority and better conditions than the prisoners. The prisoners arrived one at a time and were told only about the prison rules.

The researchers manipulated events to see the effect on behaviour, for example on the third day telling both groups that promotion to guard was possible and allowing the guards to select the most suitable prisoner. The chance to be promoted was then removed.

Six days in, the experimenters told the participants that there was actually no real difference between the guards and the prisoners, but that it was now too late to change anything.

Results

At first the prisoners adjusted their behaviour to try to get promoted. When this was no longer possible they began to show strong social identity and tried instead to change the system. The guards did not show a shared social identity and did not exert their authority. They could not deal with confrontation and gave in to demands by day four. The prisoners became more and more the dominant group.

By day six the system had collapsed and a single self-governing commune replaced it by majority decision. However, within two days the commune collapsed and the dissenters from the day before proposed a hierarchical arrangement with clear authority (they became the guards). This concluded the study as the experimenters judged it to be unworkable.

Conclusions

When groups are formed with shared norms and values, the members work together and become strong. Tyranny arises because of failed groups rather than because of tyranny of the group itself. When there was a possibility of promotion, the groups did not have shared norms and values.

Evaluation

The study can be criticised for the demand characteristics inherent in a televised observation, as participants may have managed their behaviour in order to look good. It might therefore lack ecological validity. It could also be argued that the prisoner group had the more domineering personalities in it, thus limiting conclusions about the effect of grouping. However, participants were screened to avoid individual differences being a problem.

Key issues

What you need to know

- You need to be able to describe one key issue of relevance to today's society and apply concepts, theories and/or research (as appropriate) drawn from the Social Approach to explain the issue.
- This section considers the issue of blind obedience to authority in a prison setting in detail (for example the Abu Ghraib situation) and other possible examples in less detail:
  - obedience during conflict resulting in harm to others (for example the My Lai Massacre, Vietnam, 1968)
  - football violence
  - cult behaviour.

The Social Approach looks at how elements of a social situation can influence behaviour. This includes being in a group, group norms, recognition of authority, cultural influences and so on.

Obedience to authority in a prison setting

▲ Soldiers at Abu Ghraib prison: an example of blind obedience to authority.

One issue concerns the behaviour of US military personnel during the Iraq conflict, specifically the breach of human rights for Iraqi prisoners of war held at the US-run Abu Ghraib prison. During the summer of 2004, a series of photographs detailing US military personnel abusing, torturing and humiliating Iraqi prisoners was published in the world's press. An international outcry followed and the soldiers involved were investigated and court-martialled. Eleven junior-ranking soldiers were convicted of abuse and dereliction of duty but no officers were found guilty of abuse and only two were convicted of dereliction of duty.

At the trial, two basic arguments were put forward:

1. The accused were 'corrupt cops' who tormented prisoners for fun (the personality side of the debate about influences on behaviour). This was the case for the prosecution.
2. The accused were only obeying orders given by senior officers (the situationist side of the debate about influences on behaviour). This was the case for the defence.

◆ Explaining the issue

- The defence lawyers for the accused argued that they were not bad people but rather that they were in a situation that had led to their behaviour.

- The soldiers argued that they did not have autonomy in their decisions about dealing with the prisoners, that they were following orders and that abuse of prisoners was policy in order to 'break the prisoners down' for interrogation.

- It could be argued that the soldiers operated in an agentic state to carry out the orders – both explicit and implicit – of their superiors. In that case, the responsibility for their actions lay with the authority that required the action and not the person actually committing it.

- This argument is consistent with Milgram's Agency Theory. The soldiers' behaviour does show similarity with Milgram's research participants, who also obeyed orders and harmed other people.

- There were clearly in- and out-groups, one of which (the US soldiers) had all the power.

- The US soldiers would identify with their in-group, which had a prevailing culture of mistreating the out-group. In order to establish their social identity they accepted the group norms as standard and abused the prisoners.

- Studies such as those by Tajfel (1971) and Sherif (1961) show that once you identify with a group you are much more willing to promote their interests over that of an out-group. In a war situation, where the out-group is a known enemy, this effect would be exacerbated and the behaviour towards the out-group would be much worse.

- There was very little evidence that there were direct orders to mistreat the prisoners in this way (hence the officers only being convicted of dereliction of duty, i.e. neglect),

- Not every guard engaged in the mistreatment. Indeed one of them, Joe Darby, 'blew the whistle' on his colleagues by making the photos, which were private to the group, public knowledge. This shows that there was room for autonomous action even in the high-pressure setting of a prison during a war.

◆ Summary

In conclusion, it seems that there is no simple explanation for such complex events. However, it is fair to say that explanations from social psychology do provide insights that are useful in understanding the circumstances that surround behaviour of this sort.

Taking it further

There are many articles about the Abu Ghraib situation on the internet. Try to find out more about the situation – the BBC website is a good place to start (www.bbc.co.uk).

Taking it further

Find out about the work of Philip Zimbardo. He is a very famous social psychologist who was called as expert for the defence in the court martial of Staff Sergeant Frederick, a guard at Abu Ghraib. Zimbardo used this experience as a basis for a book, *The Lucifer Effect: Understanding how Good People Turn Evil*. (2007).

OPT

Summary of three other key issues

◆ Football crowd violence

Trouble often flares up between rival sets of fans at football matches. This may take the form of actual fighting on the terraces, or a stand-off in the streets around the football stadium with two distinct groups shouting insults and throwing missiles at each other. The police become involved in order to keep the peace and may themselves become targets for this behaviour.

One issue that social psychology is good at explaining is group behaviour, so theories from the Social Approach can help us to understand why such events happen and even what can be done to minimise the violence.

- Social Identity Theory proposes that we identify with an in-group, in this case being a follower of a particular team.

- We then categorise other football fans as being members of our in-group (same team) or our out-group (rival team). We wear scarves and strips that reflect our group membership.

- In order to boost the social identity of the group – and therefore boost our own sense of self – we actively deride the out-group in order to make a favourable comparison with our in-group.

- In some people, caught up in the excitement of the match, this may go too far and lead to football hooliganism.

◆ Obedience during conflict

Soldiers are trained to obey orders, indeed their lives may depend on unquestioning obedience. The issue is, how far should this be used as an excuse for carrying out atrocities such as the massacre of a civilian population?

One such atrocity was the My Lai massacre in Vietnam. Twenty-six US soldiers were variously charged with actions involved in the massacre of between 350 and 500 women, children and old men, inhabitants of a small village in Vietnam on March 16 1968. Soldiers from Charlie Company rampaged through the village killing everyone they found. Of the 26 servicemen charged in connection with the killings, only one soldier, Lieutenant William Calley, the leader of 1st platoon, was convicted. His defence was that he was obeying the orders of his superior officer.

Calley was initially sentenced to life imprisonment but this was overturned on appeal and he served just four and a half years. The reason given by the appeal judges was that they believed that he (Calley) honestly thought he was obeying orders.

OPT

Examiner's tip

Try not to use psychology if asked to describe the issue – save the psychology for explaining it. Write like a lay-person to start with, when describing, then to move on to psychology later, backing up what you say with evidence from research where possible.

OPT

Explanations for the soldiers' behaviour include the following:

- Agency Theory can offer one explanation – that, when trained to obey, soldiers simply abdicate responsibility and become an agent for the superior authority. Calley did argue that he was an agent for his superiors.
- Some soldiers refused and ultimately it was they who brought this incident to light. This reflects Milgram's findings – most people obey, but some follow their own moral conscience and rebel.

However, it should be noted that this is an extremely simplistic explanation for a horrendous tragedy.

◆ Cult behaviour

Joining a cult is joining a group that has a strong social identity. Cults tend to be exclusive in nature and so attempt to be different from other groups in order to emphasise their own identity.

People joining a cult show strong identification with the group norms as the cult becomes a major part of their own personal identity. This may even extend to perceiving other groups as threats to the security of this identity.

One such cult was the Branch Davidian led by David Koresh at Waco, in Texas. This was a community based on very unusual religious values. Under Koresh's leadership the cult became increasingly segregated from the outside world, which was perceived as a threat. The members of the cult stockpiled food and weapons. The authorities, worried about the situation that seemed to be developing, challenged their behaviour and the US customs authority raided the compound on February 28 1993. A stand-off between the FBI and the Davidians ensued until April 19, when the compound caught fire and 74 cult members died.

Explanations for this tragic series of events include the following:

- Social Identity Theory can explain why cult members feel such a strong bond towards their in-group and why they have negative feelings towards their out-group. However, the behaviour of the Branch Davidian was clearly extreme.
- Typically, the leader of a cult is charismatic and capable of coercive persuasion. This encourages strong in-group identification.
- The authorities may well have seen the Waco community as a threat to their social identity and as such felt they had to challenge them.

◄ Social Identity Theory can explain why cult members feel such a strong bond towards their in-group.

Evidence of practice

What you need to know

- You need to devise and conduct one practical to gather data relevant to topics covered in the Social Approach. This will be a survey (either a questionnaire or an interview) and it must gather both qualitative and quantitative data. It must be conducted according to ethical principles and you must make design decisions in devising the survey and in selecting a suitable sample.
- Once the data is collected, you will analyse it and draw brief conclusions about the topic from your analyses.

Using a questionnaire to carry out a survey

In this section you will be guided through the design and conduct of a survey in the form of a questionnaire.

◆ Develop a research question

The research question used as the context for this section concerns the claims of Social Identity Theory. The theory suggests that, once someone categorises themselves as a member of a particular social group, their attitudes towards members of other (similar) social groups will be affected. Specifically, they will be more positive about those categorised as belonging to an in-group compared to those they categorise as members of an out-group.

The question is:

Do people in one age group hold negative attitudes about people in other age groups?

You will refine this to a hypothesis in the light of other design decisions.

◆ Consider the ethics

Ethically, this question seems unlikely to cause problems, but age can be a sensitive issue for some people and you will have to consider whether to ask people to state their age or ask them to place themselves in an age group category. If you are aiming to uncover personal beliefs or attitudes, participants must be assured that their responses will be kept anonymous and confidential. You should be able to get their fully-informed consent by telling them what the study entails and what your research question is. They should also be alerted to their right to withdraw at any point and to be debriefed at the end.

◆ Plan the survey

The first step is to decide on the research method, type of data and target population for your study.

Prejudice is an attitude so it lends itself well to the survey method, which aims to uncover and measure attitudes that people hold. You could choose an interview (structured or not) or a questionnaire.

Examiner's tip

Once you know what you are doing, who your sample is and the kind of questions you will be asking, you should get ethical clearance before starting. Your teacher will be able to provide this, but if in doubt you should contact the exam board.

SUM

A questionnaire can give a reasonably large sample and can give quantitative **and** qualitative data. You can get all this from self-report data from participants in a written format. You want to gather the data quickly, and do not want to have to spend time transcribing it, so opt for a questionnaire that has a variety of questions – both open and closed.

Consider the target population. It might be general, such as all adults, or more specific, such as people who are currently studying Psychology at A level. In this instance the target population is people under the age of 25.

Next, think about your sample. In a school or college a straightforward sampling method to choose is opportunity as you have access to students in the right age group. You should be aware that not all people under 25 are students and therefore may hold different views, but the ease of access may balance this consideration. The sample size should be large enough to enable generalisation but not so big as to make gathering data difficult. Around 20 is a reasonable figure for your purpose.

◆ Operationalise your question

To operationalise a research aim, you pick out the factors (or variables) relevant to the research question and define them so that they can be tested and measured.

Age group is one factor. Participants must be categorised as belonging to an age group (young, middle-aged or old, for example) and must know what is meant by other age groups. As the researcher, you decide where the boundaries are but these should be consistent with what other people would think, otherwise your research into age-related attitudes would be meaningless to the wider population. The categories used here are 16 to 25 and 60 +.

The other variable to measure is attitude. To do this you will need to ask questions that allow participants to express their views about members of an in-group and an out-group.

◆ Develop research hypotheses

A hypothesis is a testable and specific prediction (based on background research) about what you expect to find from your research. A reasonable working hypothesis for this study is:

People in a young age group (25 and under) will have more positive attitudes towards their own age group than to an older age group (60+).

This also gives the null hypothesis:

There will be no real difference in the attitudes of people in one age group (25 and under) to those in their own group compared with those in another group (60+) except that which happens by chance.

Examiner's tip

You will need to justify the choice of survey method, so think of reasons why the research method chosen is suitable for your research question in particular. You could also consider whether you are aiming for reliability more than validity, objectivity more than subjectivity, etc.

Notice also that people under the age of 16 are not included. There are two reasons for this:
- The ethics of asking young people to participate in research require that you should acquire parental or other guardian consent for them to take part.
- You could argue that they do not yet have set beliefs.

Over to you

In order to do your practical you will have selected variables to measure. Be sure you can say what they are and then specify how you operationalised them. This means how you managed to get your participants to show each variable and how you made them measurable.

Question 1

What is the difference between a null and an alternative hypothesis?

EG

Start the questionnaire with some simple instructions thanking the participant and assuring them that their answers are confidential and anonymous.

The question format can be varied so that it asks, for example, how strongly the participant agrees (or not) with a given statement.

◆ Design a pool of questions to test the hypothesis

You need some questions that allow participants to express their age-related opinions. The format of the questions must allow for both qualitative and quantitative data.

Operationalise the key variable of age group by asking participants to identify themselves with one group or other, for example:

What age group do you belong to?
Young (under 25)   **Older (over 60)**

This question is designed to set up the idea of an in-group and an out-group and allow identification with the young group.

Quantitative questions

Good questionnaires should allow for some flexibility in the participant's responses. The aim is to limit the possible responses (making analysis easier) whilst allowing a degree of choice (giving the participant room to express their real view).

A **Likert-type scale** is useful as the answers are clearly quantifiable.

How arrogant do you think older (60+) people are?

1	2	3	4	5
very	a bit	maybe	not really	not at all

Build up a series of about 10 questions (it could be more or less but must be enough to give adequate data and not so many that the participants get bored and lose interest). The questions should balance – for young and old statements, for example – allowing the measurement of attitudes towards the in-group **and** the out-group.

Qualitative questions

You are required to gather qualitative data, which means that the participant responds with their own words. This requires open questions such as:

What do you think are the most positive characteristics of the older (60+) generation?

You need to balance this in order to get a comparison for the young group, so the next question should be:

What do you think are the most positive characteristics of the younger (25 and under) generation?

Once you have enough questions, format them into a questionnaire, adding instructions and including ethical information, for example about informed consent and advising participants of their rights. A debrief statement can be included at the end of the questionnaire.

Question 2

Which kind of data do you have if it consists entirely of numbers?
a) Qualitative
b) Quantitative
c) Narrative
d) Statistical

Pilot the questions

Before using your questionnaire, go through a **pilot study** with a few people to make sure the questions are clear and unambiguous and to establish the reliability of the questionnaire and validity of the questions. It will also help you structure your data collection sheet.

Over to you

Develop a few questions related to your research question.

◆ Carry out the study

Participants can complete the questionnaire with or without the researcher present. They can also participate in one large group or alone, at a time to suit them. Ensure they understand what is required, their ethical rights and how to return the data.

Over to you

Carry out a pilot study and use the responses to develop a data collection sheet.

◆ Analyse the results

Quantitative research

Work out the scores and compile a data collection table, like this:

Participant	In-group positive	In-group negative	Out-group positive	Out-group negative
1	1	6	4	1
2	1	3	2	1
3	2	1	2	0
4	2	2	2	2
5	1	3	2	1
6	1	0	2	0
7	0	4	3	1
8	0	6	6	0
9	1	2	2	4
10	1	3	2	1
11	0	5	0	4
12	1	3	3	0
13	0	4	2	1
14	2	5	1	2
15	2	2	4	0
16	2	3	1	3
17	1	3	1	2
18	3	1	2	3
19	1	3	4	1
20	2	1	2	0

Examiners tip

In the exam you will be questioned on how you carried out your own research, so you should be able to describe what you did and justify why you chose to do this, for example describing steps you took to ensure that the ethical guidelines were met.

Table to show data from young people measuring attitudes to their age-related in-group and out-group.

Look at the data to see if you can see any patterns. In this data the highest scores seem to be in the negative to in-group and positive to out-group columns. This needs to be analysed to see if a trend is evident by finding measures of central tendency; work out the mean, median and modal scores for each column and then see what the data is showing:

	attitude of young to young (in-group)		attitude of young to older (out-group)	
attitude score	positive	negative	positive	negative
mean	1.2	3	2.35	1.35
median	1	3	2	1
mode	1	3	2	1
range	3	6	6	4

Table of descriptive statistics for scores on a questionnaire designed to measure positive and negative attitudes of 20 young people to age related in-group and out-group

Have you ever wondered?

Where do statistics like '9 out of 10 owners said their cats preferred ...' come from? They come from surveys where members of a target population are asked questions specific to a topic under investigation. You may wish to consider who the sample population were and what kind of questions were asked, whenever you hear the results of surveys in the future.

Question 3

Outline one method of analysing qualitative data.

The results of the quantitative analysis do not support the alternative hypothesis because the participants scored on average twice as much on positive statements about their out-group (2.35) as they did about their in-group (1.2). More evidence to support this shows up in the averages for negative attitude scores given —these participants were more negative about their in-group (with a score of 3) than they were about their out-group (1.35).

The mean, median and modal scores show averages (central tendencies) of data. These suggest that young people hold more positive attitudes about old people than negative attitudes and are more likely to express negative than positive attitudes about young people. You can see from the mean scores that they averaged 1.2 for their positive in-group attitude measure and 2.35 for their out-group, suggesting they were nearly twice as positive about older people as about younger people. This is true for every measure of central tendency.

The range shows the amount of variation amongst the participants in their attitude scores. The lower the range, the more consistent they were with each other. Here, they tended to score the same as each other with the positive statements about young people but were much less consistent on the negative statements.

Qualitative research

You need to look for themes in the written responses of the participants. In this survey two questions required qualitative responses. Assemble the data into two sets – older and younger. Write out the responses under each heading and then read over the data to see if there is a common theme. Look for things repeated several times, for example:

- The main point for the older group was that they are more experienced and wiser.
- For the younger group, the focus seemed to be on open-mindedness.

The dominant theme that emerged was that young people think older people are less open and more backward-looking, whereas younger people are more focused on the present and the future.

Add some quotes to support this interpretation, for example: Older people 'like to share experiences of what things were like'.

◆ Draw conclusions

Linking to the hypotheses

You need to put all the analysis together and link it to the research question and hypothesis, stating whether the findings allow you to reject the null hypothesis, and how (see left for an example).

So, although the alternative hypothesis is clearly not supported here (meaning that you cannot reject the null hypothesis), what does this say about the research question? On face value, it seems that age-related in-group/out-group attitudes do exist in the young age group but that they are biased in favour of the out-group.

Linking to the theory being tested

Social Identity Theory suggests that we will be biased in favour of people we perceive to be in our in-group. It has a lot of evidence to support it so, although the findings of this study suggest the opposite, it is unlikely that they disprove the theory. You therefore need to examine the study to see whether this is a **valid** test of in-group/out-group behaviour.

◆ Evaluate the validity of the findings

Operationalisation of variables

Think about the definitions into categories – old and young, etc. There is a validity issue here in that if you generalise these results based on one definition (of young and old), you are open to criticism on the basis of this not being a widely recognised definition (Who is to say when you become old or cease to be young?).

Type of questions

Did these actually access the participants' real views? For example, the question 'How arrogant do you think older people are?' was almost only answered with a 'maybe' response. Possibly the participants did not understand the question and therefore had no clear opinion.

Research method used

Was the questionnaire an appropriate way of measuring beliefs? As we have seen from Milgram's and Hofling's studies, people's actual behaviour differs substantially from what they believe they would do. For example, the participants in this study may have given politically correct answers and displayed anti-ageism rather than their real views.

▲ Researchers need to ensure sample groups are representative of the wider population.

Sample

Another problem arises for the population validity of any conclusions drawn. For example, a sample of students who are under 19 and in full-time education may not represent the target population – defined as people under 25 and who may be in full-time employment.

Subjective interpretation of the qualitative data

In analysing this section, it is possible that personal views and experience were used to interpret what the participants said. This could lead to a biased report being made.

Conclusion

It may be that the participants were influenced by the setting they were in – a classroom with their teacher present – to answer in a way that did not mark them out as ageist. These participants were also well used to being part of experiments in class and may have been looking for a hidden agenda and responded to that rather than to the actual questions. In order for any conclusions drawn from a study such as this to be valid, improvements must be made.

Question 4

Explain how you would decide whether findings from a questionnaire are a valid expression of an attitude that can be related to a wider population.

Over to you

What was your alternative hypothesis and did your results analysis support it? Explain why you came to this decision.

Summary

The Social Approach focuses on how our behaviour is influenced by other people.

◆ Methodology

Although the studies reported here have been largely experimental, yielding quantitative data, a major research method used in the Social Approach to study behaviour is the survey, which includes questionnaires and interviews. The survey is well suited to measuring attitudes, opinions and preferences.

Whichever type of survey is used, asking questions is at its core, and fundamental to finding useful information from the survey is asking the right questions. Questions can be open or closed:

- Open questions can be answered by the participant in any way they choose. They produce qualitative data.
- Closed questions have a very defined and limited number of responses that can be made. They produce quantitative data.

The two main types of survey are interviews and questionnaires:

- An interview can be structured, unstructured or semi-structured. This kind of method is more likely to gather qualitative data.
- A questionnaire is commonly done on a larger scale and the data is more likely to be quantitative. This lends itself to statistical analyses and enables generalisation and comparisons between groups.

The interpretation of quantitative data is objective, based on numbers. The interpretation of qualitative data is more subjective and can be open to bias.

◆ Content

Milgram

The work of Stanley Milgram on factors affecting obedience, although almost 50 years old, still holds true today. Its importance is reflected in several different ways:

- Contemporary real-life issues (such as the Abu Ghraib prison scandal) show clear echoes of Milgram's research.
- Agency Theory can explain why seemingly good people do bad things.
- His work highlighted the importance of the ethical treatment of participants.
- He graphically showed us that what people think they would do in a situation is often different to what they actually do.
- He showed us how to scientifically test an abstract concept, by designing one of the most elegant studies in psychology.

Hofling

Hofling's work builds on that of Milgram. Ethically, his study was perhaps not as good as Milgram's, because there was no consent and he was showing nurses up as rule-breakers in their professional lives. However, like Milgram, maybe the end justified the means. More crucially, the research points out ways not only to explain human behaviour but to safeguard against the worst aspects of it.

Prejudice

Tajfel's Social Identity Theory suggests that the simple act of identifying yourself with a group will inevitably lead to prejudice against others in similar but different social groupings. Tajfel suggests that we need to boost our social identity in order to benefit our personal identity and it is this boost to our social identity that leads to unfavourable comparisons with members of an out-group and which constitutes prejudice.

◆ Key issues

As part of your study of social psychology, you will have looked in depth at one key issue of relevance to today's society, using concepts and theories from the Social Approach to explain it.

◆ Evidence of practice

You will have conducted a survey to gather data to investigate an aspect of human behaviour. The data gathered will include quantitative and qualitative data and your research must have followed ethical guidelines.

Your practical needs to reflect the way psychologists use the scientific method in their research, starting with a research question and developing a hypothesis based on background theory and evidence. They then choose the most appropriate research method to test the null hypothesis and based on the data they then either reject the null hypothesis or not.

From your research, make sure you keep details of:
- how you planned it
- how you carried it out
- how you analysed it
- your conclusions
- your evaluation of it.

Examzone ——————————————————————————— Practise

Section B questions

1. Describe one or more features of the Social Approach in understanding human behaviour.
(4 marks)

2. Describe the procedure used in Milgram's (1963) original study.
(5 marks)

3. Compare Milgram's (1963) study into obedience with that of Hofling et al's (1966) study of obedience .
(4 marks)

4. Milgram used Agency Theory to explain the way that people behave when faced with a demand to obey an authority figure. Use your knowledge of Agency Theory to explain the behaviour of a prison guard who obeys an order that involves mistreating prisoners, even though it breaks prison rules.
(4 marks)

5. Outline what is meant by the term 'social categorisation'.
(3 marks)

Section C questions

6. Evaluate Milgram's research in terms of ethical considerations.
(6 marks)

7. There was a clash between fans of rival football teams in the city centre after a match. Several people were seriously injured and the damage to businesses in the centre was estimated to be over £2million. Describe Tajfel's Social Identity Theory and show how it can be used to explain the behaviour of these football fans.
(12 marks: 6 AO1, 6 AO2)

8. Assess at least two ethical issues that arise from obedience research. Your answer should relate both to participants in such studies and society.
(6 marks)

MCQ

2. Cognitive Approach

Key terms

- information processing
- memory
- forgetting
- storage
- retrieval

What you will learn about in this chapter

- How cognition/cognitive processes influence human behaviour.
- How to understand and apply methodology and design issues.
- How we remember and why we forget.
- How to apply theories to a real-life application, and explain it.
- How to devise, conduct and assess your practical investigation.

What you need to know

- The role of cognition in human behaviour and key ideas from the approach.
- The types of experiment and methodological issues relating to experiments.
- The Levels of Processing Model of Memory and the Cue-dependent Theory of Forgetting and one other theory of memory and forgetting respectively.
- Craik and Tulving's (1975) study of processing, and another study from the three specified within this approach.
- How to apply knowledge to explain key issues such as the reliability of eyewitness testimony.
- How to devise, conduct and assess a practical investigation.

Defining the Cognitive Approach

The Cognitive Approach began in the 1950s, largely because psychologists had become frustrated with previous approaches failing to explain cognition. With the arrival of computers, they could see a way of understanding and researching human cognition.

Cognition refers to the mental processes needed to make sense of the world. These include perception, attention, language, thinking, problem solving and memory. When crossing a road we perceive the traffic passing by and we pay attention to vehicles travelling towards us. We may be processing the conversation with a friend about how necessary it is to cross the road and drawing on our stored memories of road safety before we make a decision to cross. This simple task involves many cognitive processes, and demonstrates the necessity of cognition as a whole.

Cognitive psychologists believe that behaviour is influenced by cognition, so the way we perceive and think determines the way we behave. The role of the cognitive psychologist is to understand cognitive processes and suggest models and theories that help explain how humans process information, and how these mental operations influence behaviour. One area of research is the study of brain-damaged patients. Brain trauma by accidental damage or biological causes such as tumours, can affect behaviour in extreme ways. The cognitive psychologist will study the parts of the brain that have been impaired and link this to any change in behaviour, personality or ability. This has led to an understanding of how isolated or interrelated cognitive functions are and where they are located in the brain.

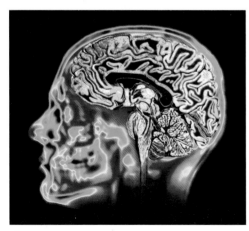
▲ Cognitive psychologists study the ways in which the human brain processes information.

◆ Information processing

The **information processing model** is used by the Cognitive Approach to explain how we receive, interpret and respond to information. It describes this flow of information using the terms **input**, **process** and **output**. Using the road crossing example, the road and cars are the 'input', putting all the information together and considering how safe it is to cross is the 'process', and a behavioural response, crossing the road, is the 'output'.

This model links to another assumption of the Cognitive Approach – that the human mind is like a computer. A computer is also an information processor: we input information via a keyboard, for example, the information is processed and can be stored on the hard drive, and an output in the form of sound, print-out or email can be made. Like a computer, the human mind is thought to have a limited capacity processor that can only deal with a restricted amount or type of information at any given time.

◆ Memory

Memory is an important cognitive function used to retain information and recall it when needed. Case studies of brain-damaged patients have shown that memory is vital – without it no learning would take place. Consider what memory is used for: relaying events to friends, remembering when to catch your bus, recalling childhood memories, faces, places, events, how to ride your bicycle. Without memory we would survive on reflexes and instincts alone, and would lose what essentially makes us human.

To store new information we must first transform it into a form capable of being entered into the memory system. The process of transforming sensory input into a memory trace is called **encoding**. Once we have encoded sensory input, we can maintain it for a while in storage. We have three storage systems: **sensory storage**, **short-term storage** and **long-term storage**.

When we register an experience it is held as an exact copy in sensory storage. This holds information just long enough to decide whether to process it further. If we do not attend to it, the information is quickly forgotten. Sensory storage is very fragile and temporary – the storage of visual images lasts half a second and the storage of sound for around two seconds. In fact, very little of the information stored here is processed further and transferred to short-term storage.

Short-term storage appears to have a limited capacity of around seven bits of information and will only be maintained for 15-20 seconds without rehearsal. Long-term storage, on the other hand, is potentially unlimited in capacity (no-one yet has been found with a full memory!) and can hold information for many years.

Retrieval refers to the process of locating and extracting stored memories so they can be used. At any of the three stages of memory, if we fail to encode, store or retrieve the information, forgetting can occur.

Have you ever wondered?

What is artificial intelligence? You may be familiar with this in the form of computer or console games but what other forms does it take? There are many artificial intelligence simulations available online. Have a chat with one of these simulations and decide whether you think humans and computers are similar. Try talking with Alicebot at www.alicebot.org/.

Taking it further

Milner (1968) reported a case of a patient who had undergone surgery to treat severe epilepsy. He had his hippocampus removed from both brain hemispheres, which left him able to recall memories prior to the surgery but unable to recall anything after it. He was able to store information in short-term memory for around 18 seconds and for up to 15 minutes if he rehearsed it. However, he was unable to place these new memories into long-term storage. It seems the hippocampus is responsible for the transfer of memories between short- and long-term storage.

Find out more about brain-damaged patients, what parts of the brain were damaged in each case and how this affected behaviour and memory function. Clive Wearing (Blakemore, 1988) is another example.

Examiner's tip

When beginning a new approach, the terms may seem confusing but the longer you spend studying the approach the easier they become. When you have found out more about this approach, try coming back to the terms and definitions. This will help you understand them and you can use knowledge of theories and studies you have learnt as examples to expand your answer in the exam.

Methodology

What you need to know

- You need to be able to describe and evaluate the experimental method (laboratory, natural, field).
- You need to be able to identify, describe and apply key terms and methodological issues.

Question 1

Which of the following examples is a field experiment, a laboratory experiment or a natural experiment?

1 An experiment was conducted to see whether more words could be recalled if the words required a deeper level of thought compared with words that required only minimal thought.

2 An experiment was conducted to see if media influenced the behaviour of children on a remote island that had previously not been connected to mainland television.

3 An experiment in obedience was conducted on passers-by to see if they would be more likely to give a stranger money for a parking meter who was dressed in uniform or in plain clothes.

Which of the experiments has ecological validity?

Which has the least control over extraneous variables?

In cognitive psychology data is usually collected in laboratory experiments. Field and natural experiments are also used.

◆ Laboratory experiment

A laboratory experiment is a study that is conducted in a tightly-controlled environment, where the independent variable is directly manipulated by the researcher and the effect of this change is measured by the dependent variable. To be a true experiment, the participants should be randomly allocated to the experimental conditions. When people think of a laboratory experiment they imagine lots of technical equipment, but this is often not the case and only basic accommodation and materials are required. More specialised rooms are needed for the study of sleep, perception and physiological responses.

◆ Field experiment

In contrast, a field experiment is carried out in a natural environment. Piliavin et al. (1969) conducted a field experiment to investigate helping behaviour by seeing how many passengers on a subway would help a person who collapses. Piliavin varied the type of person who collapsed and measured how long it would take for a bystander to help. The experimenter still manipulates the independent variable but does so in an environment typical of the behaviour being studied.

◆ Natural experiment

The natural experiment is similar to the field experiment in that it is conducted in a natural environment. The difference is that the independent variable is not manipulated directly by the researcher. Instead, the researcher takes advantage of a naturally-occurring situation where the variable is changed for one group but not another. Charlton (1998) described the effects of the introduction of live television in 1994 on an island called St Helena. He was able to compare the behaviour of children prior to the introduction of television to several years after, and also compare to children living in London.

Experiment evaluation table

Laboratory experiment	Field experiment	Natural experiment
Advantages • Extraneous variables can be controlled to such an extent that a firm cause and effect relationship can be established. • We can be fairly certain that the independent variable that is manipulated did have an effect on the measured dependent variable.	**Advantages** • Participants may not be aware that they are taking part in a psychological investigation so their behaviour may be realistic and not subject to demand characteristics or experimenter effects. • It has ecological validity, so the findings can be generalised to real-life situations.	**Advantages** • Offers ecological validity because data tends to be collected under natural conditions and, as the independent variable is naturally occurring, it could be argued that it is more realistic. • May be more ethical as participants are not unaware of taking part in a psychological study *per se*, as the situation is occurring regardless of the presence of researchers.
Disadvantages • Characterised by control over extraneous variables, making the situation highly artificial and unlike normal life. • The study outcomes may not apply to real-life situations and are only useful in explaining behaviour under artificial conditions. • Participants are often aware of being part of psychological research, which can lead to demand characteristics. • The experimenters themselves can influence the participants' behaviour (known as experimenter effects).	**Disadvantages** • No control over setting, so unexpected or extraneous variables may have an influence on the findings, which threatens the validity of the study. • Generally more time-consuming and difficult to set up. • There may be ethical problems. If a participant is unaware that they are taking part then they would not have given consent and do not have a right to withdraw from the study. In these cases a researcher may chose to debrief them after the study and offer the right to withdraw their results.	**Disadvantages** • Lack of control over the participants involved in the study and extraneous variables could affect results. For example, the researchers cannot select which participants take part in the study as they have to use those who are available and in the situation at the time. • Tends to be a unique situation, so hard to find.

◆ Experimental hypothesis

An experimental hypothesis is a statement made about the predicted outcome of the study. A hypothesis is usually based on a theory and is designed specifically to test this. For example, if a theory proposes that driving will be seriously affected by tiredness, a hypothesis will test this by stating that being awake for more than 15 hours will slow down reaction time. This is called a directional or one-tailed hypothesis, as the likely direction of the results is predicted. However, we may be unsure which way the results might go, because it has not been researched before or because previous research does not show agreement. To solve this problem we can state a non-directional or two-tailed hypothesis. This states that a difference or relationship will be found but that its direction could go either way.

◆ Null hypothesis

A null hypothesis also needs to be stated about the study. It is a statement that the results will be due to chance not to what was predicted. For example: 'There will be no difference in driving between those who have stayed awake and those who have slept. Any difference will be due to chance or some other factor.' There will nearly always be a difference in driving performance between different people, but the null really asks if the difference is big enough to accept that it is due to tiredness or is too small to be meaningful (and therefore due to chance or small differences in driving ability).

Directional or one-tailed

→

The direction of the results can be predicted.

Non-directional or two-tailed

← →

A change or difference is predicted, but not the direction it will go in.

Question 2

Look at these examples.

A directional or one-tailed hypothesis:
Participants will recall significantly more words from a categorised list than a randomised list.

A non-directional or two-tailed hypothesis:
There will be a difference in the number of words recalled from a categorised word list and a randomised word list.

Now you try: An experiment was conducted to see if there was more trolley-bumping at a busy supermarket compared with a quiet supermarket. Using this example of an experiment, devise a directional or one-tailed hypothesis **and** a non-directional or two-tailed hypothesis.

ANS

ANS

Question 3

Identify the independent variable (IV) and dependent variable (DV) in these examples.

1. An investigation was set up to examine the effect of noise on essay writing.
2. A number of first- and second-born children were given an IQ test to see if intelligence was affected by birth order.
3. One group of children were allowed to play violent computer games and another group only games that were non-violent. Levels of aggression were studied following play.

ANS

Question 4

Identify the participant design used by the following experiments:

1. Craik and Tulving (1975) conducted an experiment to see if words processed at different levels (semantic, phonetic and structural) affected recall. They presented each word one at a time and asked questions that required semantic, phonetic or structural processing. All participants had the same experience of all questions.
2. Tulving and Pearlstone (1976) gave participants either a categorised or randomised list of words to remember and recall.
3. The IQ and social skills of children attending after-school clubs for enrichment programmes were compared to those children who did not attend any after-school programmes. The researchers made sure that both groups had similar backgrounds and came from similar

An experiment always has an independent variable and a dependent variable. In a laboratory and field experiment the researcher directly controls these.

◆ Independent variable

The independent variable (IV) is the variable that is manipulated or changed in order to demonstrate a difference between the experimental conditions. A researcher who wished to investigate the influence of fatigue on driving would probably carry out an experiment involving some participants who have stayed awake for a long time and some who are rested. The amount of sleep is the IV.

◆ Dependent variable

The dependent variable (DV) is the variable that is measured or the result of the experiment. Using the fatigue experiment example, the DV is the measure of the effect of fatigue on driving performance.

◆ Operationalisation

Once you have decided on the IV and DV of a study, it is very important to make an operational definition of both. This means defining precisely how you intend to measure the DV and alter the conditions of the IV. An operational definition of driving performance might be the number of cones knocked over on a course, or reaction time in seconds. This allows the study to be repeated exactly if necessary, to assess its reliability.

◆ Participant design

Participant design describes how the participants are distributed between the experimental conditions. In the driving and fatigue example, we could make some participants get up very early and test their driving and the next day test again when they have been fully rested. Alternatively, we could wake up one group very early and let another group lie in so they are rested. There are three main participant designs:

- An independent measures design is when only one of the experimental conditions is tested on a group of participants.
- A repeated measures design means the same participants are used in all experimental conditions.
- A matched pairs design is essentially the same as an independent measures design but all participants are matched on a quality or characteristic important to the study. For example, in a non-experimental study of the effects of day care on intelligence, participants may be matched on family background to a group of children raised at home.

◆ Order effects, counterbalancing and randomisation

Order effects occur when participants take part in all the experimental conditions, as a repeated measures design is used. The two effects are practice and fatigue. Participants may become practised at the test and so improve performance, or they may become tired so that performance deteriorates.

Order effects can be controlled by **counterbalancing** or **randomising** the experimental conditions. To counterbalance, the participants need to be divided equally between the conditions and to experience them in a different order from other groups. If there are only two conditions, half of the participants are tested in condition A before condition B, and vice versa. This technique controls order effects because the first and second condition is not the same for every participant, so they are not always fresh for condition A and tired for condition B. Randomisation follows a similar principle to counterbalancing, but rather than being systematic it is purely random. Participants are assigned to condition A or B first by tossing a coin or picking a name from a hat.

◆ Experimental control

An experiment should have control over the many variables that may affect the results of the study. Some are easier to identify and control than others.

Extraneous variables

Extraneous variables are any variable, except the IV, that can have an influence on your findings. Often, the variables affect the DV and make it look as though there was an effect. In some cases the variable can confound the result. A **confounding variable** is a factor that has not been controlled and that has a direct impact on the findings.

Situational variables

An extraneous variable that might affect your results could be found in the environment or situation in which the study in conducted. Environmental conditions such as noise, lighting, time of day, location, levels of crowding, heat or weather conditions may all affect the results and should be eliminated or controlled.

Participant variables

Participants themselves may affect the results of the study. For example, some people are highly motivated, easily distracted, in a good mood, expert at a particular skill, have more experience, etc. It is fairly simple to control for participant variables such as age and gender, but others may take a little more thought. Using the fatigue and driving example, the possible participant variables would be driving skill and experience, vision and concentration level. Driving skill could be at least partially controlled by selecting those with a clean driving licence and at least five years' driving experience, and vision could be controlled by conducting a quick eyesight test if the participant agrees.

Question 5   43

A researcher was interested to see if people would recall more happy words than sad words. A repeated measures design was chosen and participants had to read and recall a list of sad words and a list of happy words. The researcher was anxious that participants would become practised or tired when reading the second list, and order effects could confound the result.

1. How might the researcher go about using counterbalancing to balance order effects?
2. How might the researcher go about using randomisation to balance order effects?

Taking it further

In the exam you may be asked to identify extraneous variables that might have affected a study's findings. Practise by assessing the experimental control of a range of studies. Identify:
- situational variables
- participant variables
- controls used by the researcher.

You may use any experiments, but here are some suggestions:

Godden and Baddeley (1975): Divers study
Craik and Tulving (1975): Levels of Processing
Schab (1990): Chocolate cue study
Pickel (1998): Weapon focus experiment

◆ Ecological validity

This refers to how well a study represents a natural situation. If a study is conducted in a highly artificial environment the results could be unrealistic and abnormal. Field and natural experiments have ecological validity as they are conducted in natural surroundings where the behaviour being studied would normally occur.

◆ Experimenter effects

This refers to the subtle cues, expectations, gender and personality type of the researcher that may influence the way a participant responds. Sometimes these effects are obvious, for example a female researcher asking a male participant about their attitudes towards women. Other effects may be less obvious, as even subtle cues given by the researcher can bias the outcome of a study.

◆ Demand characteristics

Human participants may respond to the experimental conditions in which they are involved. Humans are not passive, and they may change their normal behaviour in unusual situations. If the aim of the study is obvious this can worsen the effects of demand characteristics as participants may behave in such a way as to fulfil that aim.

◆ Objectivity

Being objective refers to being detached or neutral in terms of judgement, without the influence of personal interpretation or emotion, so that the subject matter under investigation is tested and analysed without prejudice. For example, an opinion of a painting is subjective as I might like it but you may not. However, a grain of sand is just that, everyone would agree, and it could be tested to verify it.

Cognitive psychology studies mental processes that cannot be directly observed and are therefore not directly testable. It cannot be objective. If something is not directly observable then we assume that a researcher would have to make a judgement about it that may be influenced by personal beliefs. However, cognitive psychologists would argue that, although we cannot objectively observe mental processes, we can objectively observe data produced by experimentation or brain-imaging techniques. If a cognitive psychologist conducts an experiment to test short-term memory and a participant recalls five words from a list, we can objectively infer that short-term memory has a capacity of five words.

◆ Reliability

Reliability is achieved when a study is repeated and the same results are found. This replication is possible if the experiment is tightly controlled and unexpected variables that might affect the results are eliminated. Even with tight controls, however, some studies may not be reliable, as the topic studied may be a product of a particular time or era.

Laboratory experiments are able to control participant and situational variables to ensure a cause and effect relationship can be established. This means that the results are reliable and likely to recur if the study is replicated. Field and natural experiments have little control over these variables and lack reliability.

Hofling et al. (1966) studied obedience in nurses and found that 21 out of 22 nurses would obey an order given by a male doctor to give a patient an overdose without written authorisation. This result would be unlikely to occur today, as nurses have far more autonomy than in the 1960s and women may be more likely to challenge a male counterpart, even one in authority.

Mary Ainsworth (1978) conducted a series of structured observations on children and mothers to see what type of attachment or bond they had. She found that American children were largely securely attached. Ainsworth's procedure was conducted in many other cultures, for example Japan and Germany, where it was found that children were mostly insecurely attached. This study showed good reliability in the measurement of attachment as different people assessing the same child would assign the same attachment type to the child. However, if the measurement of attachment is taken as an assessment of how normal the relationship is between the mother and child, then it is not valid, as the most prevalent attachment type differs between cultures.

◆ Validity

Validity refers to how well something measures what it is supposed to measure. If a researcher chooses to measure childhood aggression in the playground, he or she may operationalise the dependent variable to count the number of physical contacts between the children whilst playing. This could be seen as an invalid measure of aggression as the children could simply be playing tag. Construct validity is how well a measure being used is a good indicator of what is supposed to be studied.

Loftus (1974, 1975) conducted a series of experiments using slides and video footage of car accidents and gave participants a questionnaire to answer about what they had seen. These studies attempted to see if post-event information, such as leading questions, would affect eyewitness testimony. These studies were criticised for lacking **ecological validity**, as the situation did not represent what would have occurred in a natural setting. Being witness to a real car accident would involve emotions and witnesses would have a different perception of speed than participants who watched a video. Also, giving a police statement is different from answering a questionnaire and has more serious implications than being part of a psychological investigation. It could be said that the results of this study are unnatural, and that the findings are not applicable to real eyewitness testimony.

Both field experiments and natural experiments have ecological validity as they are conducted in natural surroundings where the behaviour being studied would normally occur. Laboratory experiments often lack ecological validity as participants are not in a natural environment, which will affect behaviour.

Taking it further

The link between reliability and validity is often a balancing act. Greater control ensures reliable findings but often at the expense of validity, particularly ecological validity. Similarly, greater validity often leads to a loss of control and therefore reliability is lessened.

Find four studies that have been conducted and rate them on a scale of 1 to 5 for reliability and 1 to 5 for validity.

Content

Levels of Processing (LOP) Model of Memory (Craik and Lockhart, 1972)

Why do we remember some things and not others? When we perceive a stimulus from our environment, we automatically process it. The way we process it depends upon what kind of information it is and how relevant it is to us. So, we can revise information that has little relevance to us for hours and not remember it very well or watch an interesting television programme and be able to recall virtually every scene.

◆ Types of rehearsal

Craik and Lockhart (1972) proposed that there are two different types of rehearsal. Type I or **maintenance rehearsal** means that we rehearse the information in order to preserve it for a short time, but it is unlikely to result in a strong memory being established. Type II or elaborative rehearsal refers to a deeper consideration of the information, often by giving it meaning, and is more likely to result in a more durable memory being made.

◆ Information processing

Craik and Lockhart proposed that we have a central processor that handles all kinds and quantities of perceptual information and determines how it is processed. If the information is distinctive, relevant or requires time or effort to process, it is likely to be processed at a deeper level than if it is effortless and meaningless. If information is processed on a deep level, it is more likely to be retained in the memory system. Memory is not necessarily a conscious action, but is a by-product of the way information is processed. This explains why we sometimes remember information we do not intend to.

Craik and Tulving (1975) conducted a laboratory experiment to determine whether recall is affected by the way information is processed (see also page 56). Participants were required to answer yes or no to a question about a word they were shown. There were three types of question asked that determined how deeply the word was processed:
- ones that required **structural** processing of a word (the physical structure, for example upper or lower case)
- ones that required **phonetic** processing (the sound the word made)
- ones that required **semantic** processing (the meaning of the word).

▲ Processing the meaning of words increases memorability.

They found that words processed at a semantic level were more likely to be recalled. This study provides clear support for the Levels of Processing Model of Memory, as deeper semantic processing leads to better recall.

◆ Evaluation

Advantages

- Hyde and Jenkins (1973) asked participants to learn a set of 24 words under five different conditions. They had to rate the pleasantness of a word, judge how frequently it might be used, check for specific letters, describe what part of speech the word referred to or judge if it fitted into a given sentence. These tasks required different levels of processing, as the importance of meaning varied. One group was told they would be required to recall the words later and one group was not told. There was no difference in recall between the two groups, but there was a significant increase in recall when participants were asked to judge the pleasantness of the word. Processing the meaning of words increased memorability.
- The applications are wide. They have been used to enhance learning and revision, and also applied to learning language and reading.
- It accounts for the diversity of memories stored. The Multi-store Model assumes that anything remembered for longer than a minute or so is held in LTM, but it does not account for the fact that some of these memories are strong and some weak. The LOP explains the difference in memory durability by referring to the depth of processing.

Disadvantages

- Many variables determine whether a durable memory is achieved: the relevance and distinctiveness of the information; the elaboration given; and effort and time spent on processing. It is therefore difficult to establish what is meant by depth of processing in a single given instance.
- Morris et al. (1977) found that participants recalled more words that were phonetically processed than semantically processed. This provides direct evidence against the model. Morris et al. believed that, if participants are given a word list to remember, phonetic processing is more likely to be used for this task than semantic processing. The nature of the task determines the depth of processing used, rather than depth determining retention directly.
- It can only be used to explain improved recall in explicit memory (memory that requires conscious recall). It does not really affect recall from implicit memory (memory that is recalled automatically).
- It has been criticised for being descriptive rather than explaining how memory works, and that referring to depth is circular logic.
- It does not account for all learning. That is, giving something meaning is not the only way we can leave a durable memory trace. Imagery and emotionality can also leave longstanding memories.

Taking it further

Replicate Craik and Tulving's study. Create a list of 15 words and a series of 15 questions. The questions should relate to the three levels of processing, so five questions should ask about the appearance of the word (upper or lower case, number of letters), five should relate to the sound of the word (Does it rhyme with….? How many syllables?) and the final five need to focus on the meaning of the word (Is it the same meaning as….? Is it a type of….?).
Ask family and friends to recall as many of the words as they can. Collect the data and present the findings from each question task in a table like this:

	Structural level of processing	Phonetic level of processing	Semantic level of processing
Total no. of words recalled			
Mean no. of words recalled			
Range of words recalled			

What conclusion can you draw?

Examiner's tip

In the exam, you can be asked direct questions about the theory and its evaluation. You need to have a detailed knowledge of the theory and how it might apply to situations. Practise this by explaining the following situation:
As a psychology student you have knowledge of how memory works. A friend approaches you to ask for help in revising for a history exam. Using two theories of memory, explain how you could advise your friend to revise.

Opt

Summary of four other theories of memory

◆ Multi-store Model of Memory (Atkinson and Shiffrin, 1968, 1971)

This describes memory as consisting of three separate stores:

- The sensory memory store is a buffer for all the information in the environment that bombards our perceptual system. This store holds sensory information for the briefest period until we decide to give it attention and transfer it to short-term memory.
- The short-term memory is a limited store for attended information. It is believed to hold around seven bits of information for around 18 to 30 seconds. Rehearsal is used to hold information for a longer duration and makes it more likely that it will be transferred to long-term storage.
- The long-term memory has a potentially infinite capacity and can hold memories for a few minutes or many years.

Although this theory has a large amount of supporting research, it has been argued to be an overly simplistic view of what is actually a rather complex memory system.

▶ The transfer of information through the memory system

◆ Working Memory (Baddeley and Hitch, 1974)

Baddeley and Hitch proposed an alternative theory to the short-term memory storage described in the Multi-store Model. Short-term memory was seen as a holding place for information to be interpreted by long-term memories, as well as being a place for information to pass along to long-term storage. Rather than a single storage unit, short-term memory was seen as consisting of several systems that dealt with different types of information:

- **Phonological loop:** deals with verbal information, particularly its rehearsal, and is known quite literally as the 'inner voice'.
- **Primary acoustic store:** a later addition to the theory, this holds acoustic information and is known as the 'inner ear'.
- **Visuo-spatial scratchpad:** deals with visual and spatial information and is known as the 'inner eye'.
- **Central executive:** directs the flow of information received to the appropriate system.

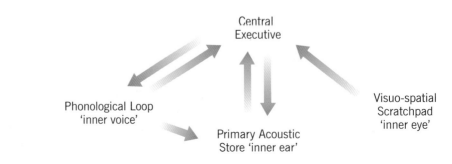

▶ A diagram of the central executive and subsystems

◆ Spreading Activation Model of Semantic Memory (Collins and Loftus, 1975)

The Speading Activation Model is an extension to Quillian's earlier theory of semantic memory. Ross Quillian was a computer scientist investigating and developing models of human memory using computer networks. He proposed that long-term memory was arranged in a hierarchical network of semantically related concepts. The concept of a 'dog', for example, is semantically linked to the concept for an 'animal' because a dog is an animal. These are built up into a network of concepts that relate to a 'dog', for example 'has paws', 'can swim', etc., and are arranged in a hierarchy. The hierarchy for a Labrador would be animal-dog-Labrador. A node represents each concept, and a neural network links each node. Once a node becomes activated, because we are thinking of it, the activation from this node spreads to further related nodes within the hierarchy.

Collins and Loftus (1975) built upon Quillian's original model but suggested that concept networks were not represented in a hierarchy. Research had shown that when we activate a concept it does not necessarily follow that we recall related concepts within that hierarchy, but rather we remember sometimes abstract concepts. For example, if we activate the concept for a dog we might also activate a node that represents a postman. This would not be predicted by Quillian's logical hierarchy, but would account for our understanding of dogs being a threat to postmen.

Collins and Loftus adopted a less rigid structure called 'semantic network' where concepts are linked by relatedness. Highly-related concepts are closer together and less related concepts further apart. This 'semantic distance' explains why related concepts are quick to recall and unrelated concepts are slower to recall.

◆ Reconstructive memory

Most of us believe that, when we remember, it is an accurate depiction of the original memory, like a video recording that we are able to replay exactly. However, we do not have the ability to replay the exact version as we often only have fragments of the original event stored. Memory then is more like a notebook where important points are jotted down, and when we come to recall the memory we use the notes and actively interpret them. Like making revision notes on a topic, we only write down the main points, as this makes it quicker to revise, but in the exam we are required to write an essay so we fill out the detail.

To make sense of the fragments of memory that are stored, we fill in the gaps of missing information by drawing upon knowledge of what is likely to fit in any given scenario. We use past experience to make sense of the memory. Bartlett (1932) described this process of active recall as reconstructive memory, as we use imagination and best guesses to complete the memory. If we take this literally, we can believe Bartlett's claim that our past is a reconstruction based on our present experience – so what we recall from our childhood, for example, is interpreted in light of our current understanding.

▲ Frederick Bartlett, 1886-1969

Opt

Theories of forgetting

- You need to be able to describe and evaluate the Cue-dependent Theory of Forgetting (Tulving, 1974).
- This section contains summaries of three other theories of forgetting.
- You need to be able to describe, evaluate and compare two theories of forgetting, one of which is cue-dependent.

One of the most frustrating and sometimes embarrassing features of human cognition is the tendency to forget. We have all experienced the forgetting of a telephone number or the birthday of a family member. Typically, we remember later, but on occasion cannot recollect even having the memory in the first place. There are two main explanations of why we forget: either the information is not available to be remembered because we have failed to store it or it has decayed from our memory, or it is available to be recalled but we cannot seem to find it.

◆ Cue-dependent forgetting

This theory explains the failure to remember as an accessibility problem. Many of us have saved work onto a CD or memory stick and when we come to retrieve this information it will not work. The information is there, so we try different ways to access the information, and it is only when the correct way is tried that the work is found. Cue-dependent forgetting is similar, in that sometimes we cannot access the memory until the correct cue is used.

When we encode a new memory we also store information that occurred around it, such as the way we felt and the place we were in. If we cannot remember, it could be because we are not in a similar situation to when the memory was originally stored. Tulving's **encoding specificity principle** explains this as: 'the greater the similarity between the encoding event and retrieval event, the greater the likelihood of recalling the original memory'. Put simply, if we encode a happy childhood memory, we are more likely to recall it when we are happy again. The mood of happiness acts as a cue to trigger the event from memory. However, if we are in a different state or context, we are less likely to remember, resulting in cue-dependent forgetting.

The most noticeable experience of cue-dependent forgetting is the Tip of the Tongue Phenomenon (Brown and McNeill, 1966). This refers to knowing that a memory exists but being temporarily unable to recall it. Participants were given dictionary definitions of unfamiliar words and asked to recall them. See if you can experience this with these questions: Who were the two lead actors in *Men in Black*?; What was the name of the dog in *The Magic Roundabout*?; Who is the Mayor of London?

Context-dependent forgetting

Context is a powerful cue to aid recall. If we are not in the same situation as when learning, we may not be able to access the memory easily. This explains why revisiting a place after many years triggers memories of being there.

Taking it further

Abernethy (1940) investigated the role of context on examination results. Research this study and suggest how the findings of Abernethy, and those of Grant and Bredahl (1998), could be applied to raising examination results within your school/college.

Godden and Baddeley (1975) demonstrated how divers recalled 50% fewer words when they were asked to recall them in a different environment from the learning. Without the same conditions being reinstated, the divers forgot the words.

It is not just location that can act as a powerful contextual cue. There are also environmental cues that can aid recall or impair it if missing. Smith (1985) gave 54 participants a list of words to learn and immediately recall in quiet, or with Mozart or jazz playing in the background. Two days later the participants were asked to recall the words, again in quiet, listening to Mozart or jazz music. This made nine conditions in which participants recalled with the same or different background noise to the first recall (see right). Forgetting occurred when the background music was not the same, demonstrating that, without the same music as a context cue, recall is impaired.

Similarly, Grant and Bredahl et al. (1998) found that memory for unrelated words declined when learning occurred in noisy conditions and testing/recall in quiet conditions, and vice versa. This was reversed for quiet learning/quiet testing and noisy learning/noisy testing.

Schab (1990) found that the smell of chocolate can be a strong cue to aid recall, and Herz (1997) found a similar effect with peppermint, osmanthus and pine (osmanthus being the most distinctive and novel, producing the best recall after a two-day delay).

State-dependent forgetting

When we learn information, we also encode details about our emotional and physical state at the time. If we wish to recall the memory, state cues may not be present, making it difficult to remember. Duka et al. (2000) gave 48 participants alcohol or a placebo, prior to a list of 40 word pairs to learn. Participants were tested in one of four learning-recall conditions: alcohol-alcohol, alcohol-placebo, placebo-alcohol, or placebo-placebo. Duka found that recollection of the words was better if the same state for learning was in place for recall. Without the placebo or drug being reinstated as a cue, participants forgot the words. (Note that it is not ethical for you to use alcohol or fear as a cue in your own practicals.)

Miles and Hardman (1998) used aerobic exercise to produce a physiological state in order to test state-dependent recall. Twenty-four undergraduates from University of Wales College of Cardiff were required to learn a list of three-syllable words whilst on an exercise bicycle. All participants repeated four combinations of learning and recall whilst pedalling or resting. They concluded that aerobic exercise did have a significant positive effect on recall when used as a state cue.

Lang et al. (2001) investigated the role of emotion as a state cue by inducing fear. Fifty-four students who were fearful of snakes and spiders had their fear induced again whilst learning a list of words. They found that when the fear was induced for recall, the scared students were able to recall more learnt words than when they were in a relaxed state. Experimental research seems to support anecdotal evidence that places, objects, smells and emotions can all be triggers to aid recall, but that without these cues present we are liable to experience difficulty remembering.

Group	Learning	Recalling
1	Quiet	Quiet
2	Quiet	Mozart
3	Quiet	Jazz
4	Mozart	Quiet
5	Mozart	Mozart
6	Mozart	Jazz
7	Jazz	Quiet
8	Jazz	Mozart
9	Jazz	Jazz

▲ A table to show the learning and recall conditions for Smiths (1985) experiment.

▲ The smell of chocolate can be a strong cue to aid recall.

Examiner's tip

When evaluating a theory you can cite research studies that support or refute it. You do not need to write out the whole study in detail, just make the findings clear and say how the study supports or goes against the theory being evaluated. For example, you might write:
Godden and Baddeley (1975) found that divers who learnt and recalled words in the same context, on land or under water, recalled 50% more than divers who learnt and recalled in different contexts. This study supports the theory of cue-dependent forgetting because, without the presence of the environment as a cue, the divers were unable to access the stored word lists.

Evaluation of cue-dependent forgetting

There is plenty of anecdotal evidence for cue-dependent forgetting, as we have all experienced the frustration of knowing something but not being able to recall it, or the feeling of memories flooding back when we meet up with an old friend. These real-life accounts are difficult to study so we have to resort to experimentation – though such experiments can be criticised for being unrealistic.

Research evidence used to support the theory of cue dependency, with a few exceptions, comes from experimental studies using word lists and unfamiliar or uncommon cues. This limits the application of the theory as these artificial situations may not reflect real-life forgetting. However, both Abernethy (1940) and Godden and Baddeley (1975) have demonstrated cue-dependent forgetting in natural environments – a college and offshore dive site – though the reliability of these findings may have been affected by a lack of experimental control.

Literally hundreds of studies have concluded that cues are a powerful aid to memory and that, in the absence of such cues, we find it difficult to remember. Who are we to argue?!

A meta-analysis was conducted by Smith and Vela (2001) on 75 experiments of context-dependent forgetting between 1935 and 1997. Across all the studies they found that reinstatement of context, such as rooms and other environmental conditions, did play an important role in remembering.

The theory of cue-dependent forgetting cannot be refuted, as it would prove impossible to tell whether a memory is inaccessible or whether it is lost. We can only rely upon accounts of experiences where we have recalled the memory later.

Most of the laboratory research cannot really tell whether what is being provided in the study is a state or context cue. Music, for example, can be both a context cue as it is an environmental feature, or a state cue as music can alter emotional state.

◆ Summaries of three other theories of forgetting

Trace decay

Trace decay theory is one of the earliest explanations of why we forget and largely tries to explain why we forget over time. The theory suggests that learning causes a physical change in the neural network of the memory system, creating a memory trace or 'engram'. Once this memory trace has been created, it must be reinforced through repetition to strengthen it. If the memory trace is not reinforced by practice it will simply weaken and decay, causing forgetting to occur. Essentially, we need to use it or lose it. Trace decay explains forgetting as a problem of availability, that is, the information is lost completely from the memory system through disuse and passage of time. This is inevitable in short-term memory due to the limited duration, but requires a significant structural change in long-term memory.

Taking it further

Hundreds of studies have investigated cue dependency and memory/forgetting, using a range of possible cues. Research to find a cue dependency study that you find interesting. Start by searching the internet using key words such as:
- 'state cues and memory'
- 'context cues and memory'
- 'cue dependency research'.

For the full article you could ask your librarian to order a copy of the study from the British Library.

Interference

In long-term memory, forgetting may occur due to interference or confusion between old and new memories. This does not necessarily mean that the memory is lost, as in decay theory, but that it may become distorted or changed as a result of conflicting memories. Both retroactive and proactive interference have been studied experimentally by learning lists of paired associate words and recalling the first or second list presentation.

In an experiment to test this, McGeoch and McDonald (1931) gave participants a list of ten words to learn until they were able to recall the whole list accurately. Participants were then required to rest for 10 minutes, learn a list of three-digit numbers (e.g. 482), learn a list of nonsense syllables, learn unrelated words, or learn a list of antonyms (opposites) or synonyms (same meaning) of the original list. They found that the more similar the new information was to the old memory, the lower recall became. This provides clear evidence for retroactive interference as similar information competes for meaningful memory space with the old memory.

Interference task	Mean number of words recalled from original list
Rest for 10 minutes	4.5
Learn a list of three-digit numbers	3.7
Learn a list of nonsense syllables	2.6
Learn a list of unrelated words	2.2
Learn a list of antonyms (opposites)	1.8
Learn a list of synonyms (same meaning)	1.3

Displacement

A friend tells us their telephone number and we rush to find a pen and paper to jot it down. Before we get the chance, another friend approaches us to ask a question – ahhhh, the telephone number is lost! This is a common experience whereby new information displaces information that is temporarily stored in the short-term memory, which has only a limited amount of storage space. As new information enters short-term memory it may overwhelm items stored and cause them to be 'pushed out'.

Taking it further

Retroactive interference test

List A	List B	Recall list A
Dog-Chair	Dog-Boy	Dog - ?
Bed-Gate	Bed-Hat	Bed - ?

Proactive interference test

List A	List B	Recall list B
Table-Sink	Table-Spoon	Table - ?
Door-Flute	Door-Pen	Door - ?

The first word in the pair is known as the stem or cue word, and the associated word is known as a target.

Try this for yourself by devising two lists of paired associate words like those above. Gather a group of participants and give them list A to learn until they can recall each target word when cued by the stem word. When they have learnt list A, give them list B to remember. Now present the stem words again to recall list A and see how many they can recall after experiencing retroactive interference. The same procedure can be used to test proactive interference by asking them to recall list B.

◄ Table showing the effect of a retroactive interference (McGeoch and McDonald, 1931)

Studies

Examiners' tip

When describing an experiment, it is important to show breadth as well as depth of knowledge. It is not enough to write how the experiment was conducted without writing about what was found or why the study was conducted in the first place. Follow this plan:

Aim: What the study hoped to find out about.

Procedure: How the study was conducted, when and on whom.

Results: What did the researchers find out?

Conclusion: A summary of the results.

The conclusion is similar to the aim, for example:

Aim: To see if a natural environment would act as a memory cue.

Conclusion: The natural environment did act as a memory cue.

▲ Divers were used in Godden and Baddeley's (1975) Context-Dependent Memory Experiment to test recall of words underwater and on dry land.

Context-Dependent Memory Experiment (Godden and Baddeley, 1975)

◆ Aim

To investigate whether a natural environment can act as a cue for recall.

◆ Procedure

Godden and Baddeley asked 18 participants from a university diving club to learn a list of 38 unrelated two- or three-syllable words underwater or on dry land and then recall them either underwater or on dry land. The divers were **randomly allocated** to one of four conditions:

1. Learn on dry land and recall on dry land (context-cued condition)
2. Learn underwater and recall underwater (context-cued condition)
3. Learn on dry land and recall underwater (no context cue)
4. Learn underwater and recall on dry land (no context cue).

The experiment took place in an open water site in Oban, Scotland. For technical reasons two participants had to be dropped from the study and were replaced by two other divers, who were tested at a freshwater site nearby. The study was conducted over four days, each diver experienced all four context conditions after a 24 hour delay, following a scheduled dive to ensure that all participants were in the same wet and cold state. Participants in all conditions were fully kitted in diving gear. Participants being submerged for learning or recall wore breathing apparatus and a communication device, whilst those on dry land sat by the edge of the water with breathing apparatus removed.

Tested two at a time, the divers were submerged up to 20 feet underwater and played a tape recording of the word list through a diving communication device. The recorded words were presented in blocks of three, with a four-second interval between each block to ensure that the noise of the breathing apparatus did not affect hearing the words. Each list was presented twice, and after a four-minute delay the participants had to write down the words, in any order, in two minutes. All participants used a pencil to write down the words on a weighted clipboard sealed with plastic.

◆ Results

Recall was around 50% higher when it took place in the same environment as learning. The mean number of words recalled in the dry land learning and recall condition was 13.5, and 11.4 for underwater learning and recall. This contrasted with 8.4 mean recall in the underwater learning and dry land recall, and 8.6 for dry land learning and underwater recall.

◆ Conclusion

Environment can act as a contextual cue for recall.

Evaluating the study

Strengths

- The experiment was conducted in a realistic open water environment for divers, so the results have greater generalisability to real-life situations than laboratory research.
- As the participants were research scientists and tested in pairs, it is unlikely that they would have cheated by writing down the words.

Weaknesses

- There was a lack of control over many parts of the procedure – equipment failure, inconsistent diving location, lack of standardisation and timing could all have affected the results. There was also no control over the fitness of the divers involved and weather conditions, and dive conditions and noise levels were variable. These factors affect the reliability of the results.
- Although it is unlikely the participants cheated, the researchers did not see them during the learning and writing stage, so cheating is a possibility.
- It is possible that participants who did not have to change environments to recall the word list were able to rehearse more.
- Participants who changed environment could have experienced interference in memory. However, Godden and Baddeley conducted a later experiment and found no difference in recall for those who experienced an interference task and those who did not.

The findings of the study have scope for many practical applications. An application of the study within educational environments could improve recall by reinstating the learning context for examinations. Abernethy (1940) found that students' test scores improved when they were examined in their usual classroom with the teacher overseeing their work. This effect also works for the characteristics of the context. Grant et al. (1998) found that students given an article to read with loud background noise or under silent study conditions recalled more when the same condition was reinstated for recall.

Context-dependent forgetting could occur when police interview witnesses as they are typically interviewed in a different environment to the event witnessed. Taking the witnesses back to the scene of the event or getting them to recreate the event mentally could cue more memories than interviewing them at home or the police station.

Taking it further

BBC's *Crimewatch* programme reconstructs crime scenes to help trigger the memory of potential witnesses in the viewing audience. How else might police help cue witness memory?

Examiner's tip

Describing a study in detail is fairly straightforward, but evaluating a study can be difficult particularly under the time pressures of an exam. Prompts or memory aids can help overcome this. Try breaking down evaluation comments in either of the following two ways:

1. A simple evaluation
   - **Methodology:** what were the advantages and disadvantages of the method used and procedure carried out?
   - **Ethics:** did the study conform to or break the BPS ethical guidelines for use with human participants?
2. The GRAVE technique
   - **Generalisability:** are the results likely to apply to people beyond the sample studied?
   - **Reliability:** are the results likely to be found again if the study was repeated?
   - **Application:** how has the study been useful in everyday life?
   - **Validity:** does the study measure what it claims to and how realistic was the study situation?
   - **Ethics:** does the study conform to BPS ethical guidelines for use with human participants?

Examiner's tip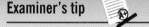

For the exam you must prepare to write about Godden and Baddeley's study and one other that you have selected. The other study must be from the suggested studies. For example:
Describe and evaluate a study of memory or forgetting from the Cognitive Approach, other than Godden and Baddeley's experiment.

Examiner's tip

Describing study results often means that you need to remember the quantities of recalled items found by the study. These quantities are easily forgotten when you are revising. To help remember (and practise drafting skills) plot a graph to represent the results visually, analyse the results and draw a conclusion.

Structural processing – a question about the typescript of a word (for example whether the word is upper or lowercase).
Phonetic processing – a rhyming question. (Does the word rhyme with…?)
Semantic processing – deciding whether a word fitted into a sentence. (The sentence had a blank space where a word was missing.)

Other studies from the Cognitive Approach

◆ The Duration of Short-term Memory (Peterson and Peterson, 1959)

Aim and procedure

The aim was to investigate how long information can be retained in short-term memory. Using a laboratory experiment, participants were presented with sets of nonsense consonant trigrams to learn. To prevent them rehearsing the trigrams and therefore retaining them for longer, they had to count backwards in threes from a given three-digit number. Participants were aware that they would be asked to recall the trigrams in the correct order. A delay of 3, 6, 9, 12, 15 or 18 seconds was introduced before recall.

Results and conclusions

After three seconds, 80% of the trigrams were successfully recalled. This fell to 50% after six seconds and around 30% after nine seconds. After 18 seconds participants found it difficult to recall even a three-letter trigram, with successful recall falling to 10%. This led to the conclusion that short-term memory lasts no more than 20 seconds, and so without rehearsal information fades quickly. This supports the theory of trace decay. The research also supports the STM-LTM distinction as LTM can retain information for longer periods.

Evaluation

• Ebbinghaus (1885) used nonsense trigrams to study memory, so that the stimuli would be meaningless and the study more objective and scientific. This has been criticised for being unrealistic, as everyday memory does not involve learning meaningless information.
• Everyday distractions are often far less focused than counting backwards and do not cause the high level of interference of the study. The findings cannot be applied to everyday memory as we would not respond to meaningful information in the same way.

◆ Levels of Processing Experiment (Craik and Tulving, 1975)

Aim and procedure

The aim was to test the Levels of Processing Theory by investigating whether words processed at different levels would affect recognition of those words. Twenty-four participants were shown 60 words via a tachistoscope and asked a series of questions about the word. The questions required structural, phonetic or semantic processing (see left). Participants were then asked to recognise the words from a list of 180 words consisting of the original 60 and a further 120 new words.

Results and conclusions

The percentage of words recognised was 17% for those processed at a structural level, 36% for words processed at a phonetic level and 65% processed at a semantic level. Overall, therefore, the deeper the processing the greater the recognition.

Craik and Tulving concluded that recognition was greater for those words that were processed at a semantic level. Deeper processing led to improved recognition, which supports the Levels of Processing theory of memory.

Evaluation

- Craik and Tulving did not inform the participants that they would be asked to recognise the words later. This ensured that they did not consciously try and remember the words but that the recall was an accurate reflection of how processing can influence remembering.
- In everyday situations we encode information at different levels according to its meaningfulness and relevance, but this rarely applies to lists of unassociated words presented for a short time. The procedure is unrealistic and presents a simplistic view of memory.
- The study ignored the role of imagery and emotion that are often associated with long-lasting memories and was contradicted by Morris et al. (1977).

◆ Age and Levels of Processing (Ramponi et al., 2004)

Aim and procedure

The aim was to investigate whether age affects the ability to process information at different levels. Ramponi et al. showed 96 participants (half aged about 72 and half about 24) a series of word pairs, presented one at a time via a computer screen. Some word pairs were strongly associated (cat–dog) and some weakly associated (cave–milk). Participants answered questions about the word pair (see right). After a distracter task, participants were told one of the words from a pair and asked to recall the other (intentional), or told to think of the first word that came to mind when given a word from a pair (incidental).

Results and conclusions

Older participants recalled fewer words than younger participants only when the recall was incidental and the association between the word pairs was weak. This age deficit was not found for strong associates or deeper levels of processing. The researchers concluded that age affects the ability to encode meaningless information that we do not process at a deep level.

Evaluation

- The study was conducted under laboratory conditions, in an artificial environment. This bears little resemblance to real life and the results cannot therefore be reliably applied to real use of memory.
- Remembering word pairs is not typically how we use memory. This again reinforces the issue of artificiality, meaning that the results of this study are not applicable to real situations of everyday memory.
- The researchers implemented many controls to ensure that word pairs were standardised and questions at each level of processing balanced. However, we cannot be entirely sure that participants did not use alternative memory strategies to memorise the word pairs.

Taking it further

Hyde and Jenkins (1973) replicated Craik and Tulving's experiment, asking participants to judge how pleasant a word was (requiring semantic processing), and Bower and Karlin (1974) used photographs of faces instead of word lists. There are many ways to make material meaningful and a variety of materials that can be used. Suggest three ways that you could make your revision notes more meaningful to prepare for the exam.

Morris et al. (1977) found that participants recalled more phonetically-processed words than semantically-processed words. Morris believed that it was the nature of the information to be learnt that affected recall, not just the task used to process the information.

The questions asked required **structural** processing (which word had more letters), **phonetic** processing (which word had more syllables), **semantic** processing (which word was more pleasant) or **imaginal** processing (which word was easier to picture).

Key issues

What you need to know

- This section focuses on three key issues that can be linked to or explained by theories, concepts and studies in the Cognitive Approach. You will only need to know one key issue for the examination. The key issue should be described and explained using ideas from the Cognitive Approach.

▲ Post-event information can distort the memory of a witness.

Taking it further

Research Loftus and Palmer's (1974) eyewitness testimony experiment and explain how this study could be used to highlight potential problems with eyewitness testimony.

Is eyewitness testimony reliable?

Eyewitness testimony refers to the recalled memory of a witness to a crime or incident. This is recorded in a police statement or given as verbal testimony to be used as evidence in a court of law. There is controversy about the accuracy of eyewitness testimony.

Why is research into eyewitness testimony so important when we have forensic evidence? Firstly, some crimes are well orchestrated and no forensic evidence can be traced. Secondly, forensic evidence is complex and jury members may lack the ability or confidence to interpret it, but when presented with a confident witness they can relate to, jurors are more likely to rely on witness testimony than scientific proof.

◆ The case for unreliability

- Bartlett believed that memory was an imaginative reconstruction based on assumptions and beliefs about a given person, object or situation. This theory poses significant problems for eyewitness recall as it suggests that the evidence may not be entirely accurate.
- Elizabeth Loftus has researched eyewitness testimony extensively, particularly the influence of post-event information that is not in the original memory but becomes incorporated into it when recalled. She conducted a series of laboratory experiments using leading questions to investigate the effect of such information on the accuracy of recall.
- Loftus et al. (1987) found that the estimated duration of an event is distorted. Showing participants video footage of a simulated bank robbery, they found the estimated duration of the footage to be five times greater than it was. This time distortion becomes a factor that affects the accuracy of witness testimony.
- Violence in the witnessed event can also affect accurate recall. Despite most of us believing that horrific events will leave an indelible memory, most research indicates that violence will have a negative effect on recall. Clifford and Hollin (1981) showed participants video footage of a man either stealing a woman's handbag and roughly pushing her against a wall or asking her directions. Recall was poorer for the violent footage. It was suggested that this might have been because violence caused interference in memory, thereby not allowing rehearsal to take place.

- Weapon focus is also believed to cause a narrowing of attention, resulting in peripheral details of the event not being recalled. Pickel (1998) investigated whether the presence of a weapon affected the ability to recall. Participants viewed a two-minute video clip of a man walking up to a hairdressers' receptionist with either nothing in his hand, a pair of scissors, a gun, a wallet or a raw chicken. Each condition was devised to test high or low unusualness and high or low threat, so the raw chicken was highly unusual but low threat, whereas the gun was high threat and high unusualness. Participants were asked what the man was doing and to recognise him from a line-up. They found that the unusual objects had the most deleterious effect on recall but not on line-up identification. As a weapon is typically seen out of context, its unusualness would explain why memory is impaired, rather than the arousal caused by the threat it poses.

◆ The case for reliability

- It is difficult to generalise the findings of most eyewitness research as typically video footage or slides are used. Participants are onlookers, so the emotion and involvement of a real incident are not achieved. This means that the study findings lack realism.
- Participants involved in laboratory experiments are aware that they need to pay attention to the video or other stimuli they are shown. Real-life events are often confusing and happen quickly, unlike laboratory studies that lack ecological validity. Similarly, the type of questioning that participants receive in laboratory studies is not as intensive and important as police interviewing.
- Most laboratory research into eyewitness testimony is drawn from limited populations of – typically – undergraduate students. Age, gender and personality types are known to be factors that affect witness recall, so drawing from a homogeneous group of people may not accurately reflect recall in the general population.
- Not all details of an event can be distorted by leading questions; it tends to be only insignificant or peripheral details that alter. Central features of an incident are not easily affected by misleading questions.
- Smith and Elsworth (1987) found that, if a witness giving a statement believes the interviewer has no knowledge of the incident or is untrustworthy, the witness will not succumb to leading questions. This would be true of an interviewing police officer who may not have any knowledge of the incident, but would not be true of a psychologist who would be expected to know what the video clip contained!
- Research into real-life eyewitness testimony has found that recall is not affected to the extremes that laboratory research suggests (see right).

◆ Summary

Evidence from research to suggest eyewitness recall is inaccurate is compelling; however, real-life witnesses cannot be ignored. The Devlin Report suggests that we should be able to use eyewitness testimony but only with significant corroborating evidence. This is a sensible solution, as dismissing it altogether would render some crimes, such as rape, untriable.

Taking it further

There are many documented cases of mistaken eyewitness identification that has led to unjust convictions. Research some of these cases and consider why an eyewitness may have got it wrong.

Try Gary Wells' website as a starting point: http://www.psychology.iastate.edu/~glwells/homepage.htm

- Yuille and Cutshall's study of statements given four months after witnessing a gun shooting found that witness recall was very accurate and not affected by the use of leading questions.
- Thompson et al. (1997) studied statements given by the survivors of the sunken river boat *Marchioness* and found that, despite extreme emotional trauma, recall was very accurate even after many months.

Opt

Summary of two other issues

◆ Flashbulb memory: a special type of memory?

The issue is whether flashbulb memory is a special form of vivid memory created because of intense emotion, or whether it is not unusual but just rehearsed.

- Flashbulb memories are detailed and particularly vivid recollections of an extraordinary or dramatic event. They could be of national tragedies like the death of Princess Diana or the London bombings, or of more personal events such as the first day at primary school. What is common is the degree of detail that can be recalled: where we were, who we were with, what we were doing at the time, how we felt, etc.

- Brown and Kulik (1982) described the flashbulb memory as a special type of memory different from the normal everyday information we store. They suggested that the emotion involved in these events activates a different way of encoding that leaves a more permanent and resilient memory trace.

- However, others argue that a flashbulb memory is no different from other stored memories, just that the experience is so unusual that it is likely to have been repeated when we retell the story to others (Neisser, 1982) or because media coverage was vast.

- Winograd and Killinger (1983) found that repetition of an event did not improve recall at all, which contradicts Neisser's repetition theory.

- So-called flashbulb memories share the same characteristics as everyday memories; they fade over time even if the confidence of recall increases over time. This suggests that they are no different from normal memories (Talarico and Rubin, 2003).

◆ The use of the cognitive interview

The issue is whether the cognitive interview aids witness recall or is actually ineffective as a tool used by the police.

- The cognitive interview is a technique used by the police during the questioning of witnesses to help them recall an incident in as much detail as possible with the most accuracy. The interview technique is largely based on psychological research into memory and forgetting and seeks to ensure that a complete and exact recollection is gained. It involves four basic concepts:
  1. Recreating the context of the incident
  2. Reporting every detail of the incident, even if it seems irrelevant
  3. Reporting the incident in any order of time
  4. Reporting how others may have viewed the incident.

    (Fisher, Geiselman and Amador, 1989)

- The interview technique is more open and less interrogatory than traditional police interviews, and is designed to encourage retrieval cues to help recall. It prevents memory contamination by keeping questioning open, thus preventing reconstruction of memory by any new information introduced by the way a witness is questioned.

Opt

- Geiselman (1984) found that the cognitive interview yielded 35% more information than standard interviewing techniques, with no difference in error rates.
- Other experts argue that the cognitive interview can actually lead to incorrect recall, as the technique of speculating from another person's viewpoint can lead to the witness guessing what someone else saw.
- Police officers may be reluctant to use the time-consuming interview techniques, particularly at the scene of a crime, where witnesses have a tendency not to wait around (Kebbell and Wagstaff, 1996).
- The police officer interviewing a potential witness may not have received the specialist training needed to administer the technique and often does not realise the significance of its use.

▲ The cognitive interview is a technique used by the police during the questioning of witnesses.

- The most damning indictment against the use of the cognitive interview is that research has failed to find significant improvement in recall when using it compared with standard interviewing (Memon, 1997). In fact, the number of reported errors is higher using the cognitive interview.
- Children have considerable difficulty with the cognitive interview, as they do not have the linguistic capacity to describe what they have experienced, or the developmental maturity to deal with the type of questioning.
- In conclusion, there seems to be mixed evidence over the accuracy of witness recall when using the cognitive interview. Clearly more research needs to be conducted to see if there are any elements of the technique that actually work.

Examiner's tip

In the exam you may be given stimulus material which requires you to use your knowledge of the theories, studies and ideas from this approach in order to explain it. Try this, for example:

Frank is driving carefully to work on the motorway when he passes a serious road traffic accident. He discusses the accident with his work colleagues but remembers very little about the incident. Use your knowledge of forgetting to explain this issue: interference, trace decay, reconstructive memory, levels of processing, etc.

Taking it further

Devise your own practical investigation to compare the cognitive interview to a standard interview technique. Show a short video clip to a group of participants and question them a few days later.

Standard interview
What did you see first?
Then what happened?
Who did you see in the clip?
What were they doing at the time?

Cognitive interview
Remember in any order what you witnessed.
Try and recall even minor details.
Do you remember how you felt at the time?
What do you think other participants saw?

Evidence of practice

SUM

What you need to know

- You need to devise and conduct one practical, which must be an experiment, to gather data relevant to a topic covered in the Cognitive Approach.
- You must be able to comment on the research design decisions.
- You must collect, present and comment on data gathered, including using measures of central tendency and dispersion.

There are many short experiments that can be conducted in the Cognitive Approach. In this chapter you will follow a practical from planning through to results analysis and discussion of findings, to investigate context-dependent forgetting. This experiment aims to test whether environment can act as a contextual cue to aid recall of a word list, and whether the absence of such a cue prevents recall.

The theory of cue-dependent forgetting states that we need the presence of cues that were encoded at the time of learning to be able to prompt the original memory. In the absence of such cues we are more prone to forgetting. The research question for this experiment is: **Will being in a different environment for learning and recall cause forgetting?**

◆ Variables and hypotheses

This experiment is investigating a cause and effect relationship between context and recall. The independent variable being manipulated is the environment where a participant will recall, whether in the same room as learning or in a different room. The dependent variable is memory recall.

To make sure that the study is clear, valid and replicable, it is important to operationalise the IV and DV:
IV: Participants will learn a list in a classroom and recall the list in the same classroom or in the library.
DV: The total number of accurately recalled words from the word list.

Once the variables for the experiment have been identified and fully operationalised, a hypothesis, or statement of prediction, can be made: **Participants will recall fewer words when they recall in an environment that is different from the learning environment, than when learning and recall take place in the same environment.**

Examiner's tip

When choosing a topic for your experiment, make sure that you do plenty of reading about it. Researching other studies into the same topic gives you ideas and insight into what can be achieved and how experiments should be conducted.

Because this experiment is based upon an established psychological theory, it makes sense to predict the direction that the results are likely to take. This is known as a directional or one-tailed hypothesis. However, if there is little supporting evidence or psychological theory it may not be possible to predict the direction of results and it is better to state that there will be a difference but that we are unsure what direction it will follow. This is known as a non-directional or two-tailed hypothesis.

All experiments require an **experimental hypothesis** and a **null hypothesis**. The null hypothesis states that the difference found is too insignificant to be able to draw firm conclusions, and is likely to have resulted from chance factors. The null hypothesis for this study is: **There will be no difference in recall of a word list recalled in the same or different environment, and any difference found is due to chance alone.**

◆ Planning the experiment

This study uses the environment as a context cue: different locations around a college provide different environments for learning and recall. Context cues are anything present in the environment, such as smell, music and colour. Alternatively, you can use state cues. These can include: mood as rated by the participant or induced by factors such as chocolate or music; level of exercise; and level of arousal (tired or alert). Above all, be practical and use cues that are readily available. If you study sports or play in a team, exercise would be an obvious choice.

Once you have chosen a cue, decide what stimulus material you will get the participant to learn and recall. A simple option is a list of words, but make sure that the words are common so they are not difficult to remember, and unrelated so they cannot be remembered by meaningful links. Also consider how the stimulus will be presented – a simple handout is fine but quicker readers may be able to read it twice. This study uses 20 words presented one at a time for three seconds each. The words are simple concrete nouns.

◆ Controls

You need to identify any extraneous variables that might affect your results and to consider how these variables should be controlled. Be aware of situational and participant variables that could, if left unmonitored, affect the experiment results. In this experiment it is important to control any distractions or interferences that might affect participants trying to learn or recall the list of words. The controls used were:
- Participants were asked to refrain from talking to each other throughout the study and mobile phones were switched off.
- Participants were seated far enough apart to prevent copying.
- The room was booked and a sign was posted outside the classroom and library area to prevent interruption.
- The length of time before recalling the list was the same for the group who stayed in the classroom and those who moved to the library.

◆ Selecting participants

Cue-dependent forgetting is possibly the most common way of forgetting, regardless of age, gender, etc. This means that a specific selection of people is not necessary; family and friends will be fine. This study has gathered 20 student participants, using opportunity sampling from around the college by simply inviting them to take part in the study.

You may want to recruit more participants to form a control group. This group should also learn and recall a list of words but without any cue.

Examiner's tip

Simple ideas are often the best. You may want to examine the effects of gender, age and ability on recall as well as the effect of context. This will often only confuse the results and you. Stick to the study aim.

Over to you

Make a list of the possible variables that may affect your experiment. Then try to find a control solution for each of these issues.

Over to you

Decide which context or state cue you will use. Identify your IV and DV.
Construct an experimental and null hypothesis for your study.

The procedure for this study was as follows:
1. 20 participants were asked to arrive at the classroom. They were all given the right to withdraw at this point.
2. They were randomly allocated to the cued and non-cued groups by drawing names from a hat.
3. Both groups were briefed about the aims and the procedure. They were given the right to withdraw, assured of confidentiality and anonymity.
4. Both groups were seated in the classroom and shown a list of 20 words one at a time via a Powerpoint™ on a whiteboard. Each word was shown for three seconds.
5. The non-cued group was asked to go to the library and the cued group to remain seated.
6. After five minutes the groups were given a blank piece of paper and a pen to recall all the words they could remember within 5 minutes.
7. Both groups were debriefed as to the study aims and thanked for their participation. They were given the right to withdraw and told that the results of the experiment would be made available.

◆ Choosing a design

This example study has adopted an independent measures design because cue-dependent forgetting is unlikely to be affected by individual differences. This means that different participants will be used in the cued and un-cued conditions of the study.

◆ Developing a procedure

To conduct your experiment reliably you need to have a schedule. This should include what is said or given to the participants and when, the time of day and place you have selected for the study, how participants are arranged there, the timings for learning and recall, and the controls you will implement during the study. Before the experiment starts, participants should be briefed on the nature of the investigation and, what is required of them and given the right to withdraw from the study. Following the experiment, the participants should be similarly debriefed, thanked and again offered the right to withdraw their data.

◆ Ethical considerations

Before undertaking any psychological study it is essential to consider any ethical implications. If the study may make participants uncomfortable, embarrassed or distressed or be in any way harmed, then the study should not be conducted. Seek advice from your teacher.

1. You must select a cue that is ethical to use (no illegal drugs, fearful or harmful cues, for example).
2. Participants should be fully informed about the aim and procedure; both when they are recruited and when they are briefed.
3. Participants should be given the right to withdraw from the study at any point. They should also be made aware that they can withdraw their results at any point.
4. No participant names should be published as this violates confidentiality. Replace their names with a participant number.
5. There is no need to use children (under 16 years) for this type of experiment, but if you do parental consent must be gained.
6. There should be no incentives or rewards for taking part, particularly if children are participants.

This example study uses a simple word list of common and inoffensive nouns and the cue is the environment. This does not harm the participants in any way as long as fully-informed consent is obtained and the participants are happy that the results of the study are not a measure of intelligence.

◆ A typical experiment testing cue-dependent forgetting

Make sure you have tested out all the apparatus and practised the instructions prior to beginning.

- Collect the participants, then brief them on the study aim and procedure. Standardised instructions can be given or read out.
- Present the stimulus material for participants to learn, and don't forget to time the learning phase.

- Make sure they are all experiencing the cue at the time of learning.
- When the learning phase is complete you may want to give them a distracter task to prevent rehearsal, or a time delay to make sure the cue is not present for one group during the recall phase.

If you are using smell as a cue, it is probably a good idea to conduct the recall phase the following day or in a different room, as the odour may linger. If location is used as a cue and one group has to change rooms, it is fairer for the group remaining in the same place to have a time delay to balance with the changing location.

- Hand out paper to recall the stimulus material or ask participants to circle those words they recognise from the original list. Recall can be recorded verbally instead.
- Don't forget that the cued condition must have the cue reinstated at the time of recall.
- Debrief participants and thank them for their time.

◆ Analysing results

Gather together the results from the cued and non-cued conditions and draw a raw data table, like this:

Participant number	Number of words recalled when recalling in the same classroom as learning	Participant number	Number of words recalled in a different place (library) from learning (classroom)
1	11	11	6
2	12	12	7
3	8	13	5
4	9	14	8
5	6	15	6
6	11	16	7
7	9	17	11
8	8	18	7
9	13	19	8
10	11	20	6
Total number of words recalled	98	**Total number of words recalled**	71

This raw data table shows that participants remembered fewer words when they recalled the list in a different environment. Only participant 17 seemed to be unaffected by the different recall location of the library. The highest recall score was 13 words, and this was when learning and recall both occurred in the classroom. It seems the raw data confirms that forgetting will happen if the context cues are not present during recall.

Descriptive statistics can help make sense of raw data as they provide a summary of the results rather than trying to analyse individual participant scores. Measures of central tendency, like the mean, median and mode, calculate a typical or common score from a set of raw data. These descriptive statistics can be presented in a summary table (see over).

Examiner's tip

Make a record of any questions participants may ask or any problems encountered when conducting the experiment. These issues may affect the reliability and/or validity of the study. When analysing your findings refer back to these problems, and be aware that they could be comments you could make in the exam if asked about validity, reliability or extraneous/ confounding variables encountered in your study.

Over to you

Decide what participant design you will use for your experiment and give reasons for this choice. Are there any problems with the participant design you have chosen? How will you overcome these problems?

Over to you

Write a bullet point list outlining the procedure of your study.

Over to you

Write a brief and debrief for your experiment.

Over to you

Make a list of the possible ethical issues with your experiment. Outline the measures you will take to ensure your study is ethical.

How to

	Number of words recalled when learnt and recalled in the classroom (cued recall)	Number of words recalled when learnt in the classroom and recalled in the library
Mean average number of words recalled	9.8	7.1
Mode of words recalled	11	6,7 (bi-modal)
Median of words recalled	11	7
Range of words recalled	7	6

From this, we can see that recall was on average higher in the classroom than the library. Participants recalled around three to four words fewer in the library, supporting the theory of cue-dependent forgetting.

All these measures of tendency and dispersion can be used to summarise the data collected. Later, you will need to understand which **measure of central tendency** is more appropriate to use, depending on the level of data collected.

◆ Presenting findings

A table of results is useful to summarise data quickly, but a graphical presentation is often better to interpret the findings of a study.

There are a number of graphs you can use to display data:
- **Bar graph:** presents discrete columns that display the cumulative mean, median, mode, total or percentage for a particular condition
- **Frequency graph:** shows the frequency of scores achieved across the data set
- **Histogram:** presents data so that the distribution of scores falling between certain ranges can be shown. The intervals shown are indicated at the mid point in each column

A simple bar graph can be used for this example:

▶ A bar graph to show the difference in the number of words recalled in the library (non-cued) and the classroom (cued).

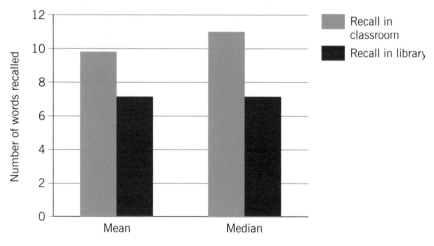

Analysing results takes time and careful consideration. Look over the table and graph and see if there are any differences, similarities, trends and anomalies between and within the cued and non-cued recall conditions. This bar graph shows a clear difference in the number of words recalled by participants. More words were recalled in the classroom than the library.

◆ Drawing conclusions

Now that your results have been collected and presented, it is time to draw conclusions. The example study seems to show a marked difference in recall, but this may not have been caused by environment acting as a context cue. Various factors need to be taken into account.

Validity

- Environment is known to be an effective cue. However, participants that were relocated to a different place to recall could have suffered memory interference when getting up and moving. This interference could account for the lower scores.
- Learning lists of words is not typical memory use and can be criticised for not representing a real task. Memory is highly complex and involves processing meaningful links between events, objects and knowledge. By giving participants lists of unrelated word to learn, it could be argued that this was not a true reflection of everyday memory.
- Moving from one classroom to the library may seem to be a change in context, but if both rooms are learning environments in that they contain a set of desks and chairs, have a whiteboard and computer, the difference between the locations may not be so significant.

Reliability

The procedure of the study was standardised so the experience was the same for all participants; they were instructed and tested in the same way. The experiment was conducted in a controlled environment to prevent noise and distractions whilst the participants were learning and recalling the word list. The procedure as a whole has good reliability as participants were not affected by uncontrolled variables.

However, there were variables that were beyond the control of the researcher and these could have affected reliability:
- The participants were friends and those who were left in the classroom chatted to each other during the timed delay before recall.
- They may have discussed the word list, which would explain better recall in the cued condition.
- The concentration levels of participants could affect how well they are able to sustain attention throughout the experiment.
- The words in the list could have been of relevance to particular individuals.

Generalisability

The example study used 20 participants for the experiment. This may not seem a large number but it is sufficient to draw conclusions from. The sample was taken from a rather restricted population of students aged 16-19 years. Normally, this would be a problem as the conclusions drawn would only be applicable to the target population of students. However, some cognitive abilities do not vary much between people and this includes cue-dependent forgetting and memory. So, despite the unrepresentative sample, it is still possible to generalise the results to the wider population.

Over to you

Refer back to your list of problems that occurred during the experiment. For example, you may have noted that a teacher interrupted the experiment, some participants were talking to each other, or that the fire alarm went off during the middle of the study. These situational variables can have a considerable effect on results, as they would have distracted participants.

Over to you

Was the independent variable an appropriate cue to use? Did it actually produce a change in context or state?

Summary

The Cognitive Approach focuses on mental processes – how we use them to make sense of the world and how they therefore affect our behaviour. These mental processes involve perception, attention, language, thinking, problem solving and memory. We input information from the world around us via the senses, we process the information and it is either stored for later or we act upon the information. The way we process the information determines how we respond to it.

◆ Methodology

Just as a gardener uses a trowel and an artist uses a brush, the tool that a cognitive psychologist uses to explore mental processes is the laboratory experiment. For the Cognitive Approach you will need to be able to identify, describe, apply and evaluate laboratory, field and natural experiments. You also need to have a good working knowledge of hypotheses, variables and participant design issues. When conducting any experiment there are important areas to consider, such as control, objectivity, reliability, validity and demand characteristics.

◆ Content

You need to be able to define, apply and evaluate the Levels of Processing approach as a framework for memory research, and one other theory of memory.

Memory is a cognitive process that enables us to store and retrieve experiences.
- The Multi-store Model of Memory (Atkinson and Shiffrin, 1968, 1971) says that memory is a series of stores that allow us to filter sensory information and store it for short or, if rehearsed, long periods of time.
- The Working Model of Memory (Baddeley and Hitch, 1974) says that memory is a more active process that allows us to hold information whilst it is being interpreted using previously stored memories.
- The Levels of Processing Model of Memory (Craik and Lockhart, 1972) says that memory is not necessarily a set of stores, but that we remember as a by-product of how we process information. The deeper the processing, the more lasting the memory will be.
- The Spreading Activation Model of Semantic Memory (Collins and Loftus, 1975) proposes a more complex system of organisation for long-term memory, regarding information as connected by meaning and meaningful distance between stored ideas and objects.
- The Reconstructive Theory of Memory (Bartlett, 1932) proposes an alternative view of memory as a constantly updating system, using new and old information and experiences to interpret stored information. We make mental notes and later have to interpret these notes to make sense of them. Memory is therefore prone to distortion.

You also need to be able to describe, apply and evaluate the Cue-dependent Theory of Forgetting, and one other theory.

◆ Studies

Key studies in cognitive psychology allow us to study in depth a characteristic of memory or forgetting. You need to be able to describe and evaluate Godden and Baddeley's (1975) study of context-dependent recall, and one other from:
- Peterson and Peterson's (1959) interference of rehearsal experiment
- Craik and Tulving's (1975) levels of processing experiment
- Ramponi's (2004) age and levels of processing experiment.

◆ Key issues

You need to be able to describe and explain one key issue relevant to the Cognitive Approach by drawing on theories, ideas and studies you have learnt. You also need to prepare to use the concepts, theories and studies you have learnt to explain an issue that you may be presented with in the exam.

◆ Evidence of practice

- You are required to plan and conduct an experiment on a topic relevant to the Cognitive Approach. Be prepared to comment on planning decisions that you have made and the data you collected. Make sure you can use appropriate psychological terminology relating to the experimental method and can justify your design decisions.
- You also need to be able to present and comment upon specific descriptive statistics, such as mean, median and mode and measures of dispersion such as range. Make sure you know how data can be presented in the form of a bar chart, histogram or frequency graph.
- A large part of your experiment will be the discussion of findings in terms of objectivity, reliability, and validity, so prepare to comment on each of these criteria in the exam.

Examzone ———————————————— Practise

Section B questions

1. Levels of Processing Theory suggests the depth of processing affects how much will be learned. Identify one level of processing and explain how it might be tested. (3 marks)

2. Evaluate the Levels of Processing Theory. (5 marks)

3. Suggest ways cue-dependent forgetting may be overcome. (3 marks)

4. Describe one theory of memory other than Levels of Processing. (4 marks)

5. Compare the Levels of Processing Theory with one other theory of memory you have studied. (4 marks)

Section C questions

6. Evaluate Godden and Baddeley's study into cue-dependent memory. (6 marks)

7. Most people can remember where they were and what they were doing when they first heard the news about the "Twin Towers" terrorist bombings in 2001. Use your knowledge of cognitive psychology to describe and evaluate explanations for how such memories are created. (12 marks: 6 AO1, 6 AO2)

8. As part of your course you devised and conducted an experiment on a topic from the Cognitive Approach. Describe the study you undertook. You must include details and justifications as appropriate regarding the design, ethical considerations and procedure of your study. (8 marks)

MCQ

3. Psychodynamic Approach: Freud

Key terms

- id, ego, superego
- oral, anal, phallic, latency and genital stages
- repression
- Oedipus complex
- defence mechanisms
- conscious, preconscious, unconscious

What you will learn about in this chapter

- Sigmund Freud – his research, theories, practices and influence on society in the 20th century and today.
- The conscious and unconscious mind (the 'iceberg' model) and theories of its workings, including neuroses, dreams, repression and memory, and the role of psychoanalysis.
- Psychosexual development, including the role of the id, ego and superego (Freud's explanation of personality), five stages of development and the Oedipus complex.

What you need to know

- You must be able to describe and evaluate Freud's theory of psychosexual development.
- You must be able to describe two defence mechanisms, including repression, and one other such as denial, regression and projection.
- You must be able to evaluate Freud's theory as an explanation of gender development and behaviour.
- You must be able to describe and evaluate research methods, including psychodynamic ones.

Defining the Psychodynamic Approach

The Psychodynamic Approach is about the mind (*psyche*) and about energy (*dynamic*). The idea is that people have a certain amount of energy, and if much of that energy is needed to deal with the past then there might not be enough left to move forward in life. It is about developing in a mentally healthy way and about curing neuroses. The way to do this is by releasing energy by exposing unconscious wishes and desires and making them conscious. Neuroses are mental problems that can be understood by the individual, as opposed to psychoses, where there is no insight. Insight is important in understanding unconscious thoughts in order to release them, so neuroses are treated, not psychoses.

Sigmund Freud, born in Austria in 1856, is the main person involved in the approach, with some of his followers breaking away to develop their own theories, such as Jung and Adler. There are also more modern versions of the approach but for this year of the course you will only consider Freud's ideas.

◆ Who was Freud?

Freud lived in Vienna, in 'high' society in Austria, and treated people who were often quite wealthy. He trained as a doctor and as a young man was horrified at the lack of knowledge and treatment for mentally ill people. He was an ambitious man with a high opinion of his own ability.

▲ The couch Freud's patients used for psychoanalysis

He developed a grand theory, focused on helping those who were mentally ill, and had the confidence to put forward what was then and is now a brave and perhaps outrageous explanation of human development.

Although you are almost sure to question some of his ideas, it is worth noting that almost 100 years after his death his views still provoke discussion. Many academics reject his explanations, but his theory is included here because it offers an alternative explanation for development and adds useful ideas about what science is – and what it is not. Freud's ideas are embedded in our society and his terms (see *Key terms*) are so well known that they are often used without question.

◆ What were Freud's theories?

Many people think that Freud's ideas are all about sex. He thought that energy could be trapped in various developmental stages over the first five years of life. Energy is an instinct, and the basic instincts are hunger, thirst, the need for warmth and a sex drive. In Freud's middle-class Viennese society people were not hungry, thirsty or cold, so the drive that he focused on was the sex drive.

He looked at an individual's need for pleasure and thought this was linked to various **erogenous zones**. The baby's need for pleasure focuses on the mouth (the oral stage), the toddler's on the anus (the anal stage), and the young child's on the genitals (the phallic stage). If a child is **fixated** at one of these stages (meaning they do not get the right amount of pleasure) then energy is used up dealing with that. This can lead to adult mental health problems.

Freud focused on neuroses, which are mental problems that the individual can be aware of (like phobias), rather than psychoses, which are mental problems where the individual has lost touch with reality (like schizophrenia). As Freud's cure was listening and analysing, helping the individual to understand their fixations, he needed to focus on people who could bring an understanding to their own symptoms.

A main focus of Freud's theory was how the unconscious is by far the largest part of the mind and has great influence on the individual, even though it cannot by definition be known. The individual does not know they are fixated, for example, and does not know that they experience the **Oedipus complex** (the idea that the boy, when aged about four, has sexual feelings for his mother in the phallic stage. He then fears his father as a rival, so to resolve the conflict he identifies with – becomes – the father and takes on his behaviour). All this and more is held in the unconscious, including material we cannot face such as traumas that we repress. Another main focus of the theory is on the first five years of life, where the main stages are worked through. The issues that can arise if this is not done successfully are covered in more depth later in this chapter.

Have you ever wondered?

Why do adults smoke, chew pens, suck their thumbs or reach for chocolate when they are anxious? The Psychodynamic Approach offers an unusual explanation for such behaviour, as well as why we have disturbing dreams and why we often choose someone like our opposite sex parent to have a relationship with.

Taking it further

Freud would ask his patient lying on the couch to tell him their worries – without censorship – and to describe their dreams. He would listen intently and analyse what they said. Dreams about climbing stairs could be about sexual intercourse, or animals might represent parents. The patient would listen to Freud's explanation. If it was accepted, the patient felt better. Freud saw this as proof for his ideas. If it was rejected, Freud saw this as proof that it was the right explanation, because why else would the patient resist? So Freud was going to be right whatever the situation.

Examiner's tip

Throughout the chapter make a list of terms that you need to explain to yourself and make up a definition for them that you understand. The glossary at the end of this book will help, but using your own words will help your revision. If you need to, make up ways of remembering them. For example, for the five psychosexual stages (oral, anal, phallic, latency and genital) you could remember them by the pretend newspaper headline 'OAP Loves Gardening'.

Methodology

What you need to know

- For this approach the main areas you need to know about are the case study research method (both in general and how Freud used it), longitudinal and cross-sectional ways of carrying out studies, and correlational designs.
- You need to know about issues of validity, reliability, subjectivity, objectivity and generalisability with regard to qualitative data. Freud's case studies have been criticised as not being credible, and you need to know about such criticisms, as well as ethical issues involved in using case study data.
- Other issues covered in this chapter include sampling methods and the use of correlational designs. You will for the first time look at carrying out a statistical test.

The case study research method

Case studies involve studying one unique individual (or small group or particular programme) and gathering in-depth, detailed and rich data about that individual. Within a case study many research methods are used, such as observations, questionnaires, interviews, experiments and case histories. Case histories gather qualitative data and find out the story of the individual. As much other data as is suitable and possible is then gathered, to achieve the required depth. Triangulation is used, which means pooling all the data from the various research methods and looking for common themes and trends.

Freud's style of case study

Freud used case studies to gather in-depth, detailed data about an individual, and to this extent he used case studies in a standard way. He used methods such as free association, dream analysis and slips of the tongue to try to uncover unconscious wishes and desires. Freud used his case studies not only as a research method but also as a therapy, as he used psychoanalysis to help his patients (analysands) to uncover their repressed memories.

◆ Research methods in Freud's case studies

- One method Freud used was free association, which is where the analysand allows a stream of consciousness out, and the analyst listens to find connections with the aim of uncovering unconscious wishes.
- Freud also used dream and symbol analysis. This is where the analysand describes a dream and the analyst looks for meaning in the dream. The manifest content of the dream is the description of the dream itself and the latent content of the dream is the underlying unconscious thoughts that are revealed through the manifest content by analysis of symbols. The analyst interprets the symbols to find the latent content.

ANS

Question 1

Case studies are useful in psychology. Describe the main features of a case study.

▲ Freud used dream analysis.

- A third method used by Freud is analysis of slips of the tongue, which is where the analysand uses the wrong word for something. Freud thought these mistakes revealed unconscious desires. An example would be saying 'erection' instead of 'election'. Much of Freud's analysis of symbols consists of sexual analysis.

◆ Strengths and weaknesses of case studies

Strengths

Case studies are useful because they are often the only way of studying a particular phenomenon and they can gather data that cannot be obtained by other means. Another strength is that they produce valid data. This is because the data comes fairly directly from the people concerned, and is usually gathered in their natural surroundings.

Weaknesses

Case studies are not replicable because the situation is unique. Also, another researcher at another moment in time might gather different data. If they are not replicable, they cannot be tested for reliability.

Another weakness is that it is hard to use the results and say they are true of other situations. This concerns generalisability – if results come from one unique individual or small group, the findings cannot be generalised.

◆ Strengths and weaknesses of Freud's case studies

- One strength is that they can be used to help the patient as well as to gather data. They are therapeutic and have a practical application.
- Another strength is that they use special means to uncover unconscious thoughts that cannot otherwise be accessed, and Freud had to develop special ways of gathering data from such a complex situation.
- A weakness is that the analyst has to do a lot of interpretation so could be subjective, whereas scientific study requires objectivity.
- Another weakness is that the concepts, such as the unconscious, are not measurable and so are hard to test in a scientific way. This means that conclusions might be drawn but there can never really be any proof.

Issues surrounding case studies – qualitative data, ethical issues, credibility

You need to look at particular issues when evaluating case studies, including issues about qualitative data, ethical issues and issues about credibility of results.

◆ Evaluating qualitative data

Qualitative data is where quality, detail and opinions are gathered, rather than the numbers which are involved in quantitative data. Case studies gather a lot of qualitative data; indeed Freud's case studies only gathered qualitative data.

ANS

Question 2

Freud's case study method was perhaps unique. Compare Freud's case study research method with the general case study research method.

Examiner's tip

Whenever strengths and weaknesses are presented in the text, make a bullet point list or make your own notes for revision so that you can easily answer questions about strengths and weaknesses. Making bullet point lists is useful, although remember in the exam to write in prose and make your points very clearly.

ANS

Question 3

Case studies can be useful but also have weaknesses. Outline two strengths and two weaknesses of case studies.

Question 4

Qualitative data is liked by some people because it seems to be about real behaviour and emotions. However, there are problems with using qualitative data. Describe and evaluate the use of qualitative data in research.

Taking it further

Look at the British Psychological Guidelines issued by the British Psychological Society (www.bps.org.uk), especially as they concern confidentiality and privacy.

ANS

Question 5

Do you think qualitative data is easily analysed? Describe and evaluate how it is analysed.

ANS

Question 6

Describe how confidentiality and privacy have been maintained in psychological research, and when they have not.

ANS

Question 7

Freud's theory is probably the one that is either loved or hated most in psychology. Describe and evaluate issues of credibility with regards to Freud's theory and ideas.

A strength of qualitative data is that it tends to be valid because it is in-depth, rich and detailed, and so 'real life'. Another strength is that using qualitative data is sometimes the only way to study the required area, as Freud found. A weakness is that qualitative data is hard to generalise to other situations, because the depth and detail of the data mean that it is unique. A further weakness is that qualitative data is gathered in a specific situation, often by one individual, and can be affected by subjectivity. Freud in particular gathered qualitative data that needed interpretation, so there was likely to be some subjectivity. This means that there is not the objectivity that is needed for a scientific body of knowledge to be built up.

◆ Analysis of qualitative data

Qualitative data is analysed by drawing out themes and trends to summarise the data and draw conclusions. Triangulation helps to draw such conclusions, where data gathered from different sources is compared for similarities. Issues of validity, reliability, generalisability, subjectivity and objectivity are important, and using different methods with triangulation helps with regard to these issues.

If data from different sources is similar, then that is a type of reliability, where data is gathered again and the same results found. Also, if data is confirmed by different means then that shows validity, as it strongly suggests that the data is 'true' and represents real life. So, although usually it is claimed that qualitative data is valid but not reliable, such data is reliable to some extent.

Drawing out themes from qualitative data can be seen as subjective, because the researcher has to interpret the data. Though when drawing out themes the researcher will always take care to present evidence to demonstrate objectivity.

As qualitative data is rich and detailed and looks at one unique individual, it is usually claimed that results and conclusions from such data cannot be generalised to other people and other situations.

As it is generally claimed that qualitative data lacks objectivity, reliability and generalisability, research methods gathering such data is usually said to be unscientific.

◆ Case studies and ethical issues

The British Psychological Society (BPS) has strict guidelines with regard to ethics and psychology. Five main ethical issues are considered in the chapter that looks at the Social Approach. Confidentiality and privacy are also very important because one unique individual (or small group or programme) is studied and they might be identifiable. Guidelines clearly state that all data must be confidential and every effort must be made to safeguard the individual's privacy.

◆ Freud's case studies and credibility

Freud's work has been criticised for being incredible – literally unbelievable. His explanations for neuroses were based very strongly on interpretations of unconscious desires, and he saw these as sexual. Many people do not find his ideas credible – for example the idea that at around five years old a boy has a sexual desire for his mother and a fear of his father (the Oedipus complex discussed later in this chapter).

Masson (1989) went further and criticised psychoanalysis in three ways:
- The interpretation of the analyst can push the patient towards certain values and goals that may not be their own, so there is an issue of the power of the analyst over the analysand.
- There is gender bias in Freud's work. For example, boys are focused on more than girls – girls are held to have a less strong **identification** and so weaker moral development.
- There is undue emphasis on sexual matters, particularly where **transference** occurs, which is about the patient having feelings for the analyst. This is ethically very sensitive.

These three ethical issues – power, gender and sexual issues – are important when considering the ethical implications and issues of credibility of Freud's work.

Correlational designs

Freud's theories are difficult to test but one way of testing them is to use a **correlational design** and **self-report data**. Freud did not use this methodology but it is useful for testing his ideas. Self-report data is data the participant provides about themselves, for example through a questionnaire. It is usual, when gathering self-report data, to include **rating scales**. Rating scales give **ordinal data**.

There are, for the purposes of your course, three main **levels of measurement**. The first level is **nominal**, where categories are recorded, such as 'yes/no' answers or gender (male/female). The second level is ordinal data, which is ranked data, such as when someone rates something on a scale. The third level is **interval/ratio data**, which is data where there is a real measurement such as height or time.

Correlational designs are not repeated measures, independent groups or matched pairs. They involve the same participant providing data for two measures, but they are not really repeated measures because correlations are a different sort of test. Correlations have two variables but both are important and there is not an independent and a dependent variable – both are measured. It is not suggested that one variable causes the other, just that they are related. In a correlation it is not a difference between two variables (the IV and DV) that is looked for but a relationship between them.

Taking it further

In gender bias, **alpha bias** is where differences between the genders are emphasised and **beta bias** is where similarities are focused on. For alpha bias, the bias is that often the differences are 'against' females, so there is a feminist argument that this is biased, and Freud's theories can be said to show alpha bias. For beta bias, the bias is that gender behaviour can be different, so these differences should not be overlooked.

Another criticism, again from Masson (1984), was against Freud's ideas about the Oedipus complex and the Electra complex – where there is said to be identification with the same sex parent in order to resolve conflict over desiring the opposite sex parent and fearing the same sex parent as a rival. At one stage Freud thought that he had uncovered real child abuse but subsequently dismissed this because he felt it could not happen to so many people and, looking back to his own childhood, felt it just could not be true. Masson claimed that what Freud found in those with neuroses did indeed stem from early abuse, which is a more credible explanation perhaps than the conflict in the phallic stage that Freud suggested.

One way of learning the three levels of measurement is to think of temperature. A day can be hot or cold, and this is developing categories, so the data is nominal. A day can be ranked according to heat such as on a scale of 1 to 5, with 5 being very hot and 1 being very cold (ordinal data). Alternatively a day's temperature itself can be recorded as a number, which is interval/ratio data.

Question 8

It is important to be able to define terms in psychology. Outline what is meant by 'self-report data' and 'rating scales'.

ANS

Question 9

What is the difference between a negative correlation, a positive correlation and no correlation at all?

◆ Positive and negative correlations

A **correlation** is a relationship between two variables measured on a scale and where both measures come from one individual. A positive correlation is where one variable rises and the other rises as well, such as: *As IQ rises, income rises.* A negative correlation is where one variable rises and the other falls, such as: *As IQ rises, a score of mental disorder falls* – the higher the IQ, the less likely you are to have mental health problems. One correlation that has been found within the Psychodynamic Approach (Bachrach et al., 1991) is that the longer psychoanalysis takes place, the better the outcome. This is a positive correlation – the longer the time (in years), the better the outcome (measured on a rating scale, where high numbers mean healthier).

◆ Testing for correlations

One way of checking for a correlation is to gather the data and then rank the scores for the two sets of data separately. Compare the ranks. If high ranks for one set of scores go with high ranks for the other set, then there is a positive correlation. If high ranks for one set of scores go with low ranks for the other set, there is a negative correlation. If the ranks don't seem to vary together at all, there is no correlation.

Another way of checking for a correlation is to draw a scattergraph of the two sets of scores and then a line of best fit. If there are equal numbers of scores on each side of the line of best fit, and the line is straight, with the scores being quite close to the line, then this is a strong enough relationship to be a correlation. If the line goes up from bottom left to the top right, it shows a positive correlation. If the line goes down from the top left to the bottom right, it shows a negative correlation.

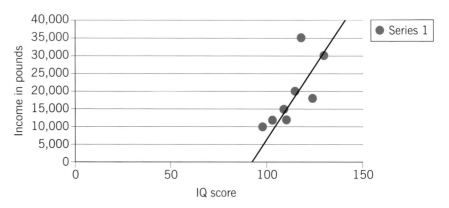

▶ Scattergraph to show the relationship between IQ and income for the 8 participants.

The final way of checking for a correlation is to carry out a statistical test. Descriptive statistics are explained in Chapter 2, the Cognitive Approach (see page 66). The mean, median, mode, and range are descriptive statistics.

Inferential statistics are statistical tests that can do more than describe the data, they can suggest how strong the difference or relationship is. For your course you will study three inferential tests – **Spearman's Rank Correlation Coefficient**, the Mann-Whitney test and the **Chi-Squared** test of association.

The Spearman's Rank Correlation Coefficient test is the one you will use for correlational data. This test relies on the rankings of the scores to see if they co-vary (are related) closely enough to draw firm conclusions. A perfect positive correlation gives a result of $+1$ and a perfect negative correlation gives a result of -1. No correlation at all gives a result of 0. So the closer the test result is to 1 ($+$ or $-$) the stronger the correlation. To see if the correlation is strong enough, the result needs to be looked up in tables.

◆ Spearman's Rank Correlation Coefficient (Spearman's rho)

There is some terminology to understand with regard to inferential statistical tests, because you need to know what the tests are for and what their 'results' mean. You will learn more about this in the next two chapters.

The Spearman's test looks at the rankings for the two sets of scores and carries out a test to see if the ranks for each score for the same person are similar enough or different. If they are similar enough, then it can be said that there is a correlation. A Spearman's test is carried out if:

- what is being tested is a relationship, not a difference, between two scores
- the level of measurement is ordinal or interval/ratio (with neither score a category such as yes/no or male/female)
- the type of design is a correlation (not a test of difference, so not repeated measures, independent groups, or matched pairs), and this means the same participant gives both scores.

The formula for the test is $r_s = 1 - \frac{6\Sigma d^2}{N(N^2-1)}$. This looks perhaps a bit confusing if you are not used to mathematical calculations, but the test can be carried out step-by-step, which makes it quite easy.

The Spearman test for correlations produces the statistic **rho** and, for the example worked through in this chapter, rho is 0.83. This is a long way away from 0 and is likely to be a significant result. As the sign is positive ($+$), if there is a correlation it is a positive one (as IQ rises, income rises).

The test here is significant, and there is a positive correlation, which would be expected with such a high figure as 0.83. The **critical value** from the tables, which is the figure to be matched or to be above, is 0.64 at a **0.05 level of significance** (one tailed). 0.83 is higher than 0.64 and so significant. Levels of significance are covered in the Biological Approach and the Learning Approach.

◆ Strengths and weaknesses of correlational designs

Strengths

- There is little manipulation of variables. Measures are often taken of existing situations with few controls needed – which can make for a straightforward design. The two measures are taken and the scores tested to see if there is a relationship. This is quite straightforward compared with some experiments, observations and surveys.
- Correlations can show relationships that might not be expected and so can be used to point towards new areas for research.

How to

ANS

Question 10

When would you use a Spearman's test?

Weaknesses

- A relationship is found but without finding out whether the two variables are causally or chance related. When looking to build a scientific body of knowledge it is usual to claim cause and effect relationships between things. For example, when a correlation was found between smoking and risk of heart disease (the more you smoke, the greater the risk of heart disease), this was not accepted by many smokers because it was not claimed at the time that smoking causes heart disease.
- Correlational designs tend to lack validity because at least one of the variables often has to be operationalised, which tends to make it unnatural. Examples are IQ or mental health score. Whenever a score is manufactured there is always the chance that it is not really measuring anything useful.

Longitudinal and cross-sectional designs, and sampling

For this part of your course you need to know about two ways of organising studies – longitudinal and cross-sectional designs. You also need to know about some sampling methods, though they are described in full in the Social Approach, so are not covered again in depth here.

◆ Longitudinal studies

Longitudinal studies are those that follow one set of participants over time, using research methods such as experiment, survey or observation. Freud studied individuals, rather than comparing groups, so did not carry out longitudinal studies in the usual way. There are, however, longitudinal studies within the Psychodynamic Approach, such as the Messinger one detailed in Bachrach et al (1991). The important points about longitudinal studies are that the participants are the same, and that measures are taken over time so that comparisons can be made. A study can last months or years. For example, a study of infants' language development over the first year would be a longitudinal one, as would the study of children through to adulthood, perhaps to see the effect of their language ability on their career paths.

◆ Strengths and weaknesses of longitudinal studies

Strengths

- Longitudinal studies are useful for looking at developmental trends. They are the main way to see how an individual's development affects certain characteristics.
- They use the same participants, which means that participant variables (variables between the individuals taking part) will not give bias in the results.

Weaknesses

In practice, it can be difficult to keep all the participants for each of the measures, and people can drop out. This means the sample can become

Taking it further

Use the internet or another source to find a longitudinal study and study the conclusions drawn. There are many studies that follow a group of children through to adulthood.

biased if it systematically excludes certain people (such as those who move house a lot, or those who are shy).

The researchers may themselves change over time, due to moving on or losing funding. This can affect the study, as relationships with the participants may differ.

◆ Cross-sectional studies

Cross-sectional studies are often seen as the opposite of longitudinal studies. They are measures taken at one moment in time instead of over a period. A cross-section of the population is chosen and then those people's results on some measure are compared. A cross-sectional study of language development, for example, would be to look at two-year-olds in an area and five-year-olds in the same area and compare their language skills. This would be instead of waiting until the two-year-olds had become five-year-olds and then comparing that group's language development, which would be a longitudinal study. A cross-sectional study uses two different groups of participants rather than the same participants.

◆ Strengths and weaknesses of cross-sectional studies

Strengths
- They gather immediate results. Immediate results are useful because they are easier to carry out in practice. They are also cheaper, because researchers only have to be in the area once, and can organise the study more easily than if they have to return, perhaps years later.
- They are more ethical than longitudinal studies because the measures are only taken once, rather than imposing on participants more often.

Weaknesses
- Different participants are used in the conditions, so participant variables can affect the results. For example, if the two-year-olds and five-year-olds are different children, their language skills might not be comparable because of different upbringing and experiences.
- There are many different variables in the two (or more) situations being tested that cannot be controlled, for example the environment of the two groups, their background or their friendship groups.

◆ Sampling – random, stratified, volunteer (self-selected), opportunity

Some different ways of sampling to get participants for studies are described in the chapter on the Social Approach, and they are mentioned again here, as you also need to know them for Unit 2. See page 10 for details.

Examiner's tip

Longitudinal and cross-sectional studies are usually compared, because to investigate areas like development you can only choose one or the other (though the research methods can vary). For example, you could carry out observations longitudinally or using a cross-sectional approach, so it is useful to be able to compare them. Draw up a table to show the similarities and differences between them, ready for your revision.

Question 11

Compare longitudinal and cross-sectional designs in terms of their strengths and weaknesses.

Content

What you need to know

- You need to know about specific aspects of Freud's work. His main theory was about psychosexual development, including the five stages of psychosexual development, the Oedipus complex, and the parts of the personality associated with the first three stages of development.
- You need to know about Freud's explanation for gender development.
- You need to know about repression and one other defence mechanism, such as displacement, denial, projection and regression.

Freud's theory of personality

Freud suggested that there are three aspects to the personality – the id, the ego and the superego. The personality develops through the first five years of childhood. The id is the first part to develop, and is the instructive part. The ego then develops, which is the rational part of the personality, and it is through the ego that the id gets what it wants. The superego is the third aspect of the personality and acts on the morality principle, developing last in the first five years of childhood. As the superego develops the ego has not only to seek to satisfy the id, but also satisfy the superego as well.

For the adult the personality should be balanced, with the ego successfully managing the needs of both the id and the superego. It is when this balance is lost, such as when the id or the superego is more in control, that neuroses occur and the individual has problems. One way of maintaining a balance between the id, the ego and the superego is to stop some thoughts and desires becoming conscious – defence mechanisms perform this function. The personality develops through psychosexual stages, These issues are explained in this section.

◆ The role of the unconscious in Freud's theory

One of Freud's main assumptions was the power of the unconscious mind, which he claimed was by far the largest part of the mind, and was inaccessible by normal means. However, he came up with some ways of 'tricking' the information out of it, as explained in the methodology section of this chapter. He suggested we have the conscious mind, which contains what we know about, the preconscious mind, which we don't know about but can access (such as memories), and the unconscious, which we cannot access.

As well as being filled with instincts and energy and being what could be called the biological aspect of the mind, the unconscious holds material from a person's everyday experiences. Some thoughts and wishes are kept in the unconscious and not made conscious. The means by which people avoid allowing (though not consciously) threatening wishes and thoughts to become conscious is by means of defence mechanisms.

Examiner's tip

Gender development is an important aspect of your course because this approach and the next two you will study (the Biological Approach and the Learning Approach) all offer different explanations for gender development or behaviour. You need to understand all three explanations and be able to evaluate and compare them.

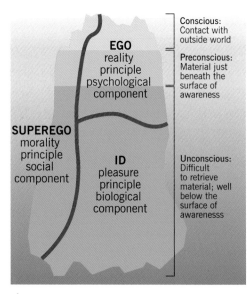

▲ Freud's 'iceberg' model of personality

◆ Defence mechanisms

Defence mechanisms (often called ego defence mechanisms) are ways of protecting the ego when there is conflict between the demands of the id and the superego, when the id itself makes conflicting demands, or when the ego is under threat from some outside force. If a person overuses defence mechanisms they can lose touch with reality, such as if denial is overused. The five defence mechanisms considered here are:

- **Repression**, which refers to not remembering something because it cannot be accessed, needing to remain in the unconscious to protect the personality.
- **Displacement**, which refers to putting unacceptable thoughts or wishes onto something or someone other than their real focus.
- **Denial**, which refers to refusing to acknowledge threatening thoughts altogether.
- **Projection**, which refers to saying that threatening thoughts or emotions are someone else's thoughts and desires.
- **Regression**, which refers to going back to a childhood state.

Freud's five stages of psychosexual development

According to Freud there are five stages that everyone passes through – oral, anal, phallic, latency and genital. The first three are focused on more as they are the ones that span those important first five years.

At each stage the libido (sexual pleasure drive) is focused on this one area. If a stage is not resolved there is fixation, which occurs when there is frustration or overindulgence. Frustration is when needs are not met and overindulgence is where needs are met too much so that the child does not move on. Either frustration or overindulgence will lock some libido in that stage, causing fixation. Normal development of personality will occur if no libido is locked into a stage, but if fixation occurs then the child will want to gain satisfaction from that stage when an adult.

◆ The oral stage

The oral stage lasts from birth to around 18 months. The mouth is the focus of pleasure. If fixated at the oral stage because of frustration, either if not nursed or if nursing stops too soon, the adult is characterised as envious, pessimistic and sarcastic. If the child is overindulged, with too much nursing, then the adult is characterised as optimistic, admiring of others and gullible. The oral character can be either of these things.

◆ The anal stage

The anal stage lasts from around one and a half to two and a half years old. Toilet training brings a focus of pleasure on the anus and with expulsion or retention of faeces. If parents are too lenient and the child gets pleasure from making a mess, the adult will form an anal expulsive character, and is messy, reckless and disorganised. If the child refuses to go and that is not overcome, the adult will develop an anal retentive character, because the child has gained pleasure from holding back. An anal retentive character is obstinate, careful and precise.

Taking it further

Visit the online Freud museum (www.freud.org.uk) to explore Freud's life further. There is a lot of information there, including historical documents. Or, if you can, visit the actual museum (or the Freud museum in Vienna, which was his home).

◆ The phallic stage

The **phallic stage** is the third of Freud's psychosexual stages and the erogenous zone or focus of pleasure is the genital region. This lasts from around three to five years. In this stage boys experience the Oedipus complex (Electra complex for girls). Through the Oedipus complex boys adopt their gender behaviour. An adult fixated at the phallic stage would develop a **phallic character** – self-assured, reckless, vain and proud. They might also be incapable of loving someone. Freud also suggested that fixation at this stage was the reason for homosexuality.

◆ The latency period

The **latency period** is not really a psychosexual stage of development because there is no sexual drive in this period. It is more of a resting period – but is usually considered to be part of the five stages. There is repression of desires. Children form same-sex friendships and focus on school and sport.

◆ The genital stage

The **genital stage** is the fifth stage (counting latency as a stage) and starts with puberty. The libido focuses again on the genitals, as in the phallic stage, and there is a formation of heterosexual friendships and relationships. If there is little libido energy being taken up by unresolved conflicts in the earlier three stages, then there is enough energy in the genital stage for 'normal' relationships to be formed. If the person is fixated at the phallic stage in particular, they will have difficulties with relationships because of repression and defence mechanisms.

Freud's explanation of gender development

Freud thought that gender behaviour is learnt during the phallic stage, which starts at around three years old and where the erogenous zone is the genital area for both boys and girls. In this stage the superego develops and with it gender behaviour. The Oedipus complex is the key to gender development for boys, and the Electra complex is the key for girls.

◆ The Oedipus complex

The Oedipus complex comes from the boy's natural love for his mother. The libido focuses on the genital area and so this natural love becomes sexual. Freud held that the father then stands in the way of the boy's feelings, because of the father's relationship with the mother, so the boy feels aggression towards the father and love for the mother. All this is at an unconscious level.

Freud also felt that, as parents tell a son off for masturbating, this causes anxiety and fear. A boy at this age will notice that women don't have a penis, and the fear is focused on **castration fear**, as the boy fears his father will castrate him. Castration fear is stronger than the desire to possess the mother, so the desire is repressed.

Examiner's tip

Prepare a definition of each stage of psychosexual development. Consider three aspects of each stage – the approximate age, the personality characteristic (such as the id in the oral stage), and the erogenous zone. Then make a note of the adult characteristic(s) too, so that you can answer a question on the characteristics of the stage and/or what fixation it is likely to lead to.

Taking it further

Jed Rubenfield has recently written a fictional novel about murder in America, which might not seem connected with your course at all! However, the novel involves Freud, Jung, Ernest Jones and others involved with Freud at the time (and some new fictional characters as well). It is about Freud's work in many ways, and much of the history is factually correct.

Read the novel to get background to Freud's ideas, but be sure to separate fact from fiction. The author explains which is which at the end of the book. The book is called *The Interpretation of Murder*. Alternatively, find a review of the book on the internet or look at related sites that explain more of Freud's theory.

This is called the Oedipus complex after the Greek legend about Oedipus, who killed his father Laius and married his mother Jocasta – though he did not know how they were related to him at the time.

Freud thought that unconsciously the boy wishes to do the same – to kill his father and marry his mother. This conflict has to be resolved by the ego to satisfy the demands of the id, and the love and fear can be reconciled if the boy identifies with his father, as if 'becoming' the father. In this way the castration fear is removed and the boy can in some way possess the mother as he wishes to. The boy, therefore, does what his father does, and in absorbing his father's approach to social rules the boy develops the superego. The boy learns to be male by identifying with his father and 'becoming' him. Once the Oedipus complex is resolved the latency period begins. Much of the evidence for the Oedipus complex comes from the case study of Little Hans (see page 86).

◆ The Electra complex

In a similar way, girls learn their gender behaviour by identifying with their mothers but Freud was more vague about the conflict for girls, which is called the **Electra complex**. Freud thought that, at around the same age, girls find out that women have no penis.

This is **penis envy**, which is similar to the castration fear experienced by boys. The girl identifies with her mother and learns her gender role in that way because she can then possess her father. However, Freud thought that this process is never complete and is not resolved as the Oedipus complex is resolved for boys. Freud believed that a girl always remains a little fixated in the phallic stage, though she does pass into the latency period once she has identified with her mother, and she develops the superego in the phallic stage, as a boy does.

Evaluation of Freud's theory

Freud's work is probably easier to evaluate in general rather than looking at specific aspects of it. For the course you need to be able to evaluate his theory of psychosexual development, including the five stages of development, the Oedipus complex, and the parts of personality associated with the first three stages. You also need to evaluate his theory about the development of gender behaviour.

◆ Strengths of the theory

One strength of Freud's theory is its completely novel approach to explaining mental disorders. In Freud's time treatment was very limited, if there was any at all. Another strength is that his methods were unique and developed specifically for his own purpose, to which they were well suited. Freud needed to find out what was in a person's unconscious and, as that person could not access that material, he needed to use special methods to uncover it.

▲ Identifying with the same sex parent resolves the Oedipus or Electra complex.

Taking it further

Freud was fascinated by how the play *Hamlet* was loved by all audiences. Hamlet famously should have taken revenge against a man who killed Hamlet's father and married his mother. However, he could not do this, as shown in his famous speech 'To be or not to be'. The play focuses around this inability to act. Freud thought that Hamlet could not do this because his unconscious wish was to kill his father and marry his mother, so in killing a man who had done just that he would be killing himself.

Using the internet or another source, look up this analysis of why the play has such universal appeal. Jones (1954) discusses this issue. Understanding the argument about Hamlet will help you to understand the Oedipus complex.

Freud also tried to be scientific and rigorous in his work. He is usually said to be rigid and to interpret data from his own ideas rather than being open-minded, and later the Little Hans study is criticised for just this reason – that it involved bias. This is because not only was Freud looking for evidence of the Oedipus complex from the start when analysing Little Hans, but the boy's father and mother were also followers of Freud's and knew about his theory before gathering the data. However, it can be seen as a strength that Freud was not as subjective as might be thought. He famously said 'sometimes a cigar is just a cigar' to show that not all symbols in dreams had hidden meaning. He was also unwilling to analyse dreams out of context, only doing so as part of a complete psychoanalysis. He agreed too that dreams did hold content from the day's events that could be used as symbols, but that were also likely to be just from those events.

◆ Weaknesses of the theory

An important weakness is the lack of evidence that could be called scientific, because Freud's methods required subjective interpretation. Freud drew his ideas from his own experiences, which is a subjective way of building a theory, involving interpretation.

Another weakness is that Freud's concepts are not measurable. Science requires data to be measurable, so that someone else can repeat a study and see if they come up with the same results. Freud's concepts are not measurable because the id, ego, superego and unconscious are not 'real' in the sense that they can be accessed and measured.

A further weakness is that Freud used case studies, so it is hard to show reliability since a case study cannot be repeated to test for reliability. Case studies are unique – and Freud's case studies were supposed to be **cathartic** so that the same problems would not occur again.

Another weakness is that Freud drew his conclusions from a small sample of case studies, mainly of middle-class Viennese women. His sample was biased in terms of gender, as he studied few men and only briefly met Little Hans, so did not really study children. There was no range of different classes and types of people. The patients were mainly middle-class and might have had specific neuroses simply because of that. It is hard to generalise from a biased sample to say that ideas are true of a whole population.

Contrasting Freud's explanation of gender development with other theories

In your course you will study two other explanations of gender development and gender behaviour. The Biological Approach looks at how gender behaviour comes from genetic and inherited characteristics. The Learning Approach looks at how gender behaviour comes from interaction with other people and experiences when growing up.

Feature	Psychodynamic	Biological	Learning
Methodology	Dream analysis, free association, case studies	Study of genes, DNA and hormones Scanning Twin studies	Experiments Animal studies
Focus on nature	Inherited focus on unconscious and stage development (nature)	Genes and hormones – born with them (nature)	Born with blank slate – ignores inherited characteristics
Focus on nurture	Parents and society give superego, morals, conscience, gender behaviour	Experience can affect hormones, etc., but generally gender is given	Parents, school, society, peers, TV, other models – all affect how we learn our behaviour, including gender
Scientific	Methods involve interpretation so are not scientific, though Freud aimed for scientific theory	Genes, DNA, hormones – all tested scientifically – focusing on physical elements and measurable	Experiments aim to isolate variables with careful controls, but behaviour as a whole is hard to measure.
Accounts for changes over time	Stage theory covers five years but development is largely fixed by then	Development fixed at birth (and before) to a large extent, but hormonal changes over time, etc.	Continuous development and people change as they are rewarded, etc. – so accounts for changes over time to an extent
Focuses on early years	The first five years and resolving conflicts are important	Biology is given at birth though environment can affect it. Maturation occurs throughout life though (e.g. hormone changes)	Early years are important in forming behaviour, lots of learning happens then, but learning is continuous over life time
Focuses on parental contribution	Parents give gender behaviour through child identifying with (becoming) same sex parent	Parents give genes (50% from each parent)	Parents are main people controlling reinforcements over early years – very important focus

The following table uses the information above to underline briefly the similarities and differences between the three approaches.

▲ Three different explanations for gender behaviour

Feature	Psychodynamic	Biological	Learning
Methodology	Different (unique)	Somewhat similar (experiments and other)	Somewhat similar (experiments)
Focus on nature	Different (partial focus)	Different (almost total focus)	Different (no focus)
Focus on nurture	Different (partial focus)	Different (a little focus)	Different (total focus)
Scientific	Different (not scientific though tried)	Similar (scientific)	Similar (scientific)
Accounts for changes over time	Different (focus on main stages to age five)	Different (focus on inherited characteristics)	Different (focus on continuous development, not stages)
Focuses on early years	Different (strong focus)	Similar (no special focus but important years)	Similar (no special focus but important years)
Focuses on parental contribution	Similar (strong – but different! – influence from parents)	Similar (strong – but different! – influence from parents)	Similar (strong – but different! – influence from parents)

Studies

What you need to know

- You need to know two studies within the Psychodynamic Approach in detail, as well as how to evaluate them in terms of strengths and weaknesses and to compare them.
- This section describes and evaluates one study in detail. Three other studies are then outlined and evaluated.

▲ Sigmund Freud (1856-1939)

Freud's case study of Little Hans (1909)

◆ Aim

Freud studied the case of Little Hans (not his real name) to try to understand the five-year-old boy's phobia of horses and to treat it.

◆ Procedure

Freud used a **case study**, including dream analysis, to research the case of Little Hans. His information came from Hans's father, not from Hans himself, as the father was a follower of Freud's work. Freud met Hans twice, and the study arose from Hans's mother and father documenting his development to test Freud's ideas.

◆ Description of themes

One theme is that Little Hans had an interest in his widdler (his penis). He dreamt about widdlers and about wiping children's bottoms. Hans denied this interest and said it was only in his dreams. When younger, Hans had played with his widdler and his mother had told him off for it.

Another theme was that Hans seemed to want his father to 'go away' on business, and when the family moved house so that his father was away less often, Hans wanted his father dead. Hans was also jealous of his sister, who was born when he was three and a half. The father reported that Hans was afraid of falling under the water when in the bath. Eventually Freud and Hans's father suggested to Hans that, when watching his mother bath his sister, he wished she would let his sister's head go under the water. Hans agreed this was true.

The phobia being treated is a third theme in the case study. Hans said he was afraid that a white horse would bite him. It appeared that he had heard the father of a girl staying with them tell her not to 'put her finger on' the white horse that was drawing the cart to take her to the station. Hans also said that he was afraid of black on horses' mouths and things in front of their eyes. Once, when walking with his mother, he had seen a horse fall down when drawing a bus.

One further theme helps the analysis. This arose when Hans was playing with dolls and 'having children'. His father commented that a boy cannot have children, and Hans said mummy is the children's mummy, Hans is their daddy and Hans's father is the grandfather.

◆ Case study analysis

This is how Freud interpreted Hans's thoughts and reactions:

- When Hans denied interest in widdlers except in dreams, this was evidence of **repression**, pushing unwanted desires into his **unconscious**.
- Hans dreamt about wiping bottoms because he had enjoyed having this done to him, which showed pleasure at the **anal stage**.
- Hans wanted his father to go away or die because he enjoyed being with his mother and having his mother's attention. His jealousy of his sister was evidence of the same desire for his mother.
- Hans's fear of a white horse represented a fear of his father. Freud thought that the fear of black around the horses' mouths and of things in front of their eyes represented adult men with moustaches and glasses on, reinforcing the idea of Hans being afraid of his father.
- When the girl was told not to put her finger on the horse, this reminded Hans of when he was told off for playing with his widdler, which Freud interpreted as **castration fear**.
- When Hans said about the doll that mummy is the mother, Hans is the father and his own father the grandfather, it showed that Hans was now cured, as this was the resolution of the **Oedipus complex**.

◆ Conclusions

Freud thought that his study of Little Hans offered evidence for his psychosexual stages and theory of how gender develops.

◆ Evaluation

Strengths

- Freud gathered information from Hans's father rather than from Hans directly. However, he did try to work on information gained directly from the little boy, when Hans talked freely about his problems (even though to his father), so the data was **valid** to that extent. The data was comprehensive, covering dreams, events, ideas and feelings.
- Freud's focus on sexual matters and unconscious processes has led to psychoanalysis and other psychotherapies being developed. The ideas of the 'talking cure' and the 'listening cure' have been built upon, as is evident in modern counselling techniques.

Weaknesses

- Writing out a case study is likely to involve **subjective interpretation**. If data is interpreted subjectively, it may be interpreted differently by another analyst or researcher, so would not be **reliable**.
- The parents followed Freud's teachings, so the data may be biased.
- There are other explanations. One comes from ideas from Bowlby (1973), who said that a child needs their mother as an attachment figure in their early years or their later development is affected. Perhaps Hans clung to his mother because she had threatened to leave the family (which it appeared was the case).
- Freud's methods are said to be not scientific because his concepts, such as the unconscious and castration fear, are not testable. Conclusions are not scientifically shown and not easily repeated, so are unlikely to be reliable.

Examiner's tip

When learning studies in detail for the exam, focus on **aims**, **procedure**, **results** and **conclusions**. Try to know enough for each of these four sections to answer a question with up to 4 marks – though this is hard for the aims, where questions are more likely to carry only up to 2 marks. (Case studies are described a little differently, as explained on page 88.)

Taking it further

Use the internet or another source to find out more about Herbert Graf, who was 'Little Hans'.

Examiner's tip

Focus on three issues when writing about a case study (like Little Hans). For the exam:

1) Remember four points describing what was done and what was found.
2) Remember four points of analysis – where the researcher(s) explains the description of the study.
3) Remember at least two strengths and at least two weaknesses, for evaluation questions.

D = Describe (4 things)
A = Analyse (4 things)
E = Evaluate (2 strengths and 2 weaknesses)

Other studies from the Psychodynamic Approach

◆ Dibs: Personality development in play therapy (Axline, 1964)

Aim and procedure

Axline, a clinical psychologist, aimed to help Dibs, a five-year-old boy, to unlock whatever was troubling him. It was clear there was a problem because he would not speak or interact with others, and could be aggressive if challenged. She wrote up a case study about Dibs and his play therapy sessions. Dibs's teachers thought they were failing him, so they asked Axline to help. At that stage, nobody really knew the story behind Dibs's silence. They just knew that his mother used to pick him up from school, they did not see his father, and he did not want to go home. The case study was a description rather than an explanation. Axline tried not to interpret what Dibs said and did.

Description of themes

Dibs showed that he was actually a gifted child who could read, spell and understand complex concepts. He used dolls and toy soldiers in the play therapy room to act out situations with his family. He showed hatred for his father by burying a toy soldier he called 'Papa' in the sand (though he did eventually dig him up again). He said he did not like locked rooms or walls. He was angry with his family.

Case study analysis

Dibs worked out his anger through play and seemed happier because of this. Axline did not analyse the case study using theory but Freud's personality theory helps to explain Dibs's behaviour. One explanation is that he had an overcontrolling superego and his ego did not manage to balance the demands of his id and superego. His father used to lock him in his room, which probably explained his dislike of walls and locked doors. His mother had pushed and tested him a lot when he was younger, and he had more stimulation than emotional support. This might have led to his reaction to the testing, which was to maintain silence.

Conclusions

Play therapy allowed Dibs's feelings to be worked through and allowed him to find himself. The overcontrolling superego would mean he had no balanced personality; play therapy allowed a balance to be found.

◆ Effectiveness of psychoanalytic therapies (Bachrach et al., 1991)

Aim and procedure

The aim was to see how effective psychoanalysis is. By using a meta-analysis of many other studies' findings, the researchers were able to draw overall conclusions. They included six studies that had gathered quantitative data and also studies using qualitative data.

OPT

Results

For patients who were suitable (who were able to have insight), there was a success rate of around 60% to 90%. However, only about 50% of those who were thought to be suitable actually gained insight so, although they may have benefited, it might not have been because of analysis as the Psychodynamic Approach sees it.

Conclusions

Those able to have insight did benefit, but so did others, so perhaps it is not the approach to analysis that works but something about the analysis itself. Judging whether someone will benefit is not very successful, so evaluation before treatment could be improved. There were problems with the studies as well. For example, defining terms such as 'suitable' or 'benefit' is not easy and was often done differently in the different studies, making comparisons hard.

◆ Identity, personality and defence mechanisms (Cramer, 1997)

Aim and procedure

Cramer wanted to see if a young person who had made a commitment to goals was less likely to use defence mechanisms than a young person who was 'in crisis'. She thought that the more anxious a person is, such as when in crisis, the more they use defence mechanisms. Ninety-one participants, all 23 years old, male and female, were asked to judge pictures to test their use of defence mechanisms. They were also asked to make judgements about statements so that Cramer could judge their levels of self-esteem and commitment to goals. She sorted participants into one of four types – diffused (not yet reached crisis), foreclosed (adopted goals without a crisis), moratorium (in crisis), and achieved (passed through crisis and adopted own goals).

Results

- Both diffused and moratorium states showed anxiety and the use of the defence mechanism denial. Diffused state also used the defence mechanism **projection**.
- Achieved state showed the least use of defence mechanisms and was low in anxiety.
- Foreclosed state showed a negative correlation with the use of denial and projection, so not only were these defence mechanisms not used but the opposite was found in the way of positive attitudes.
- Self-esteem, low for diffused and moratorium states, was high for both achieved and foreclosed states.
- There were no gender differences in the findings.

Conclusions

A period of crisis goes with the use of defence mechanisms in young people, and both also go with high anxiety and low self-esteem. A commitment to goals and beliefs goes with higher self-esteem, lower anxiety, and a very low use of defence mechanisms. An achieved state gives higher self-esteem than a foreclosed one.

▲ Students comparing their study results.

Key issues

The debate about whether dreams have meaning

Some people claim they don't dream at all; others claim they don't remember their dreams well; others claim they dream often or always. Dreams are measured by rapid eye movements taking place and, if this is a correct measure, it seems that everyone dreams – but this does not show whether dreams have meaning.

◆ Explaining the issue using the Psychodynamic Approach

- Behaviour is governed by unconscious wishes and desires. The id is in the unconscious and is the demanding part of the personality.
- The unconscious mind is powerful and controls much of our thinking and actions.
- The superego gives the personality a conscience containing the demands of society and parents. The ego is the third part of the personality and balances the demands of the id and the superego.
- One way the ego controls the id is through defence mechanisms. Unwanted thoughts and wishes are repressed. They can, however, reveal themselves, such as through Freudian slips and in dreams.
- Dreams have a content that is known, which is the manifest content. The manifest content is what the dreamer says they dream about.
- There is also the latent content, which is the underlying unconscious wish. It can be understood by interpreting the symbols that are the manifest content. The latent content can be decoded and 'means' what the unconscious wants.
- There are other explanations for dreams, such as that they are biological and have no meaning. Thoughts are left over from the day's events, for example, and the brain is still active when the person is asleep so the brain makes sense of these thoughts. This 'sense' is the dream.
- This is a physiological explanation, whereas Freud's is a psychological explanation. The biological evidence appears stronger in our society because the claims are measurable – brains can be scanned whilst the person is asleep, for example. The Psychodynamic Approach has difficulty producing measurable evidence because the unconscious, the id, dream content and the ego are not measurable.
- The Psychodynamic Approach offers little evidence for dreams having an underlying meaning other than that when an analysand is presented with an interpretation of their dream they tend to accept it.

▲ Psychoanalysis can help unlock the hidden meanings of disturbing dreams.

Examiner's tip

Make sure you can describe the issue itself and explain it using concepts from the Psychodynamic Approach.

Summary of three other issues

◆ Using psychoanalysis with abnormal and normal clients

The issue is whether such analysis is suitable for normal clients, abnormal clients, or those who have certain abnormalities only.

- Freud needed his patients to be able to have insight into their problems, so they needed to be 'normal' enough to work with the analyst.
- Freud treated people with neuroses such as hysteria, but not those with psychoses, so he only looked at certain sorts of abnormality.
- Pychoanalysis is also sought out by 'normal' people who want to have greater insight.
- However, concepts from the Psychodynamic Approach, such as the id and the unconscious, are not measurable. Effectiveness of the therapy is not easily measured either, as it has to do with whether a patient has developed an analytic process, which is very hard to judge.

◆ False memory and repression

There have been cases where a person undergoing analysis has 'remembered' traumatic events in their early childhood. Are these real memories or do they arise from suggestions by the therapist?

- The analyst listens to the analysand and then interprets their dreams or what they are saying. The analyst will be looking for interactions between the child and parent and focusing on sexual matters, so the issue of abuse is likely to be of relevance.
- A difficulty here is that the analyst's interpretation might be believed, rather than a true memory remembered.
- A problem with the Psychodynamic Approach is that it is hard to test scientifically.

> One example of false memory syndrome arising from recovered memory therapy is that of Beth Rutherford. During analysis she was asked about abuse. She started to read about abuse and then to dream about it, and her dreams were analysed as being about real abuse. It was later found that she was a virgin, so the recovered memories of sexual abuse were false.

◆ Early childhood experience's and sexual orientation

There are different sexual orientations – heterosexual, homosexual and lesbian relationships. The issue is whether sexual orientation relates to early childhood experiences.

- The Oedipus complex is when the boy, with his sexual energy focused on the genitals, has unconscious feelings for his mother.
- The father is then a rival, and the boy feels guilt, so he must resolve the complex. He does so (unconsciously) by becoming his father.
- If the Oedipus complex is resolved, the boy moves to the latency period and then the genital stage. By now, he will have adopted male gender behaviour. He will become sexual again and seek a female partner, which is what might be called 'normal' sexual orientation.
- However, if the child is fixated at the phallic stage and the complex is not resolved, later sexual orientation may not be 'normal'. These ideas are said to explain homosexuality.
- Evidence for the Oedipus complex came from Freud's case study of Little Hans. However, this case study is criticised because Hans's parents were followers of Freud and were looking for examples of behaviour that fitted the theory.

> Malinowski studied the Trobriand Islanders where boys are not brought up by their fathers in the same way as in Freud's experience. This should mean that the boys do not resolve the Oedipus complex as the family structure is different. However, the boys do develop 'normally' and have 'normal' sexual orientation, which is evidence that Freud's theory was not correct.

Taking it further

Find some websites or books that suggest meanings for symbols in dreams, and look at what is suggested. Then research other explanations of dreaming, such as the activation-synthesis theory of dreams, which suggests that our brains are active whilst we sleep to make sense of our thoughts. These are remembered as dreams. This is very different from Freud's theory.

Evidence of practice

What you need to know

- You need to carry out a practical that involves a correlation, rating scales and self-report data.
- You need to know about correlations, self-report data, scattergraphs, Spearman's test, the procedure of a study, sampling techniques, and how to write up parts of a report.

A suggested practical using a correlational design and self-report data

This suggested practical is based on an idea from Cramer (1997) to see if self-esteem and anxiety link with identity personality.

◆ Background

Cramer (1997) suggests that young people who have high anxiety and low self-esteem have not yet made a commitment to goals and beliefs – they have not get 'found' their identity personality – whereas those with low anxiety and high self-esteem have. She concludes that those with high commitment and high self-esteem use fewer defence mechanisms. (See also page 89.) Seeing if high commitment and high self-esteem go together therefore tests Cramer's (1997) claims, even though defence mechanisms, being harder to measure, are not tested here.

◆ Aim and hypothesis

The aim is to see if young people who have made a commitment to goals and beliefs have higher self-esteem and lower anxiety than those who have not made a commitment. The hypothesis is that there is a positive relationship between commitment score and self-esteem. The higher the commitment score, the higher the self-esteem score. Commitment score here includes whether the person feels they are having an 'identity crisis' and self-esteem score includes anxiety. This hypothesis is directional because a positive correlation is predicted. The higher the commitment to values, the higher the self-esteem will be.

◆ Operationalisation of variables

There are two variables, commitment and self-esteem and these need operationalising so that they are measurable. Commitment to goals, values and beliefs is the first variable. Identity crisis (the opposite of commitment) can be measured by asking questions such as whether decisions about the self are easily made. The more there is a commitment to values, the less there will be an identity crisis, so these two are measured and an overall score found.

Self-esteem is the other variable. Questions might ask the individual, for example, to judge themselves about their own worth. The more someone says they are anxious, the lower their self-esteem score will be.

◆ Procedure

The study is about young people so you need to ask their age, and it is useful to ask gender as well. You could also ask about whether they are in full-time education, part-time education, working or other, as this might be of interest.

Draw up the questionnaires

Two questionnaires must be drawn up. Self-report data are to be gathered, so the participants are asked questions about their own commitment to goals and their own level of self-esteem. For the questionnaire about self-esteem, make sure that questions are not too searching and risk making the respondent feel bad about themselves.

Participants can be asked to tick the most suitable response that gives their views, for instance SA = strongly agree, A = agree, DK = don't know, D = disagree, SD = strongly disagree.

▲ Questionnaires are an effective method of data collection.

How to

Questions relating to commitment may include:

	SA	A	DK	D	SD
a I am clear about which political party I support.	☐	☐	☐	☐	☐
b I have no idea about what career path I wish to follow.	☐	☐	☐	☐	☐
c I have different beliefs from my parents.	☐	☐	☐	☐	☐
d I am still trying to find out 'who I am'.	☐	☐	☐	☐	☐

The scoring would be:

	SA	A	DK	D	SD
Statement a	5	4	3	2	1
Statement b	1	2	3	4	5
Statement c	5	4	3	2	1
Statement d	1	2	3	4	5

Questions relating to self-esteem may include:

	SA	A	DK	D	SD
a I feel I am doing well in what I am doing at the moment.	☐	☐	☐	☐	☐
b I enjoy going out socialising.	☐	☐	☐	☐	☐
c I don't like making decisions about myself.	☐	☐	☐	☐	☐
d I am quite anxious when I am with others.	☐	☐	☐	☐	☐

The scoring would be:

	SA	A	DK	D	SD
Statement a	5	4	3	2	1
Statement b	5	4	3	2	1
Statement c	1	2	3	4	5
Statement d	1	2	3	4	5

Choose the sample

The participants need to be young people. Cramer used a mean average of 18-year-olds in her 1995 study and 23-year-olds for the 1997 study. You might find it easier to ask participants aged between 16 and 18, in which case you need to be aware of ethical issues and getting permission, as well as noting that you will possibly have different findings from Cramer. Find a sample that includes both males and females if possible. An opportunity sample is probably the easiest for you and the most ethical.

Pilot the questionnaires

Ask a few friends to do the questionnaires to check your wording and to make sure your standardised instructions are suitable. Make sure that everything you are going to do follows ethical guidelines.

Gather the data

A total of 20 participants would be useful for drawing conclusions about the correlation, but try to gather at least ten sets of data.

Taking it further

In the exam you will be asked questions based on your practical work, so keep notes in a practical notebook.

How to

Participant	Commitment	Self-esteem	Rank for commitment STEP 1	Rank for self-esteem STEP 2
1	33	30	9	6
2	25	32	5.5	8
3	18	24	2	2.5
4	34	31	10	7
5	25	33	5.5	9
6	16	18	1	1
7	22	25	4	4
8	30	28	8	5
9	28	34	7	10
10	19	24	3	2.5

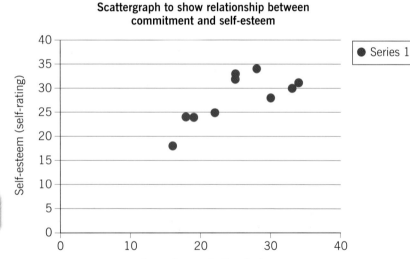

Scattergraph to show relationship between commitment and self-esteem

Results

These results have been made up to help you when presenting your own results. Using your own results, draw up a table, rank the data, draw a scattergraph and carry out a Spearman's test.

For these made-up results, Spearman's rho is 0.67, which is fairly close to 1 and appears to be a significant result. You would have to check to see, and you will find out how to do that in the following chapters. For your interest, for a one-tailed test and a level of significance of 0.05 the critical value is 0.56, so 0.67 is significant as it is greater than 0.56.

Conclusions

Looking at the ranks and comparing them, and checking using a scattergraph and the Spearman's test, all show that there is a correlation between commitment and self-esteem according to the self-report data. You would have to see what you found when you carried out your own test. Draw an overall conclusion and relate back to the background information to draw conclusions with reference to (in the case of this suggested study) Cramer's claims.

The scattergraph suggests that there is a correlation because the line of best fit is straight and there are five scores either side of it.

◆ **Writing up – the procedure, sample, apparatus, results**

A psychology research study is written up just as any science project is written up and there is a set way of doing this. For example, at the start of the report there is an abstract, which is a summary of the study setting out what was done to whom and with what result. You do not have to write up a complete report for this practical. However, over the AS course you will be writing up bits of your practicals, so that you can practise writing a report. For this chapter you need to write up the procedure, the sample, the apparatus and the results.

How to

The procedure section

For your course, the procedure of studies that you have learnt can include the research method, variables, ethics, controls, apparatus, sample and any other information about the study. However, for the practicals – but not the studies in detail – limit the procedure to what was actually done. Start the procedure section from the setting up of the environment and the setting up of the test or task.

The sample section

The sample section should describe the type of sampling and why it was chosen. The actual participants should also be described, in terms of gender and age for example, as well as how they were found. Any relevant details about the sample should be included.

The apparatus section

The apparatus section is intended to let other researchers know what they would need in order to replicate the study. For example, for this study they would need a pen, the two questionnaires, the standardised instructions and debrief and that is all. The apparatus section should also justify the tools used, in this case the two questionnaires, if that is not done in the procedure section.

The results section

For your results you need the actual scores (the raw data) as an Appendix rather than in the results section. However, a correlation can be an exception if there are not too many scores, as the scores and ranks can give a clear picture of what has been found and are useful in the main part of the report, as is done here. You then need to comment on the data in the table, to start looking for a pattern. Then produce a relevant graph, which for a correlation is a scattergraph. Comment on the graph, again to start looking for a pattern in the results. Finally, carry out a statistical test if appropriate, put the calculations in an Appendix and give just the 'answer' to the test in the results section. Give an overview of the results.

The conclusions – strengths and weaknesses of correlations

The methodology section of this chapter discusses strength and weaknesses of correlations. Using this information, consider your own correlational study and its strengths and weaknesses. For example, the results may be significant but not show a cause and effect relationship, which is a weakness. However, they may show a new area for testing, which is a strength. Your study may have used your own scoring system, which is possibly a weakness as the scoring may not validly represent a 'real' measure. The sampling method may have been opportunity sampling, which is likely to show bias, and you could explore why. This would be a weakness. The conclusions of a report needs to present arguments like this. It is useful to consider issues such as validity, reliability, generalisability, subjectivity, objectivity and credibility, as these are the areas you need to focus on for your course.

Examiner's tip

These are the headings to be used when writing up a report:

Abstract – a brief summary of the whole study

Introduction – the background theory being tested

Rationale, aims and hypotheses – more about what the study is going to do

Method – design, participants, apparatus, procedure, controls, etc. – what was actually done

Results – summary tables and graphs as well as commentary so that it is clear what is found

Conclusions – what the results mean, including their relationship to the background theory, criticisms such as about validity, reliability, generalisability and credibility, and overall conclusions

References – details of the studies and theories mentioned so others can check them

Appendices – all the other information such as questionnaires or other tools, raw scores, standardised instructions, letters to ask permission to carry out the study.

Examiner's tip

It is useful to analyse results to see how strong the findings are. You should consider criticisms of your study, including, for example, whether the questionnaires really measured commitment and self-esteem – in other words, whether the study is valid. Also, did the participants provide truthful self-report data – in other words, are the findings reliable? Would there have been demand characteristics, which is where the participants give the answers they think the study is after, or social desirability, which is where the participants give the answer they think makes them look good or is morally right? These are the sorts of questions to consider, as well as whether the sampling would have produced biased data.

Summary

What you need to know

- You need to know some key terms and a definition of the Psychodynamic Approach, some detailed methodology, some content from the approach, two studies in detail, and one key issue. You also need to carry out a practical.

The Psychodynamic Approach focuses on the unconscious, and the first five years of life. Good mental health relies on a balanced personality, with unconscious wishes being moderated by the conscience and society's rules.

Freud's ideas are central to the approach, which arose from his views about mental health and how it comes both from innate tendencies and patterns of upbringing. He thought that the personality comprises the id, ego and superego and that people were governed very strongly by unconscious thoughts and wishes – much more so than by conscious rational thinking.

◆ Methodology

The main methodology in the Psychodynamic Approach is to do with case studies and correlation designs. Specifically, you need to know about both case studies in general and case studies that Freud carried out:

- You need to know strengths and weaknesses for both styles of case study.
- You need to be able to evaluate qualitative data in terms of subjectivity and objectivity, reliability, validity and generalisability.
- You need to be able to discuss Freud's theory in terms of its credibility.
- You need to consider ethical and credibility issues with regards to case study data.
- You need to know about correlation designs, including positive and negative correlation designs and what is meant by the strength of a correlation (as opposed to the strengths of the correlation as a design), and strengths and weaknesses of a correlation design.
- You must cover cross-sectional and longitudinal designs for studies.
- You need to know four sampling methods – the same ones that you need to know about for the Social Approach – as well as their advantages and disadvantages, so revise them as well.

◆ Content

- You need to know the three parts of the mind according to Freud – the conscious, preconscious and unconscious parts of the mind.
- You need to know the three parts of the personality according to Freud – the id, the ego and the superego.
- You need to know the five stages of Freud's psychosexual theory – the oral, anal, phallic, latency and genital stages.
- You need to know about the defence mechanism of repression and one other defence mechanism.

▲ Freud has had an impact on therapy in many cultures.

- You need to know about the Oedipus complex, as well as how the phallic stage explains that people learn their gender behaviour.

You will also need to be able to evaluate Freud's theory – and to evaluate the Psychodynamic Approach's view of gender development, as well as comparing that explanation of gender with the Biological and Learning explanations.

◆ Studies

You need to be able to describe and evaluate Freud's Little Hans study and one other from:
- Axline (1964) Dibs's story
- Bachrach et al. (1991) about the effectiveness of psychoanalysis
- Cramer (1997) about using defence mechanisms and being 'in crisis' as a young adult.

◆ Key issues

You need to know one key issue that concepts from the Psychodynamic Approach can explain. Prepare one issue yourself, and be able to describe it and explain it using concepts from the approach. You must also be ready to apply concepts (research, theories, studies and so on) to an issue that you are presented with in the exam.

◆ Evidence of practice

Be ready to answer questions about a study using a correlation design that you have carried out yourself. You should have used self-report data and two ratings scales. Be ready to discuss the use of a scattergraph for a correlation design and a Spearman's test too. Make sure you can define the terms 'rating scale' and 'self-report' data. Know how to write up the procedure, sampling, apparatus and results section of a report, as you might be asked questions about that in the exam as well.

Examzone

Practise

Section B questions

1. Outline the role of the ego within the personality according to Freud's theory. (3 marks)

2. Describe the concept of fixation in Freud's theory. (4 marks)

3. Evaluate Freud's belief that the personality had three components, the id, ego and superego. (5 marks)

4. Explain how the defence mechanism of repression may be used to deal with an unsatisfactory completion of the oral stage of development. (3 marks)

5. Describe the problems (themes) that Little Hans was reported to be suffering from, at the time his father was reporting these events to Freud. (4 marks)

Section C questions

6. Freud based his theory on case studies of his many patients. Evaluate Freud's work in terms of the methodology used. (6 marks)

7. Evaluate Freud's explanation of gender development through the Oedipus/Electra complex. (8 marks)

8. Barney always arrived early for an appointment so as not to be late, but then, unable to bring himself to be seen to be early, he would wait round the corner until there was just one minute to go. At that point he would turn the corner, and enter, exactly on time. When it came to paying his bills the bill would be paid at the last possible moment and tips were never given.
Describe and evaluate how the psychodynamic approach would explain and treat these problems. (12 marks: 6 AO1 6AO2)

MCQ

4. Biological Approach

Key terms

- central nervous system
- synapse
- receptor
- neuron
- neurotransmitter
- genes
- hormones
- brain lateralisation

What you will learn about in this chapter

- The use of twin and adoption studies, and how animals are used in biological research to learn about the function of the brain.
- How different types of brain scans work and what they show.
- How genes determine gender; how hormones control gender development; and how the brains of males and females may be organised differently.
- The role of the central nervous system and neurotransmitters in human behaviour.

What you need to know

- You must be able to define and explain the Biological Approach.
- You must be able to describe and evaluate biological research methods to understand how psychologists study human behaviour.
- You must be able to describe and evaluate biological theories of gender development.
- You must be able to describe and evaluate two research studies from the Biological Approach.
- You must be able to describe a key issue that is of interest to modern-day psychologists and explain the issue from the biological perspective.

Defining the Biological Approach

This section will focus on the Biological Approach to psychology, starting with an overview of the approach as a whole, then focusing on more specific aspects. We will be looking at the research methods used in the Biological Approach, some biological theories of gender development and key issues of interest. This approach is the most scientific one we will look at in this book and is different from the other approaches. During the chapter you will come across a lot of new terms and ideas that are specific to the Biological Approach; you will need to learn these. There are a few terms that you will have to be able to define and you should make sure that you can do this.

◆ What is the Biological Approach to psychology?

The Biological Approach combines psychology and biology to provide physiological explanations for human behaviour, from the basic differences between males and females up to more complex phenomena such as memory, language and perception. The Biological Approach has been very influential in psychology since the 1950s, after the publication of D.O. Hebb's book *The Organisation of Behaviour* in 1949. Hebb's book outlined a very detailed theory of how behaviour could be explained by brain activity.

The book was based on research he conducted using both animals and humans. He moved away from previous theories which held that many human behaviours are too complex to be reduced to chemical changes in the brain or basic physical make-up. Hebb's theory sparked off a great deal of debate about where human behaviour comes from, and has led to a lot more research being conducted to test the idea that biology determines behaviour.

◆ Advances in the Biological Approach

The Biological Approach to studying psychology is still in the early days of its development compared with other approaches such as the Learning Approach and the Psychodynamic Approach that have been around for many, many years. This means that, while the approach has made a lot of progress in its short life, there is still a long way to go.

▲ Identical twins are often used in psychology studies within the Biological Approach.

Psychologists in the biology field have used brain scans that allow us to see the living brain and how it works. Every new type of scan that is developed offers the chance to see a clearer picture and acquire more information about the brain. Surgery has been used to disable parts of the brain to see how this affects behaviour (lesion studies), and new techniques are now being created so that damage caused to the brain in animals for research purposes does not have to be permanent.

The Biological Approach has been involved in many other things such as the use of drugs to treat mental illness, research into the genetic basis of academic ability and research into the causes and effects of stress. Because of the scientific nature of the approach, the research methods used by psychologists within the Biological Approach are also scientific, with an emphasis on control. Research conducted in this approach therefore tends to take place in a laboratory setting, with strict controls over the variables being studied.

The Biological Approach focuses on two assumptions about where our behaviour originates from: that our behaviour is the result of the genes that we possess from conception; and that our behaviour is controlled by the activity in the central nervous system – specifically, the brain.

Have you ever wondered?

Have you ever wondered why you get angry even when you try not to, or why you get scared of something even though you know you shouldn't? Some psychologists believe that a lot of who you are is pre-determined at conception because it depends on the genes you inherit from your parents. Your genes determine all your main characteristics – from hair and eye colour to your gender – but some people believe genes can also determine more complex things like mental disorders you might develop or how easy you are to scare.

Taking it further

Research has found that illnesses such as schizophrenia can be the result of genes passed on through families. This means that, if one person in a family develops schizophrenia, there is an increased chance others in the family will also have it or will develop it in the future. Some research has found that things like IQ can be genetic and that family members will have similar levels of intelligence. Look for some research that has found support for the idea that disorders like **schizophrenia** or **traits** like intelligence run in families.

Examiner's tip

When learning new terms that are very complex, as many of the ones in the Biological Approach may seem, you need to make sure that you understand them and can define them in your own words in order to demonstrate that understanding. As you go through the course, keep a 'diary' or glossary of key terms, with a definition in your own words of every new term you come across. If you are not sure you do understand the terms, ask your teacher to check your definitions.

Methodology

What you need to know

- You need to be able to describe and evaluate twin and adoption studies as research methods.
- You need to be able to describe PET and MRI scanning techniques.
- You need to be able to describe and evaluate the use of animals in laboratory experiments, including strengths and weaknesses, validity, reliability, generalisability, credibilty, ethical and practical issues.

Have you ever wondered?

Why do some twins look and behave the same but others don't? Monozygotic (MZ) twins, or identical twins, are two babies who develop from the same egg and are therefore genetically identical to one another as they have 100% of their genes in common. Dizygotic (DZ) twins, or fraternal twins, are two babies who share the same womb at the same time, but develop from two separate eggs. They therefore share 50% of the same genes – the same as any siblings.

◆ **Seeking genetic explanations**

Psychologists working within the Biological Approach look for genetic explanations for who we are, to support the argument that our behaviour is biologically determined. One of the best ways to do this is to study identical twins, as they have exactly the same genes, or to study children who have been adopted and not brought up by their biological parents. Any similarities in behaviour between those with a close genetic relationship can be attributed, at least in part, to that relationship.

◆ **Twin studies**

Twin studies are used to see if behaviours are shared by those who are genetically similar. Psychologists look at twins to see what traits they share by looking at concordance rates between them (the likelihood that, if one twin has a certain trait, the other twin will also have the same trait). For example, if one twin develops **schizophrenia**, psychologists would look at whether the other twin develops the disorder. By doing this on large numbers of twin pairs they can work out the likelihood that, if one twin has schizophrenia, the other will also develop it.

If there is a high concordance rate for any traits between MZ twins, there may be a genetic cause for that trait. By then comparing the concordance rate of MZ and DZ twins, it is possible to see if there is a genetic cause because MZ twins share more genes in common than DZ twins. If the concordance rate is higher for MZ twins than for DZ twins, then it is likely that genes play a strong part in the behaviour being studied. However, most twins also share the same environment, so the similarities in behaviour may be due to environmental factors and not genes. To overcome this, psychologists try to study twins who are reared apart in order to separate nature and nurture effects on behaviour.

◆ **Adoption studies**

Studying children who have been adopted is another way of looking at whether behavioural traits are the result of nature (genetic) or nurture (environmental) factors. Adopted children share no genes in common with their adoptive families but share the same environment. They also share 50% of their genes with each of their biological parents, but no longer share the same environment.

By studying children who were adopted at birth or very soon after, psychologists can separate genetic and environmental influences on behaviour by looking for similarities in behaviour between the children and their biological and adoptive parents. If there is a similarity between the behaviour of a child and their biological parents, and not between the child and its adoptive parents, that supports the idea that the behaviour being studied has some genetic cause. For example, if a child has a very high IQ and so does his biological mother, but both adoptive parents have an average IQ, a psychologist may determine that the child's IQ is the result of a 'Genius' gene.

◆ Evaluating twin and adoption studies

Both the methods described above are good for testing genetic causes of behaviour, as they try to study people who share a close genetic link but do not share the same environment, thus isolating genetic causes from environmental ones. Studying MZ twins reared apart is the best way of doing this as the twins have identical genetic make-up, but if they have been raised separately, similarities in their behaviour cannot be due to sharing the same environment and could therefore be the result of genetic influences.

There are many problems with using twin and adoption studies, however. Even twins separated at birth shared the same pre-natal environment, as for 9 months they shared a womb. This could account for some similarities in behaviour. Likewise, even children who were adopted from birth share a pre-natal environment with the biological mother and this could influence the child's development. For example, the mother's general health and nutrition, and any drug-taking whilst pregnant, could affect the child's development and account for similarities in behaviour between biological mothers and their children.

Further issues are that:
- Twins who are adopted and reared separately often share similar experiences in the environments in which they are brought up. Adoption agencies often try to find similar families to bring up twins who are to be separated, in order to make their developmental experiences as alike as possible. This means that any traits that they share could be the result of their similar upbringings and not simply the genes that they share.
- The number of twins reared apart is minimal, so sample sizes are small and it may be difficult to generalise the results.
- Many participants in twin and adoption studies are gathered using advertisements asking for suitable people to volunteer to take part in research. This may result in bias in the sampling, as the type of people who would come forward to take part in a study may be very different from those who would not.

▲ Identical twins are often used in biological psychology studies because their genetic make-up is exactly the same.

Taking it further

Plomin et al. (1997) found that during infancy and early childhood children's cognitive abilities, such as language skills and memory, are very similar to that of their adoptive families. However, as they get older their cognitive abilities become more and more like that of their biological families, suggesting a strong effect of genes in cognitive development.

Brain scanning techniques

One way that psychologists can study our behaviour and the biological influences on it is by using brain scanning techniques to study the brain and what it does. Prior to developing brain scans that can penetrate skin and bone to look at the brain, the only ways to study the brain were to operate on people or look at the brains of corpses.

Brain scans fall into two main types, **structural scans** that show images of the brain, and functional scans that show you what parts of the brain are the most active at different times.

◆ MRI (Magnetic Resonance Imaging) scans

An MRI scan is a way of seeing a picture of the brain inside the skull, just like an X-ray. It allows you to see the structure of the brain and therefore whether there is damage or tumours that may need treatment. During an MRI scan, the patient is placed in a large scanner which passes a very strong magnetic field through their head. The **nuclei** of some atoms in certain molecules spin a particular way when they are placed in a magnet, which allows a detailed picture of the brain to be produced on a computer. In the scanner, electromagnetic waves are passed through the body by the magnet, and the nuclei in hydrogen molecules emit their own radio wave at a frequency that the scanner picks up. Because hydrogen concentrations vary in different areas of the brain, a very detailed image of the brain at cross-sections can be seen.

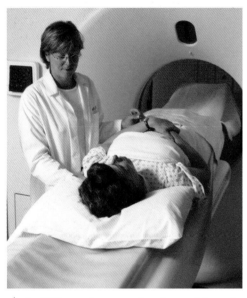

▲ An MRI scan is a way of seeing a picture of the brain inside the skull.

◆ PET (Positron Emission Tomography) scans

A PET scan is a way of seeing a picture of a 'working' brain. It can also show any malfunction, therefore helping to identify damage or tumours. Patients are injected with glucose or water that has been labelled with a **radioactive tracer** while they lie with their head inside the scanner. Once the substance reaches the brain, the brain cells start to uptake the oxygen in the water or glucose and the tracer begins to decay. When the tracer decays it emits positrons, and the more glucose or oxygen the cells in the brain use up, the more positrons there will be emitted in that area of the brain. When the positrons are emitted, they collide with electrons and form gamma rays which are detected by the scanner to produce an image of the activity in areas of the brain.

Laboratory experiments and the use of animals

The use of laboratory experiments was discussed in Unit 1. They are also used by psychologists within the Biological Approach to study behaviour in controlled environments, using specialist equipment.

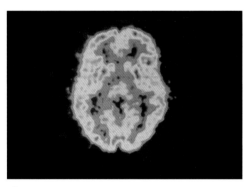

▲ PET scans can help to identify brain damage or tumours.

◆ Issues of validity, reliability and generalisability

In the Biological Approach, animals are used a lot in research, including lesion studies, where damage to the brain is caused and the resulting change in behaviour is measured. Brain damage can be caused permanently in animals by surgically cutting or burning away a part of the brain, or by using drugs and other techniques to 'shut off' parts of the brain temporarily. Causing damage to the brain would be the independent variable and the resulting changes in behaviour that may occur would be the dependent variable.

ANS

Question 1

List the key features of a laboratory experiment, making sure you refer to the variables involved.

By comparing the behaviour of those animals with brain damage with a **control group** who have fully-functioning brains, it is possible to see which parts of the brain control which types of behaviours.

◆ Evaluating lesion studies using animals

Strengths	Problems
• Small animals like rats and mice are often used for lesion studies as they are easier to 'house' and monitor during research than humans. • Large samples can easily be bred in a short period. • It is possible to cause a level of harm to animals that is not possible with humans, as long as the knowledge gained is likely to be of significant benefit to others. • Animals are more likely to be naïve participants. This means that the overall validity of the experiment will be higher as there will be a truer picture of how the brain damage affects behaviour, without the problem of participants behaving differently in the experimental conditions.	• Using animals rather than humans may be more expensive to the researcher as only the highest level of care is acceptable, whereas humans can go home and look after themselves. • Human and animal brains are different, so measuring the effect of brain damage on an animal's brain may not tell you anything about the effect of the same damage on a human.

◆ Evaluating the use of animals: credibility, ethical and practical issues

Animal research in psychology has low credibility with many people as there are so many differences between animal and human behaviour. Studying lesions on animal brains may be of limited use when there are large differences in the structure and functioning of their nervous systems compared with ours. Many people would give more credibility to research using humans as it may be more capable of explaining the behaviour of other humans. It is, however, possible to create more damage to the brain of an animal than it would be with human participants, for ethical reasons, so more extensive research is possible with animals. Another factor is that animals are unlikely to have any prior knowledge or experience that will affect their behaviour in the experiment, thus making the research findings more valid and credible.

When using animals in any experiment, the ethics must be considered carefully. It is against ethical guidelines to cause pain or discomfort to animals in any research, unless the findings are likely to have significant benefit to humans. Any researcher using animals must be licensed to do so and must follow strict government guidelines. The natural behaviour of the animals must be taken into account so that the caging environment mirrors their natural situation as much as possible, to reduce any possible stress.

Because animals can be caged in a way that humans cannot, it is possible to have more control over animals in research. It is possible to isolate animals from other variables, so that measurement of any effect of the independent variable on the dependent variable is more accurate. It is also possible to strictly control the environment in which the animals are kept, so that even when the animal is fed is controlled by the experimenter. This means that, practically, it is easier to control an experiment using animals than one with human participants.

Question 2

Describe the issues of validity, reliability and generalisability arising from laboratory experiments.

Examiner's tip

When answering questions on research methods, be sure to read the question carefully before you start writing. If the question asks you to **describe** a method, you just need to give its main features. If it asks you to **evaluate** a method, do not describe it but explain what the strengths and problems of using it are.

Content

The central nervous system and human behaviour

The central nervous system (CNS) is made up of the brain and the spinal cord. The Biological Approach focuses on how the brain specifically, as part of the CNS, controls our behaviour. The brain contains billions of nerve cells called **neurons** which pass information around inside the brain. It then communicates with the rest of the body through the nerve cells in the nervous system, telling different parts of the body what to do.

Neurons communicate with one another through **synapses**, which are small junctions between neurons where **neurotransmitters** are released and passed from the **terminal button** of one neuron to the **dendrite** of the receiving neuron. Some synapses are excitatory and encourage the neuron to 'fire' (lead to the release of another neurotransmitter), while other synapses are inhibitory and tell the neuron not to 'fire'. The decision over whether to 'fire' or not depends on how many excitatory and inhibitory messages the neuron receives from its thousands of synapses. If the number of excitatory messages far outweighs the number of inhibitory messages, it is likely to fire, and vice versa.

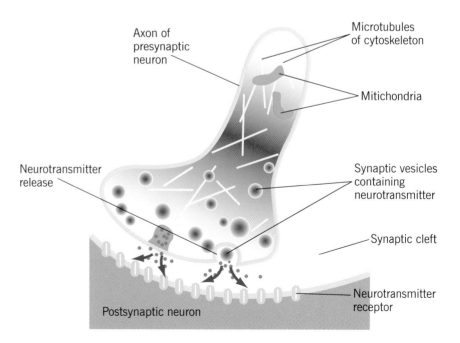

Synaptic transmission ▶

Genes and human behaviour

Genes are made up of DNA (deoxyribonucleic acid) which is responsible for the protein synthesis which influences our development. They are contained on chromosomes which are found within the nuclei of cells; we inherit 23 chromosomes from each parent, which is thought to account for shared behaviour traits between family members. These genes are thought to dictate everything from our eye and hair colour to our gender, and many people also believe that many of our personality traits are determined by our genes.

All humans share certain behaviours, such as the need for sleep or the drive to eat, and we also share a lot of the same genetic make-up, so many people believe that these shared genes account for the shared behaviours. At the same time, the differences in our genetic make-up may account for differences in our behaviours. This makes up part of the basis of the nature-nurture debate which has been a huge issue in psychology for many years. **Nature** refers to the idea that our behaviour is determined by our biological make-up and is therefore beyond our control. **Nurture** refers to the influence of the environment and experiences after birth on our behaviour. The debate is over how much nature and/or nurture actually controls who or what we become.

The role of biological factors in gender development

We all inherit 23 pairs of chromosomes from each parent. Twenty-two of the 23 pairs determine physical appearance such as hair colour, eye colour and height, but the final pair determines gender. In females, the final pair of chromosomes is XX, where the foetus inherits an X chromosome from each parent. In males, the final pair of chromosomes is XY, where the foetus inherits an X chromosome from the mother and a Y chromosome from the father.

A Y chromosome must be present for a foetus to develop into a male. For the first few weeks of pre-natal development, every foetus develops identically and the only difference between them is the single sex chromosome inherited from the father. At about 6 weeks of pre-natal development, the gonads, or sex organs, begin to develop but at this point there is no difference between the developing sex organs of males and females. Further on in the development of the foetus, the gonads begin to develop differently according to whether they are male or female.

A gene in the Y chromosome called **SRY** produces a protein called 'testis-determining factor', which turns the developing gonads into testicles rather than ovaries. So, if there is no Y chromosome the foetus will develop into a female with full female sex organs, but if there is a Y chromosome testicles will develop and the foetus will develop fully into a male. It appears that the default setting for all foetuses is to develop into a female unless there is a Y chromosome.

Taking it further

As you are looking over the different approaches, consider where each one stands on the nature-nurture debate. The Biological Approach explains behaviour from a mainly nature standpoint by looking at the influence of biology on behaviour, but other approaches take a very different view on this. Draw a continuum of nature to nurture and add where you think each approach lies.

Have you ever wondered?

Ever wondered what makes males male and females female? There are many different explanations as to why we develop the way we do but psychologists in the Biological Approach focus on explaining gender differences by looking at the physiological differences between males and females, starting from genetic differences. The genes people have influence the hormones their body will release, and the hormone levels will then influence how their body develops. This is what creates the physical differences between males and females.

Hormones

From the point at which the gonads of a foetus have formed, the influence of genes on gender development ceases. The role of the Y chromosome is to ensure that the gonads of males develop into testes rather than ovaries, so that the male will then be exposed to male rather than female hormones. It is exposure, both before and after birth, to these hormones that is responsible for the physical differences between males and females.

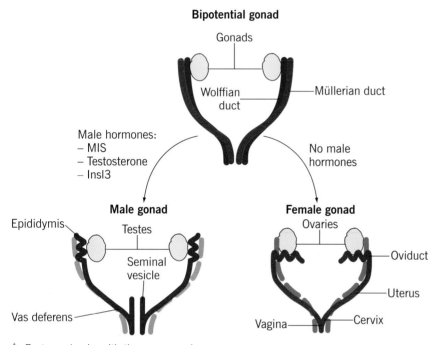

Bipotential gonad

Foetuses begin with the same sex hormones but develop differently according to the Wolffian or Müllerian system and exposure to the different hormones involved.

Before we are born, exposure to sex hormones has a permanent 'organisational' effect on the development of sex organs so that males develop testes and a penis, while females develop ovaries and a vagina. Six weeks into foetal development, a protein hormone called **H-Y antigen** is released if there is a Y chromosome present in the foetus's genes. This encourages the development of testes whilst stopping the development of ovaries. For the first few weeks of pre-natal development all foetuses have the same undeveloped sex organs, both male (called the Wolffian system) and female (called the Müllerian system). After three months of pre-natal development, if there has been development of testes and therefore production of male sex hormones, the male Wolffian system will develop fully into male sex organs – or the absence of male sex hormones will result in the full development of the Müllerian system into female sex organs.

The first hormone to be released by the testes is called the **anti-Müllerian hormone**, which prevents the further development of female sex organs. The testes then produce androgens, which work to masculinise the male foetus by stimulating the development of male sex organs. It is the absence of male sex hormones, rather than the presence of female hormones, that leads to the development of complete female sex organs.

Brain lateralisation

Brain lateralisation refers to the extent to which each hemisphere of the brain is involved in different activities. Some evidence suggests that there are differences between males and females in terms of how their brain works and which hemispheres control the same behaviours. Most research on the influence of hormones, and therefore gender, on brain development has been done on rats, because rats are born 22 days after conception at the point at which hormones no longer influence sex organ development and begin to influence brain development.

Examiner's tip

When discussing biological influences on gender development, you should be able to describe the individual influence of genes, of hormones and of brain lateralisation on gender differences. Genes influence hormones, and hormones influence the development of the brain, but all three aspects play a different role in creating differences between males and females. The examiners will expect you to be able to explain all three.

Pfeiffer (1936) removed the sex organs of genetic male and female newborn rats and found that they all developed into adults with female hormone release patterns from the pituitary gland. Some of the rats who had their gonads removed had testes transplanted onto them and when this happened, even to female rats, there was a steady release of male sex hormones from the pituitary gland. This suggests that the presence or absence of testosterone from the testes accounts for sex differences in the **hypothalamus** (the part of the brain which controls the release of sex hormones from the **pituitary gland**). If there is testosterone present in the body, the hypothalamus will tell the pituitary gland to release male hormones, but if there is no testosterone then the hypothalamus will tell the pituitary gland to release female hormones.

However, human evidence may go against this, as in the case of Daphne Went. Daphne is chromosomally male but has both the appearance and the behaviour of a female (see also page 108). Also, Dorner (1976) found that damaging a small part of the hypothalamus of newborn male rats resulted in them showing female behaviour as they grew up, suggesting that there was disruption to the normal release of male sex hormones.

There has been some evidence to suggest that females show less brain lateralisation for language abilities than males do. In males, the left hemisphere of the brain is more active than the right during linguistic tasks, but in females there is more likely to be **bilateral activity** in the brain during the same tasks. This means that, in females, left-hemisphere brain damage is likely to result in fewer problems with linguistic abilities than the same damage would cause in males.

LEFT SIDE:
Speech
Analysis
Time
Sequence

Recognises:
Words
Letters
Numbers

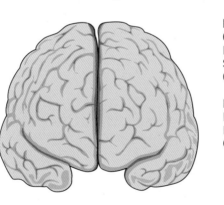

RIGHT SIDE:
Creativity
Patterns
Spatial
Context

Recognises:
Faces
Places
Objects

◄ Each hemisphere of the brain is responsible for different functions.

Similar differences are seen between males and females during spatial tasks. In males, the right hemisphere is shown to have high levels of activity during tasks requiring spatial ability, but in females both hemispheres are activated during spatial tasks.

All this evidence suggests that brain damage, such as that caused by a stroke, that only affects one hemisphere of the brain, is likely to be more detrimental to males than females, as in females the unaffected hemisphere may be able to take over from the damaged area.

Evaluating biological influences on gender development

The case of David Reimer supports the argument that biological factors influence gender development significantly. When he was born, David was chromosomally and physically male. However, after an accident during his circumcision, he was raised as a female. Other than his family and the doctor, no-one was aware of the fact that he was actually male. Yet many people reported that his behaviour was very 'male' and David himself said that he always felt very masculine and did not feel he was a girl.

It appears that, even though his upbringing was that of a female, his biological status as a male was strong enough to override this. There is also lots of evidence from animal research, such as Pfeiffer's studies on rats, that has shown significant biological differences between males and females, suggesting that our sex may be determined by our biology.

◆ Use of animal research

A lot of research into the influence of hormones and biology on sex has been done on animals, as it is clearly not feasible for ethical reasons to alter hormones levels or perform gonad transplants on human infants. Studying animals in this way gives us new knowledge about how human sex may also be determined, as long as we are willing to assume that humans and animals develop it in the same way – though many psychologists would argue that it is not safe to extrapolate information from animal research in order to explain human behaviour, as there are too many differences. Using animals is also useful for studying biological influences on gender development because, unlike humans, they are born shortly after conception (22 days). Studying the pre-natal development of rats is therefore much faster and more practical.

◆ Pseudo-hermaphrodites

Cases of pseudo-hermaphrodites may both support and refute the influence of biological factors on gender development. True hermaphrodites are born with both male and female genitalia and are therefore both sexes to some extent. Pseudo-hermaphrodites are chromosomally one sex but appear physically, and are therefore raised, as the opposite sex.

Daphne Went, for example, is chromosomally male but was born with the physical appearance of a female and was raised as such. Into adulthood, Daphne lives successfully as a female despite having a Y chromosome that makes her genetically male. This evidence would refute the genetic explanation of gender development, as if a person has a Y chromosome they should develop male sex organs, be exposed to male sex hormones, and develop male brain lateralisation. The fact that Daphne Went has the Y chromosome but has developed into a female suggests that something else must have played a part in her gender development.

◆ Problems with hormones

There is some evidence to suggest that the discrepancy that occurs between genetic and physical gender happens due to hormonal problems during pre-natal development. For example, in androgenital syndrome, a foetus that is XX is exposed to excessive amounts of androgens – male hormones which masculinise the female foetus and result in the development of male rather than female sex organs. This results in a baby who will appear physically to be male, but who actually has two X chromosomes. In the case of androgen insensitivity syndrome, a foetus that is XY becomes feminised by a lack of exposure to male hormones and female sex organs therefore develop, resulting in a baby who will appear female but is chromosomally male (Daphne Went, for example). Both of these syndromes support the argument that pre-natal exposure to certain hormones determines gender development, as it appears that hormone exposure can even override genetic sex.

◆ Social learning theory

Another theory of gender development is social learning theory, which emphasises the role of observational learning and reinforcement in developing gender roles. It is thought that children observe and imitate the behaviour of same-sex role models such as parents, and are reinforced for showing gender-appropriate behaviour by being given praise and encouragement. For example, boys may be encouraged to help Dad in the garden and be given praise for doing so, while girls may be asked to help Mum cook the tea and be told they are very helpful. This encourages the same behaviour to be repeated in the future, creating a gender identity for the child. This means that gender role is created by others and occurs due to experiences we have after birth, suggesting that biological sex plays a lesser role. However, we know from looking at the case study of David Reimer that the biological sex of a child can have an overriding effect on their gender identity. David was raised and treated as a girl by all who knew him from a very early age, but still he felt and acted very much as a male, his true biological sex.

◆ A combination of biology and environment

Whilst many psychologists argue that gender must be caused either by nature or by nurture, there is also an argument that it may be the result of an interaction between both biology and environment. For example, we will treat a child differently if they are male or female, and the way we treat them will influence how they behave in the future. So, if a child is dressed in blue and playing with trucks we assume that it is male and encourage male activities such as play-fighting or building with blocks, and male behaviours such as aggression and competitiveness. When the child behaves as we expect he will be praised and told he is a 'good boy' which then strengthens his identity as a male. His future behaviour is therefore shaped by the way he is treated by others, which is influenced by the gender others perceive him to be, which will depend on his physical gender, which is dictated by his biology.

Freud's psychodynamic theory of gender development states that the resolution of the Oedipus/Electra complex occurs through identification with the same sex parent, at 5 to 6 years old. However, we know from observing the behaviour of young children that they usually show gender-appropriate behaviour and preference for gender-specific toys well before this age. Psychologists working within the Biological Approach would argue that this could be explained by a biological impact on their gender, which will influence their behaviour long before the age of 5.

Taking it further

Try listing the main physical, psychological and biological differences between males and females and working out whether they are the result of genetic, hormonal or brain differences between the two sexes. By doing this you will be putting into practice the theories on the development of gender differences, which should help to build your understanding of them.

Studies

What you need to know

- You will be expected to be able to describe and evaluate the study by Money (1975) into the case of a genetic male who was raised as a female, and one other study to be chosen from Gottesman and Shields J (1966), Raine et al. (1997) and Bellis et al. (2001) .

Ablatio Penis: Normal male infant sex-reassigned as a girl (Money, 1975)

◆ Can you raise a boy as a girl?

Gender is a complex phenomenon and there is much debate over what makes us male or female. Psychologists working within the Biological Approach argue that our gender is determined by our genetic and biological make-up, whereas others may argue that our gender develops as a result of our upbringing. This study aimed to test the idea that gender can be **learned**, in a unique case study of a small boy whose penis was destroyed in an accident and who was brought up as a girl.

◆ Aim

The sexologist John Money, working at the John Hopkins University in the US, strongly believed that gender is determined by social experience after birth and is therefore the result of our upbringing. He believed that all children are born 'gender neutral' and are created as males or females through the way that they are brought up. He tested this theory in the famous case study of Bruce/Brenda.

◆ Procedure

In 1965, identical twins Bruce and Brian were born. At 10 months they were sent for circumcision becuase of a problem in urinating. The technique involved using a hot wire to cut away the foreskin. Bruce was treated first, but a mistake during the procedure meant that his penis was burnt almost completely off, and Brian's circumcision was cancelled. The skin gradually flaked off almost entirely until Bruce's penis was unrecognisable.

Bruce's parents were distraught and unsure of how best to bring Bruce up to deal with his 'disability'. They saw Dr. Money talking on television about intersex children being brought up as either male or female. His argument was that the sex of a child is determined by the process of their upbringing. They contacted Dr. Money and the decision was made to bring Bruce up as a female, as it was felt that dealing with his masculinity in the absence of a penis would be too difficult for him later in life.

In 1967 Bruce was surgically castrated, his name was changed to Brenda, and his parents began to dress 'him' only in dresses and encourage him to play with dolls. From the age of 12, Brenda was given oestrogen to encourage female rather than male puberty. Money tracked the progress of Brenda over many years as he felt it would be invaluable to measure the development of identical twins who were being brought up into different gender roles.

◆ Analysis

Dr. Money believed she was all right, but Brenda's transition to 'female-hood' was not easy and she was often described as having very masculine traits. She liked to play with guns and other masculine toys, was often involved in playground fights and was described by many people as a tomboy. Brenda even urinated standing up as a male would, despite the lack of a penis. She had many behavioural and emotional difficulties throughout her childhood and at the age of 15 was so unhappy with being raised as a girl that the decision was made to allow her to live as a boy. 'David', as he now became known, had phalloplasty to create a penis, with a later operation to make the penis more realistic.

David became much happier after he decided to live as a male and in his 20s he was introduced to, and later married, a divorcee who had three children to whom he became step-father. Sadly, in his late 30s David's twin, Brian, killed himself and David blamed himself because of the trauma that his case had caused the family during their childhood. He became increasingly withdrawn and unhappy, leading to the breakdown of his marriage. His depression worsened and in 2004, at the age of 38, David shot and killed himself. It has been argued that the strong, natural force he felt telling him that he was male, being then overridden by the upbringing he received, was a significant factor in the depression leading to his suicide.

▲ A photograph of David Reimer (formerly Bruce/Brenda) taken in February 2000.

◆ Conclusion

While Dr. Money wanted to try to prove that biological gender can be easily overwritten by the upbringing of a child, he seems to have actually supported the counter-argument that biological gender is more determinate of the child's sex role.

Evaluating the study

Dr. Money originally used the case study to support his theory that gender is determined by socially-learned factors rather than by biology. However, follow-up evidence provided by Diamond and Sigmundson (1997) on the true effects of the case study on David, suggested that gender is probably more likely to be determined by natural biology. David said that throughout his life he felt strongly that he should be male.

In terms of ethics, the negative effects of David's case study on his life are huge, as many people believe that the stress put on the family was a significant factor in both twins' suicides.

Taking it further

Cases such as that of David Reimer are very rare but there have been cases of children whose sex organs appear to make them one sex when in fact they are not. Do some extra research into cases of hermaphroditism or intersex children whose biological sex does not match their sexual appearance. You might also like to start thinking about the ethics of conducting transgender surgery on children. For example, whose choice is it to have surgery and who decides what gender the child should be raised as?

There is also some argument over the decision to raise Brenda as female simply because of the damage to the penis. It is argued that it is more difficult to build a penis than a vagina, so many intersex children have a vagina created because it is easier. Many would say, however, that gender is determined more by exposure to hormones in the womb and the biology of the child and that more thought should therefore be given to the raising of the child so that they do not suffer problems adjusting to a gender they do not feel is natural to them.

There was also some question over the ethical treatment of the twins by Dr. Money as he showed them sexually-explicit material to try and strengthen their gender identities. On the other hand, one very good point about the study was that it was possible to compare the behaviour of twins who share the same genetic make-up but have different experiences of being brought up as either male or female. This means that there was a good matched control to compare 'Brenda's' behaviour with after her upbringing as a female. The fact that both boys developed as males even after having different upbringings provides strong support for the argument that gender is determined by genetic or biological, rather than social, factors.

Other studies from the Biological Approach

◆ Bellis et al. (2001)

This study used MRI scans to look for sex differences in the maturation of the brain, by looking at volumes of cerebral grey and white matter and corpus callosal areas in groups of healthy children and adolescents. Comparing the older and younger groups, it could be seen that, with age, there was a reduction in grey matter volumes, but an increase of white matter and of corpus callosal areas. By looking at differences between males and females, it was obvious that males showed a more prominent difference between the decrease in grey matter and the increases in white matter and corpus callosal areas with age.

One of the problems with this study is that it is cross-sectional and only shows age-related differences in brain structure by looking at different groups of children and adolescents. To get a better view of brain maturation and give the research more validity, it would need to follow the same group through childhood and adolescence to study the brains in the same group over time. This research does have its strong points though, as using MRI scans to measure brain structure is objective and therefore not open to bias in interpretation.

◆ Raine et al. (1997)

The researchers aimed to study whether there were brain differences between 41 violent offenders and a group of 'normal' controls, using PET scans to compare the brain functioning of the two groups of participants. A group of prisoners convicted of murder was sent for brain scanning for various reasons related to appeals over their guilt/innocence on the grounds of insanity, and this group was matched with a group of non-offenders on age, sex and schizophrenia where appropriate.

Murderers showed lower levels of activity in the **pre-frontal cortex**, **corpus callosum** and parts of the **limbic system** than non-offenders, all of which are areas of the brain associated with self-control and inhibition of violent behaviour. This was thought to show that the murderers found it hard to control their behaviour. It was also found that the murderers had a lower level of activity in the **parietal cortex** which could link to low verbal ability and therefore lower educational attainment, which may also account for their criminal behaviour.

One of the biggest problems with this piece of research is that, whilst PET scans are objective measures of brain activity, they are difficult to interpret accurately. It is also difficult to say whether the differences in brain function are the only factors in the murderers' criminal behaviour. There could, for example, also be social factors that were not considered in the research. Strengths of the study were that the sample size was quite large and that there was a matched control group, meaning that conclusions could be made quite confidently.

◆ Gottesman and Shields (1966)

This study aimed to investigate the relationship between genetic make-up and schizophrenia, by looking at whether the twins of schizophrenics are also likely to develop the disorder. The researchers studied both identical and fraternal twins where at least one of the twin pair had been hospitalised and diagnosed with schizophrenia. They found that identical twins of schizophrenics had a high incidence of schizophrenia, and almost three quarters of them were thought to have some kind of abnormal behaviour. The rate of schizophrenia in fraternal twins of schizophrenics was lower than for identical twins, but was still higher than in the general public. The research concluded that there appears to be a genetic component in the cause of schizophrenia and that, while the evidence may not suggest that genes are the only cause of schizophrenia, they may be an important factor.

Problems with this kind of research are that twins share at least some environments for some time, even if just during pre-natal development, and things that happen in any shared environment may affect their behaviour. This kind of research was important in the study of the causes of schizophrenia as it was part of the early investigations into a biological cause. It led to our modern understanding of the disorder and the very successful treatments that have been developed to help control its symptoms.

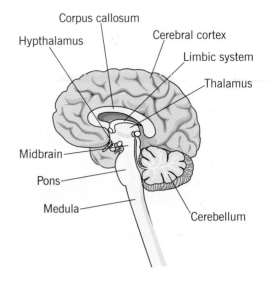

▲ The corpus callosum

Examiner's tip

When evaluating a study, try to focus on some key factors that could apply to any piece of research that will help to jog your memory in an exam. Factors to focus on include:

- Are there any problems with the methodology used?
- Were there any ethical issues raised that may have put the participants at risk?
- Have the results of any other studies supported or refuted the findings of the study being evaluated and, if so, how do their findings compare with the study you are looking at?

Key issues

What you need to know

- You need to be able to outline the key points of the issue you are going to discuss, and why it is of interest to psychologists in the Biological Approach.
- You must be able to explain the issue using concepts, ideas and theories from the Biological Approach. One example of an issue is outlined in detail here to show you the sort of detail you need to include, followed by some ideas for concepts that you could use to explain the issue in more detail.
- Some other ideas are introduced in brief to show you other points you could discuss. In the exam you may be given an issue which you will be expected to explain using suitable concepts, so you need to think about this when preparing for the exam.

Is autism an 'extreme male brain' condition?

Autism is a developmental disorder which affects a child's ability to interact and build relationships with others, including parents. It is not usually diagnosed until the age of 3 or 4 years, but autism is thought to be present from birth and many parents of autistic children report noticing problems with the child well before an official diagnosis is made.

▲ Certain activities can help autistic children improve relationships with others.

Symptoms of autism can include:
- often, lower than normal language abilities
- low levels of imaginative thinking
- problems with communicating and building social relationships
- a preference for order and organisation
- a resistance to change.

About three quarters of all autistic people are male, so it is a predominantly male condition. Baron-Cohen et al. (2005) suggested that the brain structure of autistic people is an 'exaggeration' of normal male brain structure. They argue that there are many similarities between the brain structure of an autistic person and the brain structure of a normal male, and that in the autistic person the brain structure is a more extreme version of the male brain.

◆ Explaining the issue using the Biological Approach

Suitable examples of concepts you could use include the following.

Male brain structure is different from female brain structure

- The normal male brain is heavier than a female brain, as males on the whole are heavier than females. In people with autism, the brain is even heavier than a normal male brain (Bailey et al., 1994).
- Male brains grow more quickly than female brains during early development. In people with autism this early growth is even more rapid.
- Normal males have a smaller corpus callosum than normal females. In people with autism the corpus callosum has been found to be even smaller than in normal males.
- In males, the amygdala is slightly larger than in females. Brain scans of toddlers with autism have shown that their amygdalas tend to be abnormally large when compared with toddlers without autism.

Male brain function is different from female brain function

- Males are generally stronger at spatial tasks such as map reading than females, and tests with autistic people show that they seem to be even better at spatial tasks than normal males.
- Males develop language more slowly than females, and people with autism are very slow to develop language.
- Males tend to show more lateralisation of brain functions such as those related to language skills than women, who generally show more bilateral brain activity when performing linguistic tasks. If the extreme male brain theory were to be believed, we would expect that people with autism would show stronger than normal brain lateralisation, but they do not.

Male hormones affect development

- There are three times more males than females with autism.
- Males have more exposure to male hormones than females do, as the male hormones are produced by the testes. However, a low level of male hormones is produced by the adrenal glands in females so there is still some possibility of male brain structures in females. This would therefore account for some females developing autism.

Autism may be genetic

- Research using twins has found a strong concordance rate of 60-90% for autism in monozygotic twins, but only 5% in dizygotic twins.

Autism may be the result of other biological causes

- There is also some evidence to suggest that autism could be the result of damage caused by undiagnosed phenylketonuria (PKU) in some cases. A build-up of phenylalanine in the body prevents normal brain development so if PKU is undiagnosed it could result in abnormal brain development.

Taking it further

The extreme male brain theory of autism was developed by Baron-Cohen in 2005 and was discussed in detail in an article in *Science* magazine. Baron-Cohen believes that the brain of an autistic person is an extreme version of the brain structure and function of a normal male brain. Try having a closer look at his ideas by going to the following link and having a look at his full theory.
http://www.autismresearchcentre.com/docs/papers/1999_BC_extrememalebrain.pdf

Have you ever wondered?

What does 'et al.' means when it appears after a psychologist's name? When psychologists publish a piece of work they often work together in groups to develop an idea or conduct a piece of research, but rather than list every person's name they use the abbreviation 'et al.' after the first person's name. It is short for the Latin *et alia*, meaning 'and others'. For example, this study by Bailey et al. means that the research was carried out by Bailey and a group of other psychologists.

Examiner's tip

When explaining a key issue from any approach you should outline what the issue is, starting with a clear question that has been of interest to psychologists from the approach, and developing this to define any key ideas and explain why it has been researched. You should then answer the question about the issue you set out at the start, using ideas from the approach to give a detailed discussion of the issue.

Taking it further

A hermaphrodite is an individual who has been born with both male and female sex organs at the same time, meaning that they are neither male nor female. True hermaphrodites have one gonad that has developed into a testis and another that has developed into an ovary, meaning that they can potentially fertilise an egg themselves without the help of another individual. There are many other forms of intersexuality affecting the gender identity of individuals which you can look into.

Taking it further

Research other cases of hermaphrodites who have been treated with transgender surgery, to see how the surgery affected their development. Money did a great deal of research into children who were born with abnormal genitalia and many of them had surgery to remove one set of sex organs or to create new sex organs. By looking at other examples you will be able to see various different possible outcomes. This will help you to assess the ethics of this type of surgery.

Summary of three other issues

◆ Are transgender operations ethical?

A transgender operation involves changing the physical sex of a person. It may involve removing a male's penis and creating a vagina and feminising the male, or vice versa to change a female to a male. These operations may be done in adulthood because an individual feels that they have been born into the wrong body; while they appear to be one sex they feel strongly that they are the other.

The operation may also be conducted on children in cases of indeterminate sex or hermaphroditism, where a child is born with sex organs that are unrecognisable as one sex or the other or where complete sex organs of both sexes are present. In this case parents make the decision over which sex the child should be raised as, and sex organs are 'created' accordingly. In cases where an adult patient requests surgery, ethical issues are of less significance, as the patient can be briefed about the effects and make an informed decision about whether to have the operation. In the case of children, however, some argue that there are serious ethical questions that should be addressed.

◆ Explaining the issue using the Biological Approach

Suitable examples of concepts you could use include the following.

The case of David Reimer

- The decision to raise Bruce as a girl after his botched circumcision did not prove to be a good decision, as Bruce always felt more like a male and this affected his self-esteem growing up.

Other cases of males raised as females

- Reiner and Gaerhart studied 16 genetic males born without (or with a very small) penis, but normal testes and XY chromosome, 14 of whom were raised as girls after surgery. The majority of those raised as girls still felt as if they were male, which raises some ethical questions about whether the parents should have had the power to make that decision.

Surgery decisions

- It is easier to create a working vagina and feminise a body than it is to create a working penis, and it is thought that this drives decisions over which gender to raise a child.

Biological development

- For a transgender operation to be truly successful, so that sex organs can be created as functional, it has to be done in infancy when the body is still developing.

◆ Is it safe to use drugs during pregnancy?

During the late 1950s and early 1960s many pregnant women were prescribed a drug called Thalidomide to help reduce morning sickness. The result was that over 400 babies of those women were born with severe physical disabilities, including missing or malformed limbs.

Evidence has also suggested that the use of Thalidomide during pregnancy led to a higher rate of autism than in the general population. This has led to many pregnant women avoiding use of any kind of medication or drug while carrying a developing child, and many doctors are cautious about prescribing drugs to pregnant women for fear of the same thing happening again.

A report by the BBC in January 2006, however, suggests that in some cases this may actually be putting the lives of pregnant women and their unborn children more at risk. The issue therefore centres around how safe it is to use drugs during pregnancy, and what risks there might be to the developing foetus if the mother uses drugs of any kind. In some cases, it is more damaging to the mother's health, and therefore the overall health of the child, if medication is not taken during pregnancy. For example, not taking anti-epilepsy drugs whilst pregnant will increase the risk of having a seizure. In many cases, doctors can prescribe safer alternatives to any drugs thought to be of risk to pregnant women or developing foetuses.

▲ Thalidomide, used by many women during pregnancy in the 1960s, often caused birth defects.

◆ Explaining the issue using the Biological Approach

Suitable examples of concepts you could use include the following.

Mother and foetus linked through the placenta
- The main problem with drug use in pregnant mothers is that anything that is taken into the body of the mother may pass to the foetus through the placenta, so the drug itself will pass to the foetus. Drug use may also affect the passage of nutrients from the mother to the foetus, or it may affect the health of the mother which in turn will affect the health of the foetus.
- No clinical trials use pregnant women, for obvious reasons, and so the actual effects of many drugs remain unknown.

Smoking during pregnancy
- Babies of women who smoke during pregnancy are usually smaller and are more likely to have birth defects affecting the face, brain and heart than babies of non-smokers.

Drinking alcohol during pregnancy
- Alcohol is another drug with well-documented effects on developing foetuses. Excessive alcohol consumption by the mother during pregnancy can lead to Foetal Alcohol Syndrome (FAS). This results in:
  - poor growth both before and after birth
  - malformed head and brain resulting from poor growth
  - possible facial defects
  - mental retardation.
- Goodlett, Marcussen and West (1990) found that exposing rats to alcohol during the main foetal brain growth spurt affected their adult brain weight.

Using sex hormones during pregnancy
- The use of certain sex hormones during pregnancy can affect the normal development of sex organs in a developing foetus.

Evidence of practice

- You need to be able to devise and conduct one practical, which must be a test of difference collecting ordinal or interval/ratio data using an independent groups design.
- You must be able to carry out a Mann-Whitney test and interpret the findings.
- You must be able to write up the hypothesis, results and analysis of the study, using an appropriate graph and a table of the results, and to draw conclusions.

One theory developed by psychologists working within the Biological Approach is the idea that males have better spatial ability (judging space and distance, etc.) than females. This section is going to show you how to develop a study to test this theory, and how to analyse the results to see how significant they are. If the theory being tested is that males have better spatial ability than females, the research question will be: **Do males have better spatial ability than females?**

Planning and designing the experiment

◆ Research method

For this piece of research you will be conducting a **quasi experiment** because the variable that will make one group different from the others is what gender they are. Since gender is something that cannot be altered, the groups are pre-determined by their biological sex, thus making it a naturally-occurring variable. Any experiment that involves the investigation of a variable like the effect of gender on behaviour is called a quasi experiment because the groups will be based on a natural phenomenon.

The most suitable environment for conducting research of this sort is a laboratory, where the environment can easily be controlled. By getting the participants together in this way, you can easily divide them into two groups: males and females. Because the setting will be controlled, you can also be more confident that the only factor creating a difference in the scores of the two groups is whether they are male or female.

In order to test whether males have better spatial ability than females, you need to have a test that all participants in the experiment will do to see how good their spatial ability is. An easy activity to use in this experiment is a mental shape rotation task. The task requires participants to mentally rotate pictures of objects in order to match each picture with another picture that shows the object in a different position. They can choose the correct match from a selection of four possibilities.

◆ Controls

Because the study is in a laboratory setting, controls can be put in place to prevent other variables affecting the results. It is therefore possible to be more confident that any difference between the results of the males and the females is only due to their gender.

A list of controls that could be put in place includes:
- Make sure that all participants are the same age.
- Have all participants do the same task.
- Have all participants do the task in the same environment.
- Make sure that the experiment is carried out in the same way for all participants.
- Seat participants away from each other to stop them copying answers.

◆ Variables

In any experiment, you have to define the variables you are testing so that someone looking at your work knows exactly what you were trying to find out. It is important that the variables are fully **operationalised** so that it is clear how you changed or manipulated the independent variable, and how you measured your dependent variable.

In this experiment, the independent variable (IV) is whether each participant is male or female. The dependent variable (DV) is the number of correct answers given by participants on the mental shape rotation task.

◆ Hypotheses

Before doing any research a psychologist has to give a prediction, or hypothesis, about what they think is going to happen, based on the theory they are testing. In any experiment, you have to write an **experimental hypothesis** which describes exactly what you expect will happen in the experiment. Here, your experimental hypothesis will probably be: **Males will correctly identify more shape pairs than females in the mental shape rotation task measuring spatial ability**.

Because this study is based on a theory that lots of other psychologists have tested and supported, it is possible to be fairly sure that you will find that males perform better on the mental shape rotation task than females. This makes it a **directional hypothesis**.

Whenever you conduct a piece of research you should be carefully evaluating whether the alternative hypothesis is truly better supported than the null hypothesis. You need to show beyond reasonable doubt that what seems to be an effect of the IV on the DV is not a matter of chance. If in doubt the null hypothesis stands.

In this piece of research the null hypothesis will be: **There will be no difference in the number of right answers achieved by males and females in the mental shape rotation task of spatial ability, except due to chance**.

◆ Sampling

In order to carry out the experiment you need participants, so you need to think about the best way of collecting the sample. You need a group of males and a group of females – about 10 in each group to give a good representation of those groups.

Over to you

What design decisions will you be using to gather your data and why?

Over to you

List the controls you will put in place and say why you need them.

Over to you

Identify and operationalise your variables.

Over to you

Decide whether your hypotheses should be directional or non-directional (one- or two-tailed), then write suitable alternative, experimental and null hypotheses.

Over to you

Decide on your sample size and what groups you will need, and choose a suitable sample of participants.

Over to you

Decide on a suitable design for your experiment and justify your choice.

Question 1

Why is it important to have controls in place when conducting an experiment?

Question 2

Why is it important to debrief participants after they have taken part in a piece of research, and what information should be given to them at this point?

Over to you

Once you have decided how you will conduct your experiment, it is time to gather your data.

To collect a sample quickly you need to conduct an opportunity sample. This involves choosing people to take part in the experiment based on those who are easily available at the time the experiment will take place, but making sure that they fulfil the needs of the experiment. In this experiment, you need both male and female participants in equal numbers (your participant quota). Once you know when the experiment is going to take place, you can ask suitable participants to take part if they happen to be free.

◆ Design

You need two groups of participants, one male and one female, so that you can compare the scores of the male group with the scores of the female group. This means that your participant design is independent groups, as each participant is only in one group. Clearly, a participant cannot be in both the male and the female group, so the two groups are independent of one another.

This also makes the experiment a quasi experiment, as in other types of experiment the researcher can choose how to group their participants. In a quasi experiment there is only one way to group the participants because the independent variable is decided by something beyond the experimenter's control.

◆ Design decisions

In order to make it easier to record how well each participant performs in the test, you should give each one their own sheet containing the activity. They can then record on the sheet which of the four shapes is the same as the sample shape seen first in a different position, for each part of the activity. This makes it easier to collect and check the data. It also means that all participants will have a clear view of each set of shapes which may not be possible if you used a computer screen to display the shapes.

The participants will have 5 minutes to choose as many matched shapes as they can. This should be enough time for participants to have a go at a few pairs, but will not be enough time for them to learn what they should be doing. If they have too long to work on the activity they may start to guess exactly what you are trying to do and then try harder, which would give us a false idea of their spatial ability.

Carrying out the experiment

1. Set up the classroom, which will be the controlled 'laboratory' setting for this experiment, so that the desks are arranged in an exam-style formation, making sure the participants will be far enough apart to prevent copying when doing the task.
2. Choose 10 male and 10 female participants, bring them to the classroom and seat them separately at the pre-arranged desks.

3. Give the participants a brief explanation about the research that they are taking part in, explaining what they will have to do, and make sure that they consent to take part and have their data used for further analysis. You should inform them of their right to withdraw at any point. Telling the participants the full aim of the experiment may change the way they behave, so revealing the full aim should be left until after the experiment.

4. Distribute the sheets.

5. Allow participants 5 minutes to complete as many as they can.

6. When the 5 minutes is up, stop the participants and collect in their completed sheets, marking on top of each one whether the participant is male or female.

7. Give participants a full debrief about the true aim of the experiment and how their results will be used, then allow them to leave.

8. Mark the participant answers and collate the data.

Analysing the results

Once the results have been collected, you need to analyse them to see if you have found any support for the hypothesis that males have better spatial skills than females. The raw data collected from the experiment is shown on the right. It shows that, in general, the males seem to have higher scores than the females.

To look further into the difference between the two groups you need first to look at a summary of the data for both groups, in order to compare them. If you put this summary data into a table, you can see an overview of the data for each group, which may give a clearer picture of the differences between the spatial ability of males and females.

By looking at the data in this table (see right), you can see that in general males scored more highly than females as all the measures of central tendency are higher for males than for females. This suggests that males have better spatial ability than females because males, on average, correctly matched more shapes. If you put this data into a graph, it makes the picture of the differences between the two groups even clearer.

Now, if you look at the comparison in scores between the male and the female groups on the spatial task, you can see that males do tend to score higher than females on all measures.

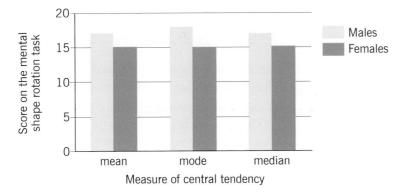

Measure of central tendency

Table of raw data

Participant	Male spatial score	Female spatial score
1	15	
2	22	
3	16	
4	20	
5	18	
6	18	
7	15	
8	16	
9	18	
10	14	
11		12
12		19
13		15
14		17
15		12
16		15
17		14
18		15
19		13
20		16

Over to you

First draw a raw data table to show all your data. Then draw a summary table for your data and identify any trends.

Measure of central tendency	Males	Females
Mean score	17	15
Mode score	18	15
Median score	17	15

Over to you

Draw a graph to display your data and describe any trends.

◀ Graph to show the average score of spatial ability for males and females.

How to

ANS

Further analysis

The data seems to show that males have better spatial ability than females, but this is only a summary picture of the results and the difference between the groups is not very big, so perhaps you need to analyse the data further in order to come to some firm conclusions. To do this, you use **inferential statistics** to test the probability that the results are showing a large enough effect of the independent variable on the dependent variable.

Inferential statistics are used to test the **significance** of results, which will indicate whether or not to reject the null hypothesis. Using an inferential test will indicate the probability that the results are due to chance. If the probability is high, you cannot reject this null hypothesis and assume that there is no difference between the spatial ability of males and females. However, if the probability that this is true is low, you can reject the null hypothesis, accept the alternative hypothesis and assume that there is a difference between the spatial abilities of males and females.

Before you can do an inferential test on the data, you need to work out which test is appropriate to use. To do this you need three pieces of information about the data:

1. the level of data measurement collected
2. the participant design of the experiment
3. whether the research is looking for a difference or a correlation between the two groups.

In this case, the test to use is a Mann-Whitney test because the data gathered is interval/ratio, it is an independent groups design and you are looking for a difference in scores between the two groups of participants.

The result of the Mann-Whitney test is **U=23.5**.

Now you have to interpret what this means for your findings. You need to work out if your results are **significant** and, if so, how significant they are, based on the **probability** that the results are due to a real effect of the independent variable on the dependent variable and not due to the group of participants chosen.

Drawing conclusions

Now you need to make some conclusions about your study by thinking back to the original hypotheses. You need to compare what you set out to find out, to the result of the inferential test.

The results, when analysed using the Mann-Whitney test, were significant at the 0.05 (5%) level. You can therefore reject the null hypothesis and accept the alternative hypothesis. This means that you have found support for the idea that males do have better spatial ability than females, but it does not prove that the hypothesis was true in all situations. (Levels of significance and seeing if a test result is significant are explained in Chapter 5.)

Question 3

What does the term 'significance' mean when referring to the outcome of statistical tests on the results of psychological research?

How to

Over to you

You need to carry out a Mann-Whitney test on your data to decide whether you should reject your null hypothesis and to make a decision about the significance of your results.

Over to you

Work out the significance of your results.

Over to you

What conclusions can you draw from your data?

Here are some issues that may affect the strength of the results.

◆ Validity

The mental shape rotation task is not really a true reflection of how we normally use spatial information. The test itself may not be a realistic measure of spatial ability, as the mental shape rotation task is only looking at one specific type of spatial information. We use our spatial ability in many everyday activities, such as driving or writing, and these specific forms of spatial ability would not be measured by the task used. The validity may also be questioned because of the controlled, artificial setting used, as the participants knew that their performance was being monitored and this may have influenced their behaviour. Males are possibly more competitive when they know they are being watched, which may explain why males performed better than females.

◆ Reliability

Each person who took part in the study had their spatial ability measured using the same test scored in the same way, so the internal consistency of the test is good. Because all participants were tested at the same time, in the same room, and received the same instructions on what to do, the procedure was fully standardised for all participants. This makes it is likely that the study results are reliable. The fact that the study can be replicated means that the reliability can be tested.

◆ Generalisability

The overall number of participants used is adequate to draw conclusions from, but only having 10 in each group does not give a broad enough sample to allow a comparison of the male and female groups to be considered strong. Also, all the participants used in the study were students at college, which means they were not representative of the population as a whole, being all within approximately the same age group.

◆ Credibility

The overall credibility of the experiment may be questioned as the research took place in an artificial setting and the results could have been the result of where and how the research was conducted rather than the result of the difference between males and females in terms of spatial ability. Because the experiment may have some validity issues, this fact, combined with the generalisability problems caused by the limited and unrepresentative sample, would lead many psychologists to argue that the results lack credibility. More evidence may therefore be needed to support the hypothesis that males have better spatial ability than females.

Over to you

What issues might there be with the validity of your results?

Over to you

How reliable are your results?

Over to you

Can you identify any problems there may be when generalising your results?

Question 4

What factors might affect the generalisability of the results of an experiment?

Taking it further

Although psychologists will consider their findings to be significant enough to be able to accept their alternative hypothesis if the probability of the results being due to chance is at 0.05, they also look at lower levels of probability to render their results highly significant. If the result of an inferential test was actually showing that the probability of the findings being due to chance was only 0.01 (1%), for example, they would accept their alternative hypothesis as being highly significant.

ANS

Summary

The Biological Approach focuses on explaining behaviour in terms of people's biology, for example:

- how the genes they are born with determine who they will become
- how the way that their central nervous system works influences their behaviour.

◆ Methodology

To study genetic influences on behaviour, psychologists use methods such as twin and adoption studies to look for similarities in behaviour between close family members.

- Twin studies can be used to see if siblings who share a lot of genes in common (100% if the twins are identical; 50% if the twins are fraternal) also have similar behaviour.
- Adoption studies can isolate genetic factors from environmental factors in determining traits.

Biological psychologists also study the brain and how it controls behaviour, using brain scanning techniques and by looking at how brain damage affects behaviour.

- Structural scans such as Magnetic Resonance Imaging show pictures of the brain to show areas of damage.
- Functional scans such as Positron Emission Tomography show how active certain areas of the brain are during different activities.
- Lesion studies on animals, where brain damage can be caused deliberately, mean that any changes in the animal's normal behaviour can be attributed to the change in brain structure.

In the exam, you will be expected to be able both to describe the main features of the research methods used within the approach and to evaluate their strengths and weaknesses.

◆ Content

Psychologists working within the Biological Approach look at various aspects of human behaviour but this chapter focuses on biological explanations of gender:

- How genes influence gender
- How hormones influence gender development
- How brain lateralisation is linked to gender development.

These three explanations can be summarised as follows:

- We are all born with a series of chromosome pairs which contain genes that tell our body how to develop. One of those pairs contains the genes that influence gender development. Females have an XX pair that cause female body parts to develop, while males have an XY pair that result in male body development.
- Once the genes are in place, it is the introduction of hormones during body development that helps to determine how the sex organs develop.

High levels of testosterone lead to testes developing, and an absence of testosterone means that the body develops with female sex organs.

- Evidence has shown that, as well as the obvious differences between males and females in terms of the sex organs, there are also differences in the brain structure and functions of males and females. Psychologists working within the Biological Approach look in detail at the differences between male and female brain structure to learn more about how the two genders are significantly different.

◆ Studies

The famous case study of Bruce-Brenda-David, by Dr. John Money, gave us great insight into the involvement of biological factors in gender development by looking at how a genetically normal male reacted to being raised as a female after a failed circumcision left him without a penis. It was found that 'Brenda' did not grow up to be a normal female just because she was raised as a girl, and her behaviour was still very masculine. The child's genetic make-up was the stronger factor in determining gender and he remained male. As well as describing the case study by discussing what happened, you also need to think about the strengths and problems associated with this study, and one other.

◆ Key issues

As part of your study of the Biological Approach, you will have looked at a key issue. You must be sure that you can describe the issue in some detail and produce it as a question, and that you can then go on to answer the question using ideas and explanations from this approach. You should keep details on:

- how you **planned and carried out** your experiment
- how you **analysed** your results
- any **conclusions** you made.

Examzone _____ Practise

Section B questions

1. Describe how information is transmitted between neurons in the Central Nervous System. (4 marks)

2. Genes determine biological sex; assess the extent to which gender is based on our genes. (4 marks)

3. Animals are frequently used to gather evidence for the Biological Approach in psychology. Evaluate the use of such studies. (4 marks)

4. You have studied the case of David Reimer who was raised through childhood as a girl. Outline the actions that were taken in order to establish a female identity. (3 marks)

5. Outline one way in which researchers may produce a scan of the brain. (3 marks)

Section C questions

6. Compare the explanations offered by the Psychodynamic and Biological Approaches to the development of gender. (8 marks)

7. Evaluate twin and/or adoption studies as a means of understanding the nature – nurture debate in the Biological Approach. (6 marks)

8. Describe and evaluate evidence for psychological differences between males and females being determined by biological factors. (12 marks: 6 AO1 6 AO2)

MCQ

5. Learning Approach

Key terms

- classical conditioning
- operant conditioning
- social learning
- stimulus and response

What you will learn about in this chapter

- How conditioning, reinforcement and social learning influence human behaviour.
- How to understand and apply some methodology and design issues.
- The mechanisms that underlie our learning.
- How some behavioural therapies work and whether they are useful.
- How to apply a theory to a real-life application and explain it.
- How to devise, conduct and assess your practical investigation.

What you need to know

- The role of conditioning, reinforcement and social learning in human behaviour and key ideas from the approach.
- Observational research and methodological issues relating to laboratory experiments.
- Inferential statistics and levels of significance.
- Ethical guidelines for the use of human participants in psychological investigations.
- The three mechanisms of learning: classical conditioning, operant conditioning and social learning theory, and associated key terms.
- One behavioural therapy that is based on the principles of either classical or operant conditioning.
- How learning theory can explain gender development, including a comparison with the Psychodynamic and Biological Approaches.

Examiner's tip

There are many new terms to learn in this approach. Try to practise them by relating them to your own experiences. Develop a glossary of terms with definitions and examples to help you revise later.

Defining the Learning Approach

The Learning Approach proposes that behaviour is acquired by learning experiences. Learning theorists examine how we acquire these behaviours and study the mechanisms that underlie learning. Unlike the Cognitive and Biological Approaches, this approach sees mental processes and genetics as relatively unimportant in determining our behaviour. Instead, the focus is on **observable** behaviours, viewing the investigation of mental processes and unconscious forces as unscientific and untestable.

The early 20th century saw a rejection of the unscientific methods used to understand human emotion and thinking, and a shift towards a more scientific study of human behaviour. The Learning Approach uses laboratory experiments on humans and animals to investigate the mechanisms of behaviour acquisition by observing responses to given stimuli. This is known as **conditioning**.

The approach considers the role of the environment to be of greater importance than genetics and cognition in determining behaviour. Essentially, we are not restricted by our genetic make-up; we are only constrained by the environment we are brought up in. The approach clearly therefore falls on the nurture side of the **nature-nurture debate**.

The approach puts forward three mechanisms of learning: **classical conditioning**, **operant conditioning** and **social learning**.

◆ Classical conditioning

This is learning through **association**. When we pair a new stimulus with an existing **stimulus-response** link, we learn to associate the two stimuli and respond similarly to both. For example, our mouth waters when we bite into a lemon, and if we associate the taste of a lemon with the colour yellow, we will also experience mouth-watering at the colour. The taste and the colour have been paired and now both create the conditioned response of salivation.

◆ Operant conditioning

This is learning through **consequence**. If we perform a behaviour that is punished, we will not repeat the behaviour as it is associated with something unpleasant. However, if we perform a behaviour that is reinforced by a pleasant experience, we will repeat it because it is linked to something positive. Similarly, we will repeat behaviour in order to avoid something unpleasant, such as handing in an essay to avoid being told off.

Thorndike (1911) demonstrated that behaviours could be repeated (and therefore learnt) by providing a positive consequence for those behaviours. Similarly, behaviours could be stopped by providing a negative consequence. He demonstrated this using a **puzzle box** in which he placed a kitten; the puzzle was that the kitten had to escape to receive food as a reward. Initially, the kitten clambered around the box and through trial and error happened upon the escape latch. Once the kitten escaped it received food and then was placed back in the box.

Over several trials, Thorndike observed that the kitten escaped faster. He reasoned that the escape behaviour was not a flash of inspiration or rationalisation on behalf of the kitten, but rather it was trial and error learning, whereby a number of different attempts were made until the correct response (pulling the latch) was made. The kittens then made an association between the correct response and their escape and this association was rewarded with food. The stimulus-response link (latch-escape) is repeated when reinforced with food; this is known as the **law of effect**, meaning that the effect/consequence of a behaviour determines whether the behaviour is repeated.

◆ Social learning

This is learning by **observation**. This theory does not fall under the **behaviourism** banner, as it moves from the conditioning of behaviour (association and reinforcement) to the copying of behaviour. Social learning proposes that we imitate the behaviour of a person, called a **model**. The behaviour is not immediately imitated, but is stored in memory until required (therefore involving cognition). According to this theory we imitate or copy the behaviour of models who are similar to us, who we may respect or admire, or someone we can identify with. We are more likely to copy the behaviour of a model if they have been reinforced for their behaviour. This is known as **vicarious reinforcement**, as we are learning from the consequences of others' actions.

Have you ever wondered?

Why are you the way you are? What makes you motivated, shy, tearful, skilled? List some behaviours that are unique to your personality. Reflect on the list and try to give a reason why you have these attributes.

You may have listed shyness as an attribute that you have learnt from your parent, or maybe that it runs in your family. The Learning Approach believes that all behaviours are learnt, not inherited. Look back at your list and see if your attributes can be explained through learning from experience or from another person.

Taking it further

Skinner (1904-1990) is famous for putting his own daughter Debbie in an adapted 'child-friendly' Skinner box and for writing the books *Walden II* and *Beyond Freedom and Dignity* to endorse communities functioning on the principles of operant conditioning to manage behaviour.

Research Debbie and some of the moral objections to environmental control proposed in Skinner's publications.

▲ Daughter Debbie in the Skinner box

Methodology

What you need to know

- You need to be able to describe and evaluate observation as a research method, including different types.
- You need to be able to describe inferential tests, including levels of measurement, reasons for choosing a chi-squared, Mann-Whitney or Spearman's test, and be able to compare observed and critical values to judge significance.
- You need to be able to describe and evaluate laboratory experiments as used with both animals and humans.
- You need to be able to describe and assess ethical guidelines for using humans in research.

> One rule about observations is that they can be carried out without getting consent, debriefing or giving the right to withdraw, as long as they are done in a public setting when the person is expecting to be observed in general by others. If someone is not expecting to be watched, the study cannot be done without permission.

Taking it further

Investigate Mary Ainsworth's work where she uses the Strange Situation to try to understand patterns of attachments between mothers and their children. The situation is set up but all the data is collected by observation.

Question 1

Explain the difference between participant and non-participant observations, and between overt and covert observations.

Examiner's tip

If you are asked to outline what is meant by some of the types of observation, be ready with an example as that will show your understanding of the concepts after you have defined them.

Observation as a research method

Many research methods use observation. Milgram watched the behaviour of his participants when they thought they were giving dangerous electric shocks to others. However, observation as a research method involves all the data being gathered by observing and does not involve manipulation of the independent variable (IV). Milgram's study was a laboratory experiment, not an observation. Case studies can involve observations but the case study is the main research method. So observations can be defined as being when watching is the main way of obtaining data and when there is no manipulation of the independent variable. Observations can be structured but are usually naturalistic.

◆ Types of observation

Sometimes, the behaviour to be observed is carried out in a structured setting, where observation can be by using a one-way mirror or screen. Apparatus is available and a structure for the behaviour is laid down. This is usually in situations such as childcare or observations of other relationships. These are called **structured observations**. Most observations are naturalistic because natural behaviour is what is required.

Naturalistic observations take place in the participants' natural setting. There can be non-participant observations, where the observer is not part of the situation, and participant observations, where the observer is also a participant. Observations can be overt, which means the participants know they are being observed and possibly why, or covert, which means the observation is kept secret from the participants. Observations usually include **tallying**. Tallying produces quantitative data, whereas if observations include writing down quotes or telling the story of what is happening, that is qualitative data.

The first stage of an observation, after access has been obtained and decisions made about the type of observation, is to watch the situation to note down behaviours ready for tallying. For example, if you want to see whether women drivers jump traffic lights more often than men, you need to decide what 'jumping the lights' means.

Probably, you would record every driver that crossed the lights on amber and note their gender. If you were watching to see if boys and girls choose different toys, you would focus on certain toys only, to make the observation manageable. A chart is then drawn up, arrangements made, ethical issues adhered to, and decisions made about the mechanics of the observation. The final task is to make the tally marks.

◆ Evaluation of observations as a research method

Naturalistic and structured observations
Structured observations can be useful because there are controls, which means that cause and effect conclusions are more easily drawn as there are fewer factors to affect what is observed. It also means that such observations can be tested for reliability, as they are replicable.

Naturalistic observations may be seen as not very reliable because they take place in the participants' natural setting, which is hard to replicate. Behaviour at one moment in time is not likely to be repeated. However, if the procedure of the observation is fully documented, another researcher could repeat it and it might be found reliable. The more controlled the observation, the more likely it will be found to be reliable.

Naturalistic observations are valid in that they take place in a natural setting, and the observations are of naturally-occurring behaviour. Structured observations can lack validity.

Overt and covert observations
Overt observations are good because informed consent can be obtained and the right to withdraw can be given. Covert observations are less ethical because the participants are not aware the study is taking place.

Regarding validity, covert observations are good because the participants do not know they are being studied. Their behaviour should therefore be as usual, which makes it valid behaviour. Overt observations, however, might lead to unnatural behaviour simply because the participants know they are being watched.

Non-participant and participant observations
Participant observations have validity because there is no 'strange' observer affecting behaviour. The observer is already part of the group. Non-participant observations can lack validity because the observer affects behaviour.

On a practical level, non-participant observation is good because the observer can concentrate on time sampling and tallying, which is hard to do if you are also trying to take part in the group or behaviour. Participant observation is hard because there is no time to make notes or actually observe. Also, if you are a participant it might be hard to step back and watch. On the other hand, the participant observer has shared understanding with the group, and so understands the data in a way that a non-participant observer might miss.

A difficulty when tallying is that if, for example, one child you are watching stays in the book corner for ten minutes whereas another child moves around, you would make more tally marks for that second child but this would not represent their behaviour appropriately. **Time sampling** is used, where a tally mark is made at regular intervals.

Question 2

Evaluate naturalistic observations in terms of their reliability and validity.

▲ In covert observations, participants are not aware the study is taking place.

Question 3

Discuss one way in which observations can be said to be ethical and one way in which they might not be ethical.

Question 4

Compare the four types of naturalistic observation (participant, non-participant, covert and overt) in terms of their strengths and weaknesses.

ANS

ANS

ANS

ANS

Question 5

Outline three guidelines you have studied in your course.

Ethical guidelines for the use of human participants

The chapter on the Social Approach considers the guidelines for informed consent, debriefing, right to withdraw, competence and deceit. Check that you understand these five ethical guidelines and that you can define them, explain them, apply them, and give an example of each. You will also have looked at privacy and confidentiality when considering other approaches, such as the Psychodynamic Approach.

◆ Studies and assessing the guidelines

One way to assess the guidelines is to look at studies to see whether they used the guidelines. Two studies suggested for the Learning Approach use human participants and can be assessed for ethics.

The prescribed study for this approach is Bandura et al. (1961), who did an experiment using children. They used models to show children aggressive behaviour and then watched to see if the children imitated the models, which in general they did. Parents appear to have given consent and there was theoretically the right to withdraw. There was no real deceit involved and the researchers carried out the study competently. The level of violence that the children watched was not too high, as the adults simply 'bashed bobo'. There did not appear to be a thorough debriefing, however, and the children were exposed to watching aggression, so it might be said that the study had some problems regarding ethics. Guidelines have been tightened since 1961.

Another study suggested for this approach is the Little Albert study, done in 1920, where a very young child was made to jump by banging a metal bar hard enough to make a loud noise. Little Albert learned to associate the loud noise with his pet rat and other white furry things, and developed a phobia. There was no informed consent, as it does not seem that Little Albert's mother knew clearly what was going on. The researchers were competent up to a point, because the baby seemed to come to no direct harm, but it is not known what the lasting effects were, which raises questions. The baby did not really have the right to withdraw and there was no debriefing. This was before the guidelines were enforced strongly.

Taking it further

Find some more modern studies where guidelines seem more appropriately enforced. These studies do not have to be within the Learning Approach. Consider studies you have already looked at that were done after the year 2000 and note whether they adhered to guidelines or not. You should find that more modern studies are less unethical.

Question 6

Referring to at least one study, show how two ethical guidelines have been either adhered to or breached during psychological research.

Another study, Milgram's (1963) is always useful when it comes to assessing guidelines, as there were many ethical issues involved (see pages 10-11 and 15, where such issues are discussed). Note that in 1963 there were some guidelines but they have been greatly developed since then. Consider studies you have covered for your course where ethical issues are better focused on, so that you can give a balanced argument. You will find that studies from the 1990s are less likely to break current guidelines.

Laboratory experiments

The Learning Approach uses laboratory experiments a great deal as well, with both animal and human participants. Make sure you understand all the features and terminology in the following table.

Features of laboratory experiments using human participants	Evaluation of laboratory experiments
• An independent variable is manipulated. • A dependent variable is measured. • An experimental hypothesis explains what is predicted. • The hypothesis is directional or non-directional. • There is often an experimental group and a control group. • Extraneous variables are controlled for, so there are no confounding variables. • A cause and effect relationship is claimed. • Behaviour is reduced to a measurable concept by operationalising the IV and the DV. • Sampling is careful to avoid participant variables. • Controls are careful to avoid situational variables. • Care is taken to avoid experimenter effects. • With a repeated measures design, counterbalancing or randomisation is used to avoid order effects. • Laboratory experiments tend to gather quantitative data.	• They tend to be reliable because controls mean they are replicable. • They tend not to be ecologically valid because the setting is usually unnatural. • They tend not to be valid with regard to the task, because of all the controls. • They tend to be fairly generalisable because sampling is careful and representative. • They can lack credibility because of the artificial setting and artificial task. • The data is gathered objectively, usually because someone other than the researcher can often run the experiment and also because the IV is tightly controlled and the DV follows – there is then little need for interpretation. • There can be ethical problems because of the controls and the artificial tasks and setting.

Additional features of laboratory experiments using animals:

• Ethical issues concerning use of animals must be adhered to, such as suitable caging, use of anaesthetics, not using endangered species, not causing unnecessary pain and suffering, having a licence when required, using as few animals as possible, always looking for an alternative first.

• Studies must pay attention to features of the species used, so that conclusions are appropriate given the natural tendencies of different species.

• Generalising from animal studies to humans is problematic – to the point where animal studies may not be useful.

• Findings from animal studies can benefit animals with regard to their care – though this may not be a strong enough argument for their use.

Question 7

Describe four main features of a laboratory experiment using humans.

Taking it further

Use the BPS (British Psychological Society) website to check their ethical guidelines. The most recent are in the Code of Conduct 2006. Make notes from this code, referring to the seven guidelines listed in this section and add some more that you find interesting. Consider special issues such as when doing observations and when using children.

Examiner's tip

The methodology that is new in this approach concerns observational research methods and there is some new material on inferential statistics. Apart from that, the specified material on ethics, laboratory experiments and using animals is covered elsewhere. Be ready to answer questions on any area of methodology by this stage in your course, because this is the last approach and you are expected to have fully understood all the methodology terms by now.

SUM

EX

Inferential testing

You will have looked at inferential testing if you have already studied the Psychodynamic or Biological Approach. The Learning Approach covers the third inferential test required, the Chi-Squared test, following a brief review of the features of inferential testing.

◆ Levels of measurement

There are three levels of measurement you need to know about:

- **Nominal data** is when categories are recorded, such as the number of yes/no answers.
- **Ordinal data** is ranked data, such as judging on a scale of 1 to 5 how anxious someone is.
- **Interval/ratio data** is where scores have equal intervals between them and are mathematical scores, such as time.

The chi-squared test can only be used for nominal data. Note that interval/ratio is the highest level of measurement in terms of giving information. Ordinal is the next highest and nominal the lowest. A level of measurement can be reduced to the lower levels. For example, degrees Celsius is interval/ratio but can be converted to ranks of temperature, which again can be converted to hot/cold categories.

◆ Participant designs

You have studied three participant designs – repeated measures, matched pairs and independent groups. **Repeated measures** designs involve using the same people for all parts of the study. **Matched pairs**, though they involve using different people, are treated as repeated measures when it comes to statistical testing because those different people are matched as if they are the same people. **Independent groups** designs involve different people for each part of the study and they are not matched. The other design is a correlation, which requires a different test.

◆ Testing for a difference or a relationship

When choosing a statistical test, you need to look at the alternative hypothesis and see if it is predicting a difference or a relationship. For example, if the hypothesis is that people over 50 drive more slowly than those under 50, it is predicting a difference in speed of driving between the two groups. If the hypothesis is that the older you get the slower your driving, it is predicting a relationship between age and speed of driving. It is important to check whether a hypothesis looks at a difference or a relationship.

◆ Choosing an inferential test

Three tests are specified for your course. It is easier to explain how to choose a test if others are included, so eight tests are included in a table on the CD-ROM to help you understand how to choose the right test. Use the table to see how to choose the three highlighted tests, which are the ones for your course, following a step-by-step approach, as outlined opposite.

ANS

Question 8

What is meant by the terms 'levels of measurement' and 'participant design'?

ANS

Question 9

What three features of a study need to be considered when choosing an inferential test?

Examiner's tip

You could be asked to give reasons for choosing a particular test, and you can use the table on the CD-ROM to work out the reasons. Alternatively you might be given some information and asked to choose the test. The table will enable you either to work from the information to the test or work from the test back to the information you need.

How to

1. Test of difference or relationship
2. Repeated measures/matched pairs or independent groups (if test of difference)
3. Level of measurement of the data
4. Choose the test.

Choosing a level of significance

Choose either p≤.05 or p≤.01. 0.05 means 5% of the results can be due to chance but that is acceptable for an alternative hypothesis when there is not already a lot of evidence to say the predictions are likely to be true. 0.01 means 1% of the results can be due to chance and that is acceptable. This is used when there is previous research suggesting that the alternative hypothesis is likely to be found true. If the observed value is found to be significant (you compare it to the critical value to find out) then the null hypothesis, which says the results are due to chance, can be rejected (they are not due to chance any more than is acceptable).

Using critical value tables

You will by now have carried out a Spearman's test, a Mann-Whitney test and a chi-squared test. All three have critical value tables that can be found in statistics textbooks and are not all reproduced here. When you have the result of the test, which is the observed value, find the relevant critical value tables. For Spearman's and Mann-Whitney you need to know N, which is the number of participants in the group(s) and for chi-squared you need to know df, which is the degrees of freedom. For a two-by-two table (two columns and two rows) df is 1, and for a three-by-two table, df is 2.

You need to choose a level of significance and p≤.05 is suitable. You also need to know whether the alternative hypothesis was directional (one-tailed) or non-directional (two-tailed). For the Spearman's and chi-squared tests the observed value must be equal to or larger than the critical value and for the Mann-Whitney test the observed value must be equal to or less than the critical value, for it to be significant.

	Levels of significance (one-tailed test)			
	0.05	0.025	0.01	0.005
	Levels of significance (two-tailed test)			
df	0.10	0.05	0.02	0.01
1	**2.71**	**3.84**	**5.41**	**6.64**
2	**4.60**	**5.99**	**7.82**	**9.21**

An example of a critical value table (for a chi-squared test)

Df 1 and 2 are shown as they are relevant to a two-by-two table or a three-by-two table. Numbers in bold are the critical values, which in this test the observed value must be equal to or more than, to be significant.

Question 10

What is meant by p≤.05?

Examiner's tip

You may be given a section of a critical value table and then asked whether an observed value would be significant or not, and why. Practise this sort of question by making up observed values and the other details you need in order to check for significance.

Examiner's tip

Make up some studies so that you can work out which test you would choose out of the three for your course. You will find that you can only work with correlations (when the test is Spearman's) or studies using independent groups design (when nominal data means you use a chi-squared test and any other data means you use a Mann-Whitney test).

Taking it further

For the Psychodynamic Approach you will have done a Spearman's test but you may not have looked to see if your result was significant. Go back now and use critical value tables to see if what you found was significant. You probably did check for significance when you did your Mann-Whitney test but, if not, check that as well.

Question 11

If the result of a chi-squared test is 6.20 and the hypothesis of the study was directional, with df = 1, would the null hypothesis be rejected? In other words, is the alternative hypothesis 'significant'? Explain your answer with reference to the critical value table given here.

ANS

Content

What you need to know

- You need to be able to describe the key features of three theories of learning: classical conditioning, operant conditioning and social learning theory.
- You need to be able to describe and evaluate one treatment/therapy for either classical or operant conditioning. One therapy is detailed here, with a brief outline of two others.
- You need to be able to describe and evaluate learning theory as an explanation of gender development and compare this theory with that of the Biological and Psychodynamic Approaches.

Key terms

Neutral stimulus (NS): Any environmental stimulus that does not naturally produce a behavioural response, e.g. a computer does not naturally produce a fear response.

Unconditioned stimulus (UCS): Any stimulus that produces a natural, unlearnt behavioural response, e.g. a lemon naturally produces a mouth-watering response.

Unconditioned response (UCR): Any response that occurs naturally without learning, e.g. blinking in the sunlight.

Conditioned stimulus (CS): A stimulus that has been associated with a UCS so that it now produces the same response as the UCS on its own, e.g. the colour yellow makes you feel ill because the taste of school custard once made you ill.

Conditioned response (CR): A learnt behaviour that is shown in response to a learnt stimulus (CS), e.g. being scared of dogs is a response that was learnt when one bit you.

▲ Terms and definitions used to understand the process of classical conditioning.

Classical conditioning as a theory of learning

Classical conditioning refers to the process of learning through associating a neutral stimulus with an unconditioned stimulus, which produces a natural response (unconditioned response). If the association between the neutral stimulus and unconditioned stimulus is maintained, the same natural response will be shown when the neutral stimulus is present. The neutral stimulus is now a learnt association and becomes known as the conditioned stimulus. The result is that we respond in the same way to the unconditioned and the conditioned stimulus.

◆ Pavlov's theory

Ivan Pavlov (1849-1936) developed the theory of classical conditioning from his research on the salivary response of dogs. Pavlov had designed apparatus that allowed the saliva of dogs to be collected in response to food being presented to them. Dog naturally salivate at the sight and smell of food, but Pavlov noticed that the dogs were salivating before food was presented; they were salivating at the sight of the technicians who gave them food. The dogs had learnt to associate the technicians with food. This observation led to the development of **classical** or Pavlovian conditioning and he started a series of experiments to test the theory.

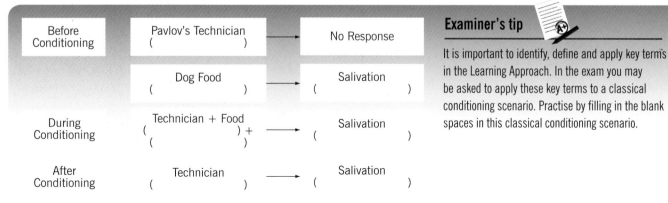

Examiner's tip

It is important to identify, define and apply key terms in the Learning Approach. In the exam you may be asked to apply these key terms to a classical conditioning scenario. Practise by filling in the blank spaces in this classical conditioning scenario.

First Order Conditioning	Bell (CS 1)	$\longrightarrow$	Salivation (CR)
	Bell + Buzzer (CS 1 + CS 2)	$\longrightarrow$	Salivation (CR)
Second Order Conditioning			
	Buzzer (CS 2)	$\longrightarrow$	Salivation (CR)

◀ Higher order conditioning

Pavlov conducted a series of experiments to investigate whether a bell could induce salivation by associating the noise with food. The food (UCS) and bell (NS) were paired on a number of occasions, then the bell presented alone. Pavlov found that the dog salivated at the sound of a bell, which had become a conditioned stimulus (CS), which produced the learnt response of salivation (CR). He then paired the bell with the sound of a buzzer several times and found that the dog would salivate at the buzzer too. This further conditioning is known as **higher order conditioning**, and can explain why some behaviours can be triggered by rather abstract and unrelated stimuli.

Pavlov also found that the dogs would salivate at any stimulus that closely resembled a conditioned stimulus, for example the dogs conditioned to salivate at the shape of a circle would also salivate at an oval shape. This extending of association is known as **stimulus generalisation**. Generalisation is an important mechanism – if we are bitten by an adder we need to steer clear of other similar-looking snakes in case we are bitten again. The opposite can also be true. If you condition a dog to salivate at the sight of a circle and never present food when an oval is presented, the dog will learn to **discriminate** between the two shapes and not salivate when an oval is presented.

Pavlov found that he could weaken a learnt behaviour by dissolving the link made between the conditioned stimulus and conditioned response. Dogs that were trained to salivate at the sound of a bell were no longer given food and the bell alone was presented many times. Eventually the dogs stopped salivating at the sound of a bell. This process is known as **extinction**. However, it does not mean that the behaviour has been unlearnt, rather that it has become dormant. If a dog is taken out of the experiment and then brought back later, it may salivate spontaneously at the ringing of the bell. This is called **spontaneous recovery**.

◆ Fear as a conditioned response

It is widely accepted that we acquire a fear or phobic response in the same way that Pavlov conditioned his dogs to salivate at different stimuli. In this case we learn to associate a neutral stimulus with the response of fear. For example, it is possible that a person can get stuck in a lift, experience anxiety and maybe fear the lift will drop. The next time the person approaches a lift they exhibit a similar fear response.

Some behaviours are acquired quickly after only one pairing of the CS and UCS. This is known as **one-trial learning**, so repeated pairings/ associations are not necessary. Taste aversion is an example of one-trial learning – when we eat something that makes us ill we tend to avoid the food in the future. This is an important survival mechanism.

Taking it further

Watson and Raynor (1920) demonstrated how a fear could be acquired in a classic experiment on a child called Little Albert. They introduced Albert to a white rat and observed that he was interested in the rat but not afraid of it. They then made a loud noise with a steel bar behind Albert's back, which startled him and made him cry. After repeated pairing of the white rat and the loud noise, Little Albert eventually came to fear the rat on its own.

Using the diagrams of classical conditioning shown here, draw a diagram to illustrate how Little Albert became scared of the white rat. Use all the key terms.

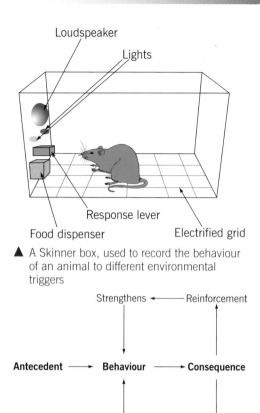

▲ A Skinner box, used to record the behaviour of an animal to different environmental triggers

Strengthens ◄——— Reinforcement

Antecedent ——→ Behaviour ———→ Consequence

Weakens ◄——— Punishment

▲ 'Behaviour is shaped and maintained by its consequences' (Skinner, 1938).

An example of negative reinforcement:
• A child associates a spider with fear.
• The fear continues because the child avoids spiders by running away.
• The fear is therefore avoided.

Reinforcement and punishment are not always clear cut. For example, a naughty child may be punished by a parent. The parent assumes that punishment will prevent the naughtiness from recurring but actually the child sees the punishment as attention, so repeats the behaviour. Punishment and reinforcement are therefore subjective and different for every individual.

Operant conditioning as a theory of learning

Unlike classical conditioning, which is learning through association, operant conditioning involves learning through **consequence**.

B. F. Skinner (1874-1949) developed the theory of operant conditioning and recorded the behaviour of animals in response to different consequences. The Skinner box, which he designed, contained a lever for an animal such as a rat or pigeon to press for food to be delivered. It also had a speaker and lights that could be used to trigger a behaviour, and a shock generator was connected to the floor to deliver an electric shock in response to a behaviour.

Skinner described the ABC model of operant conditioning to illustrate how this theory of learning works:

Antecedent: the chamber could present a stimulus (lights, noises) that triggers behaviour.

Behaviour: a response that could be observed and measured as a result of the antecedent (lever pressing).

Consequence: a reward or punishment followed the behaviour (food, shock).

The stimulus–response association is only repeated or learnt if the consequence of the pairing is a positive one. A negative consequence would weaken the stimulus-response link.

• Positive reinforcement is giving something pleasurable to the animal following a desired behaviour, to make sure the behaviour is repeated, for example giving a rat food for pressing a lever. The consequence of lever pressing is desirable, so is repeated to gain more food.

• Negative reinforcement is removing something nasty or uncomfortable in response to the desired behaviour. This also results in the behaviour being repeated, in order to escape the nasty stimulus. An example would be to give the rat an electric shock until a lever is pressed. The lever pressing stops the shock so the rat presses the lever again to ensure it avoids it in the future.

Both types of reinforcement produce repeated behaviour. Although fears are typically acquired though classical conditioning, they are maintained through negative reinforcement. **Punishment**, on the other hand, weakens the behaviour by presenting something unpleasant or painful whenever the behaviour is shown. For example, when a rat presses a lever it is given an electric shock; it ceases lever pressing at that time to make sure that it does not have another shock.

◆ Types of reinforcer

It is important to identify a reinforcer that will encourage the behaviour in question to be learnt.

There are two types:

• Primary reinforcers are used to satisfy a basic survival need, such as food, sex or water.

• Secondary reinforcers are only fulfilling because they are associated with a primary reinforcer, such as money that is used to buy food.

Sometimes reinforcement is unintentional, that is, we produce a chance behaviour that happens to be given reinforcement. This can lead to rather odd behaviour being displayed. See pages 144-145 for an example.

◆ Behaviour-shaping

The principles of operant conditioning can be used to develop complex behaviours that would not be displayed naturally. This is achieved by reinforcing any behaviour that closely resembles that of the desired target behaviour. Reinforcement then gradually becomes more selective by reinforcing more and more closely-related behaviours until the target behaviour is produced. This process is known as **behaviour shaping**, as reinforcement is given for **successive approximations** until the desired response is achieved.

Social learning theory

Social learning is learning through **observation**. An observer learns a new behaviour by watching and **imitating** another person, or role model. Both humans and animals learn through this **modelling** process. Cook (1988) found that reared Rhesus monkeys, which initially displayed no fear of snakes, displayed alarm after watching the anxious reactions of wild monkeys to the presence of snakes.

Bandura (1977) believed that social learning was achieved only if four criteria were met:

1. **Attention** to the role model – if we do not pay attention we will not learn.
2. **Retention** of the observed behaviour – essentially, the capacity to remember it.
3. **Reproduction** of the target behaviour – if the behaviour is beyond our capability, we cannot reproduce it.
4. **Motivation** to imitate the observed behaviour – a reward we anticipate we will receive if we reproduce the behaviour.

For example, a child watches an older sibling eating with a spoon. The child remembers this the next time they are eating and imitates the behaviour by using a spoon to eat food. The parent notices and praises the child for eating correctly. Of course, the child may learn the behaviour but choose not to display it. Just because we observe behaviour does not necessarily mean that we reproduce it, otherwise we would have a great many children doing housework after watching their parents!

Role models

The type of role model helps determine whether a behaviour is copied. Effective role models are typically the same-sex as the observer, are admired or respected and have status power. It is important that the role model can be identified with.

We often do not need direct reinforcement to reproduce behaviour. If a child is praised for eating with a spoon, the younger sibling may copy, but not if the role model is punished for eating with their hands. This is known as **vicarious reinforcement**, which essentially means that we learn through others' mistakes or successes:

Taking it further

▲ David Beckham is seen as a role model.

Why might David Beckham be seen as a role model?

Who is he a role model for?

What behaviours will be copied?

Treatments/therapy used in the Learning Approach

◆ Aversion therapy: a treatment based on the principles of classical conditioning

(UCS) Emetic drug ⟶ Vomiting (UCR)

(CS) Alcohol + (UCS) Emetic drug ⟶ Vomiting (UCR)

(CS) Alcohol ⟶ Vomiting(UCR)

▲ Aversion therapy to treat alcoholism

Aversion therapy is based on the principles of classical conditioning in that it aims to remove undesirable behaviour by associating it with an aversive stimulus, conditioning a kind of phobia of the undesired behaviour.

Aversion therapy has been used to treat alcoholism. The alcohol is paired with an **emetic drug** which causes nausea and vomiting, so that vomiting becomes a conditioned response to alcohol.

Note that it is necessary to give the patient other non-alcoholic drinks without the emetic drug during treatment, to prevent stimulus generalisation.

Aversion therapy has also been used to prevent a number of **sexually-deviant behaviours**, ranging from homosexuality (clearly very controversial) to fetishism. Shocks have been paired with sexually-inappropriate literature, photographs or film to condition avoidance of sexually-deviant behaviour.

Taking it further

The film *Clockwork Orange* portrays aversion therapy in an extreme form. The leading actor is given an emetic drug when shown film footage of sadistic and sexually-violent acts (offences that he had previously been imprisoned for doing himself). Following this therapy, the violent behaviour previously enjoyed by the character is replaced by extreme nausea and sickness every time he witnesses sexual or violent behaviour. **Note:** *Clockwork Orange* is an 18 certificate.

Evaluation

There has been some success using aversion therapy for alcoholics, but typically only when it is one treatment alongside others. Relapse rates can be very high, as the therapy depends upon the patient being able to avoid the undesired stimuli. If an alcoholic undergoes aversion therapy and is ill at the taste of alcohol, the alcohol is avoided. However, if they are exposed to alcohol again without the emetic, they may feel ill but do not vomit, so they will eventually lose the association and relapse.

Aversion therapy today is not popular because there are ethical issues to consider when deliberately conditioning aversions by making people ill or uncomfortable. Giving electric shocks or emetic drugs is distressing for the patient; some also question the degree of control the therapist has over the treatment, and therefore the lack of control the patient has. Clearly, a patient has to be very unhappy or unhealthy to want to undertake this form of therapy, and it may be seen as a last resort.

During the 1970s aversion therapy was used to treat homosexuality. Not only does this label homosexuality as a deviance or illness, but it puts pressure on to perfectly healthy people to try and change their sexual behaviour in order to conform to what is socially accepted.

A more recent variation of aversion therapy, called **covert sensitisation**, involves the imaged association with the undesirable behaviour. This is seen as more ethical because, for example, a patient would have to imagine being sick or feeling shocks, rather than actually vomiting or being electrocuted.

OPT

◆ Systematic desensitisation: a treatment based on the principles of classical conditioning

Systematic desensitisation is a treatment based on the principles of classical conditioning in that the aim is to extinguish an undesirable behaviour, such as a phobia, by substituting the response. For example, the response to a phobic object (spider, snake) is fear; systematic desensitisation substitutes fear with the response of relaxation. This is known as reciprocal inhibition, as two contrasting emotions cannot co-exist – you cannot be relaxed and scared at the same time.

The treatment involves a series of steps to achieve this goal, hence systematic – step by step. This is achieved by the patient forming a list of fears or anxieties that begin with the least feared or anxiety-provoking through to the most fearful situation. This hierarchy of fears is then worked through, starting with the least fearful situation, getting the patient to relax using relaxation techniques. The patient only progresses through the hierarchy as he or she becomes sufficiently relaxed at each stage.

The treatment has been very successful with specific phobias but not with social phobias or agoraphobia (fear of open spaces). Unlike aversion therapy, the patient has greater control over their own treatment as they decide when they are sufficiently relaxed to progress further through their hierarchy of fears.

◆ Token economy: a treatment based on the principles of operant conditioning

OPT

Token economy is a treatment based on the principles of operant conditioning in that it aims to use reinforcement to encourage desirable behaviour. Tokens given to patients act as secondary reinforcers – they are exchangeable for primary reinforcers when a sufficient number of tokens has been saved. This treatment has been widely used in psychiatric institutions to encourage self-sufficiency and in prisons to encourage non-aggressive, compliant behaviour. Tokens can be saved and exchanged for permission to purchase wanted items, watch a television programme, etc. The intention of the treatment is that more natural reinforcers, such as praise for desired behaviour, will eventually replace the tokens.

The use of tokens has shown considerable success in psychiatric institutions (Paul and Lentz, 1977) with improvements reported in self-care and pro-social behaviour. However, the tokens can lead to dependency, whereby patients only produce the desired behaviour in order to receive a token. There can be a serious problem when attempting to transfer the behaviour to the 'outside world', as everyday reinforcement is subtle and often delayed, whereas a token is immediate and obvious. It could also be argued that it is the increased attention of staff that leads to desirable behaviour rather than the token itself, and that staff using tokens develop a more positive attitude to the patients, which leads to improvements in how they are treated.

Learning theory as an explanation of gender development

Social learning theory and operant conditioning can provide an explanation for how boys learn to be boys and girls learn to be girls. According to these theories, gender development is formed through the processes of observation, reinforcement, modelling and imitation of gender-appropriate behaviours in parents, peers and others.

Children observe their parents as role models and are encouraged to engage with the same sex parent when performing stereotypical activities such as housework or fixing a car. Even if parents do not engage in stereotypical roles themselves, the children are still exposed to the way in which the media and literature portray men and women, and there are significant others such as grandparents, teachers and peers who may encourage and display gender-appropriate behaviour.

Gender-appropriate behaviour is often encouraged from birth, with the choice of clothing given to girls and boys; even the décor of a bedroom can encourage feminine or masculine behaviour. Gender development occurs at a very early age. Cramer and Skidd (1992) found that pre-school girls made reference to female stereotyped concepts of affiliation and caring, and boys to male stereotyped concepts of domination and intrusion, when conducting a story completion method.

The Learning Approach considers that children are treated differently according to their biological sex, and that it is the way they are treated that determines which behaviours they display. Gender-stereotypical behaviours are encouraged through reinforcement, and gender-appropriate behaviour will be rewarded with praise and attention. Gender-inappropriate behaviour, on the other hand, may be punished. This punishment is more pronounced when boys display feminine behaviour in the view of their father (Langlois and Downs, 1980). Even the choice of toys bought for children encourages gender-appropriate behaviour; dolls reinforce quiet, nurturing behaviour in girls, whereas cars and tools encourage noisy, physical play in boys. Recent research by Karniol and Aida (1997) found that children adopted gender-stereotyped toys as their own and, when they were asked to judge a punishment for a child who broke a same sex or opposite sex toy, the children gave greater punishments to opposite sex toy breakers. This study demonstrates the level of gender ownership over stereotypical toys.

Evaluation

Learning theory as an explanation of gender development appeals to our common sense, as it makes sense in terms of the available role models and reinforcement given for gender-appropriate behaviour. However, the explanation ignores biological evidence that gender development is caused by biological determinants such as the presence of the Y chromosome and masculine hormones that encourage development of male sexual organs.

Bussey and Perry (1982) recorded the behaviour of children who were asked to watch a same or opposite sex model play with a variety of objects. They found that all children played with the objects selected by the same sex model, but that boys showed a rejection of objects selected by an opposite sex model. The children were found to imitate the same sex model and to show a preference for the objects selected by these models. This may explain why boys show a strong preference for 'masculine' objects, such as trains and tools, and girls for 'feminine' objects, such as dolls and household items.

Taking it further

Research children's classic nursery rhymes, such as Little Miss Muffet and Little Jack Horner, and see how many references there are to stereotypical gender-appropriate behaviours. Explain how a child may be influenced by these nursery rhymes.

Taking it further

Look back through this chapter and Chapters 3 and 4 for a full comparison of the three explanations of gender development. Each chapter tackles the comparison of the three explanations in a different way, so draw all the information together and study it in a way that suits you.

David Reimer was born a male and, due to unfortunate circumstances, was turned into a female (see pages 110-111 for a detailed account). Despite his upbringing he always felt he was masculine and, even though he was treated as a female, he rebelled and acted as a male. This case contradicts the learning theory of gender development because, if gender is learnt, David Reimer would have been satisfied with his new ascribed feminine gender. The fact that he was not, and always felt himself to 'not fit' with this ascribed gender, evidences the idea that gender is biologically determined rather than wholly learnt.

Comparing explanations of gender development

Psychodynamic explanation	Biological explanation	Learning explanation
Freud believed that children in the phallic stage of psychosexual development need gratification from the opposite sex parent. This manifests itself as wanting to eliminate the same sex parent so that the desire to be with the opposite sex parent can be realised. However, the same sex parent is 'in the way' and poses a threat to the child (particularly the male child who fears castration anxiety), and the only way that this threat can be resolved is through identification with the same sex parent (keep friends close but enemies closer). A child simulates the same sex parent in order to be able to 'possess' the other parent.	Gender is determined before birth. Both parents contribute 50% of their genetic make-up to their offspring. The mother gifts the X chromosome and the father the X or Y chromosome. It is the father who determines the sex of the offspring. If the father passes on the X chromosome the child will be female, and if he passes on the Y chromosome the child will be male. It is the presence of the Y chromosome that determines testes development. Testosterone is released and male characteristic develop, and this affects brain hemisphere specialisation and hypothalamus action.	By observing significant others, gender-appropriate behaviours are modelled and imitated by children. Bandura (1961) found that children tend to pay more attention to and imitate same sex role models, which means that boys will copy men and girls will copy women. Once gender-appropriate behaviour is displayed, it is reinforced with praise and attention. This positive reinforcement is operant conditioning and encourages gender-appropriate behaviour to be repeated.

Examiner's tip

Comparing these explanations is tricky, so try the following ways to help link ideas from each explanation:
• Compared to...
• Which is different from...
• Similar to...
• Contrasting with...
• Unlike...
• Matches with...
Don't forget that comparison points can be made into evaluation points for any explanation.

Taking it further

Malinowski's study of the Trobriand Islanders found that boys developed normally despite not having a father figure in the traditional way. Review the Learning, Psychodynamic and Biological explanations of gender development and consider which can explain the Trobriand Islander boys.

Studies

▲ Children in Bandura's (1961) study acting aggressively towards the bobo doll

Physical aggression displayed by the model included:
- Sat on bobo doll and punched it on the nose.
- Raised bobo doll then hit it on the head with a mallet.
- Tossed bobo doll into the air.
- Kicked doll around the room aggressively.

The physical aggression was accompanied by verbal aggression:
- "Sock him on the nose…"
- "Hit him down…"
- "Throw him in the air…"
- "Kick him…"

Transmission of aggression through imitation of aggressive models (Bandura, Ross and Ross, 1961)

◆ Aim

To investigate whether exposure to a real-life aggressive model increases aggression in children.

◆ Procedure

Bandura et al. tested 72 children enrolled at Stanford University Nursery School, 36 male and 36 female, between the ages of three and five. The participants were divided into eight experimental groups of six children, with the remaining 24 children forming a control group. The children in the experimental groups watched an aggressive or non-aggressive role model of the same or different sex to themselves. The children in all groups were matched for physical and verbal aggression from ratings made by the experimenter and a nursery school teacher.

The children were individually brought in by the experimenter, who then invited the model to come in. The child was placed in one corner and shown how to design a picture. The model was taken to the opposite corner which contained a table, chair, tinker toy, mallet and 5-foot inflatable bobo doll. The experimenter then left the room. The child could only watch the model and overheard the experimenter tell the model that it was 'their' play area and that the child had no access to it.

The model played with the tinker toy for a minute, then began to act aggressively towards the bobo doll. In the non-aggressive condition, the model continued to play with the tinker toys.

After 10 minutes the child was taken to another room and given toys to play with, which were then taken away. All children were therefore in an equally frustrated mood. The child was then taken to an experimental room where they were allowed to play with a variety of aggressive and non-aggressive toys. The child had 20 minutes of free play in the room whilst being observed through a one-way mirror.

◆ Results

The children were rated for 'imitative aggression' and 'non-imitative aggression'. Children exposed to an aggressive role model displayed significantly more direct imitation than children exposed to the non-aggressive model. Watching an aggressive role model had a greater effect on boys than girls, particularly when observing a same sex model.

	Aggressive adult role model		Non-aggressive adult role model		Control group
	Female model	Male model	Female model	Male model	
Female child	5.5	7.2	2.5	0.0	1.2
Male child	12.4	25.8	0.2	1.5	2.0

◄ Mean number of 'imitative physical aggressive acts' (physical and verbal aggression copied from from the adult model).

	Aggressive adult role model		Non-aggressive adult role model		Control group
	Female model	Male model	Female model	Male model	
Female child	21.3	8.4	7.2	1.4	6.1
Male child	16.2	36.7	26.1	22.3	24.6

◄ Mean number of 'non-imitative aggressive acts' (physical and verbal aggression directed at targets other than the bobo doll).

Both boys and girls displayed more non-imitative aggression after observing the aggressive role model. The effect was stronger after watching a same sex aggressive model.

◆ Conclusion

A child exposed to an aggressive model is likely to display aggression and to imitate aggressive acts. Boys are more aggressive than girls overall, but are less likely to copy aggressive behaviour from a female model.

◆ Evaluation

Strengths
- The study has contributed greatly to the understanding of how children acquire behaviour through observing others. Further research has led to censorship and certification laws. The study also highlights how non-aggressive role models in the media can encourage helpful behaviour.

- Observations of children's behaviour are potentially subjective. However, there were a number of observers and only shared and agreed behaviours were presented, so reliability was established.

Weaknesses
- Although the experiment took place in a familiar type of environment, the conditions were not normal so the study does lack ecological validity.
- The children may have been simply showing obedience to the adult.
- As the children were from an American nursery, it is unlikely that we can generalise the results beyond the sample.
- The children were made to feel aggressive and probably distressed by withdrawal of the toys. Exposing children to an aggressive role model and effectively teaching them aggressive acts is also unethical.

Taking it further

Investigate tragedies such as:
- Columbine High School Murders (1999)
- Virginia Tech University campus shooting (2007)
- Tuusula, Finland shootings (2007).

All involved a young person committing murder. Find newspaper footage or search the internet and see how many references are made to the aggressor watching or being influenced by violent TV, films or songs.

We should maintain caution over accepting the view that children learn purely through observation, particularly the link with media violence, as it ignores the genetic basis for aggression. Not all children copy aggression from violent media, so there must be several factors at work, and watching violence can actually be cathartic by aiding the release of aggression rather than causing it.

EX

Summary of three other studies

◆ Cocaine-reinforced behaviour in rats: effects of reinforcement magnitude and fixed-ratio size (Pickens and Thompson, 1968)

Aim and procedure

The aim was to investigate cocaine as reinforcement for rats, and whether different doses and different fixed-ratio schedules affect responding behaviour. Three albino rats were laboratory-reared individually in a cage, with free access to food and water. Each rat was fitted with an intravenous device that allowed it to self-administer a cocaine solution when a lever was pressed. Each time a rat pressed a lever, an infusion of cocaine and saline was administered (continuous reinforcement). The number of lever presses was recorded. The rats were then given different doses of cocaine ranging from 0.25mg to 3.0mg, and a fixed-ratio schedule (number of responses) was varied from FR5 to FR80.

Results and conclusions

A fixed-ratio schedule should produce a high rate of response leading up to the delivery of cocaine. However, as the dose increased the response decreased. Overall, it was found that the same level of drug was administered over the same time period, regardless of actual dose administered. Cocaine therefore reinforces behaviour, but when the dose of cocaine increases, the response behaviour decreases.

◆ Superstition in the pigeon (Skinner, 1948)

Aim and procedure

The aim was to investigate whether superstitious behaviour can develop in response to food reinforcement. Eight pigeons were individually placed in a cage for a few minutes each day. The cage had a food hopper that would swing into the cage at timed intervals for the pigeon to eat from. The food was given no matter what the pigeon did.

Results and conclusions

Cocaine was a reinforcer for lever-pressing behaviour in the continuous reinforcement study. However, the size of dose had an inverse effect on response rate. After several days six of the pigeons were seen to display bizarre behaviour just before the food hopper was presented. One, for example, exhibited a thrusting of his head into one of the upper corners of the cage, a second tossed its head as if lifting an object, and two pigeons displayed pendulum-swinging motions of the head. Following the initial experiment, Skinner ceased the food reinforcement and observed this behaviour until it gradually disappeared. The pigeons had associated a chance behaviour they happened to be performing as the food was delivered with the food reinforcement itself. They continued to exhibit these bizarre behaviours to receive food. Skinner believed that the pigeons had developed a superstitious behaviour.

Evaluation
- The generalisability of the findings may be narrow, as animals and humans respond and behave differently.
- There may be moral objections to the use of animals in drug research, but they were caged and fed appropriately. This experiment has directly informed the role of drugs as reinforcers, which can be applied to help understand addiction in humans.
- There is a suggestion that rats act differently in a caged environment than in a natural environment, but this is not the case with laboratory-reared animals that have no other experience.

Evaluation
- There is a general acceptance that superstitious behaviour is learned through operant conditioning of chance behaviours. However, the experiment was performed on animals, so the results may not be applicable to humans.
- Gambling and sporting rituals also develop by a similar learning mechanism. A sportsperson may associate wearing a special pair of trainers with winning, or a gambler may blow on a dice to ensure a win. This study could be useful to gain a better understanding of gambling addiction.

◆ Conditioned emotional responses (Watson and Raynor, 1920)

Aim and procedure

The aim was to investigate whether emotional responses, such as fear, could be conditioned. Little Albert was a healthy and unemotional child of a nurse at a local children's home. At nine months, he displayed interest but no fear response to a variety of neutral stimuli. At 11 months, he was presented with a white rat. He initially showed no fear and reached out to the rat. At this point the researchers loudly struck a steel bar behind Albert. He jumped at the noise and buried his head in the mattress. After a short time Albert reached out for the rat again, and the same loud noise was presented. Albert leaned forward and began to whimper.

The rat and noise were paired together a few times and Albert showed increasing distress. He was still distressed when shown the rat without the noise. Albert was then presented with a range of furry stimuli (rabbit, dog, seal pelt, Santa Claus mask). He demonstrated various degrees of fear response and negativity towards each. Seven weeks later, he still demonstrated some fear towards the furry stimuli.

Results and conclusion

The results after one week demonstrated convincingly that Little Albert had acquired a fear of rats as a learnt emotional response. The pairing of rat and loud noise created an association resulting in the rat alone being a conditioned stimulus, producing fear as a conditioned response.

The fear response exhibited when the rat was presented seemed to be shown when Albert was exposed to other similar furry objects. This is known as stimulus generalisation. The last time Albert was tested showed a marked reduction in the intensity of response to the stimuli. The researchers concluded that it is possible to classically condition the emotional response of fear, although this response seems to diminish in intensity over time.

Evaluation

- Albert was due to leave the nursery, so there was no chance to recondition him and ensure he did not suffer a long-term fear. However, it is unlikely, as the experiment clearly demonstrated a reduction in the intensity of his reaction.

- Albert was certainly not protected from distress as current guideline would ensure. Even at the time, the study was open to criticism on these grounds.

- It is a single case experiment, so the findings may be limited to Albert. In fact, replications of the experiment failed to reproduce the findings.

Have you ever wondered?

Why you do you have fears? List your fears and ask your parents or guardians how they came about. Can any of them be explained in a similar way to Little Albert's fear of rats?

Have you ever wondered?

Do you have routines and rituals that play a part in your everyday life? Many of us feel out of sorts if these routines are broken. We may have rituals to perform before a sporting event, before we go to bed at night or while walking down the street. They are not abnormal behaviours, and often develop as a result of chance reinforcement.

- List your routines, rituals or superstitious behaviours.
- How do you feel if you cannot perform these routines?
- What do you think will happen if you break a routine?

EG

Key issues

- This section focuses on three key issues that can be linked to or explained by theories, concepts and studies in the Learning Approach. You will only need to know one key issue for the examination. The key issue should be described and explained using ideas from the Learning Approach in your explanation.

▲ Thin models are often blamed for teenage eating disorders.

The influence of role models on anorexia

Billie Piper is a well-known actress who admits to suffering from anorexia and who speaks out against role models who are size zero. (Size zero is a very small size, almost certainly not a healthy size, and one that is very difficult to achieve.) One girl in every 100 is said to suffer from an eating disorder, according to a survey quoted in the *Daily Telegraph*.

The survey also said that only around 8% of 14-year-olds were happy with their bodies, with seven out of ten saying they would be 100% happier if they could lose half a stone. Two-thirds of the 2000 girls in the survey blamed celebrities with perfect bodies for their own negative body image.

The source of the evidence was not given but the point is that media articles suggest that media images are to blame for girls wanting to be thin. *Girlguiding UK* carried out a survey of over 3000 girls and found that over half said the media made them feel that 'being pretty and thin' was 'the most important thing'. Kate Moss and Victoria Beckham (both very thin) were said by 95% of the girls surveyed to be the most influential role models.

The issue is: Do role models encourage eating disorders such as anorexia because they lead to teenagers wanting to be 'impossibly' thin?

◆ Explaining the issue using the Learning Approach

- Social learning theory states that people learn by imitating role models whom they see as important. They are likely to be similar to them – of the same gender for example.
- Role models are usually perceived as having prestige as well, such as celebrities who have money, power and fame.
- Behaviour that is modelled by those perceived as important is likely to be imitated.
- This is particularly true if the observed behaviour is seen to be rewarded as well. Media role models tend to be celebrities and in some way successful, which can be seen as a reward, so their behaviour is particularly likely to be imitated.

- If role models are punished for their behaviour, Bandura and others have shown that behaviour is less likely to be copied. Size zero models are now being banned by some advertising companies; if this is perceived as punishment, perhaps they will soon no longer be imitated.
- The Psychodynamic Approach suggests that anorexia is a result of wanting to remain a child and not wanting to move into an adult sexual role. This goes against social learning theory as an explanation.
- Evidence for social learning theory comes from Bandura, who developed the concept of social learning. His studies show that behaviour tends to be copied if it is rewarded and is carried out by someone similar to the observer.
- However, studies such as Bandura's were carried out in an unnatural setting, using unnatural behaviour, so the findings were not very valid.

Summary of two other issues

◆ The influence of advertising on people's behaviour

Products are advertised in places which give access to a lot of people. How does advertising work?

- Classical conditioning suggests that, by associating something with a stimulus that would naturally give a certain response, what was associated with the stimulus will give the same response. For example, a product associated with something that naturally gives excitement will give excitement, and so might be bought for that reason.
- Operant conditioning suggests that behaviour is repeated if it is rewarded, so if a product rewards someone it will be bought again.
- Advertising can suggest that a product is rewarding, and observational learning suggests that, if behaviour is seen to be rewarding, it will be repeated.
- Social learning theory suggests that role models are imitated and that, if celebrity role models are seen being rewarded (perhaps by having fewer wrinkles because of using a cream), their behaviour (using the cream) will be imitated.

◆ The increase of female violence related to changing role models

There is a suggestion that there has been an increase in female violence over the last ten years or so. Violence, which used to be seen as a male behaviour, is now linked to females and female gangs as well.

- Social learning theory suggests that modelled behaviour is imitated – if female violence is portrayed in the media, it is likely to be imitated.
- There are more 'violent' females in the media, such as Lara Croft (the character that started as a computer game) and the female role in *Kill Bill*. If such models are not punished, which they tend not to be, social learning theory suggests that they will be copied and will become role models. This is particularly true if their behaviour is seen as rewarding.

Examiner's tip

Make sure you can describe the issue itself and explain it using concepts from the Learning Approach. It is a good idea to describe the issue as a question to be answered. Make sure you don't use concepts from the approach when describing the issue.

Taking it further

Investigate the size zero issue for yourself, as it is currently a very topical debate. Do you think the debate is talked about in the media as an excuse to show thin models? Or do you think the media are really willing to change so that they portray more rounded women as being attractive?

OPT

OPT

Evidence of practice

What you need to know

- You need to devise and conduct one practical, which must be an observation using independent groups and collecting nominal data, such as by using tallying.
- The observation must focus on some aspect of learning.
- You must be able to carry out a chi-squared test and interpret the findings.
- You must apply issues of validity, reliability, generalisability and credibility to the results.
- You must adhere to ethical principles – as always with practicals.

Taking it further

Watch a few TV advertising segments at around 9.00 p.m. and study the car adverts. Note down whether large or small cars are being advertised, then note down some information that suggests the target market, for example:
- the gender of any people shown in the adverts
- the gender of any voice-over
- the type of setting
- other information, such as any technical information given.

Come to a conclusion about whether larger cars are targeted at males and smaller cars at females. For example, Renault Clio adverts are targeted at females and the new larger Audi adverts are targeted at males.

Examiner's tip

You will need to know your design decisions, as you might be asked about your procedure and why you made the decisions you made. Make sure you know about your ethical decisions as well, and can justify them.

◆ Hypothesis, IV and DV for a suggested practical

A suggested practical is included here, though you can choose your own. The hypothesis is that there will be a difference in gender of drivers depending on the size of the car they drive – there will be more males driving big cars and more females driving small cars. The IV is gender and the DV a judgement on what size of car they are driving, which is explained in more detail below. This is a directional hypothesis.

◆ Background and links to learning theories

Adverts aiming to sell cars focus on different markets depending on the car. There is a tendency to show large cars in such a way that a man might be reinforced to buy one, while small cars are 'for women'. This can be seen by the people shown in the adverts, for example smart 'career' women driving small cars and 'business men' driving larger cars – though there are exceptions. Social learning theory suggests that people imitate those they see as having prestige or those they see as similar to them. Those that are seen as similar are likely to be the same gender. Adverts for 4x4s and sports cars, as well as people carriers, are marketed a little differently, so these are not included in this study.

◆ Participant design and design decisions

This is an independent groups design, because each participant can only be in either the male or the female category. Data is gathered by **tallying**, since that is convenient, and the study involves only nominal data. The study looks at whether the driver is male or female, and whether they are driving a large or small car, so the data is quantitative.

A pilot observation took place whilst walking along the streets in a small market town, where there was quite a bit of traffic but not too much – every car could be used in the observation, which meant there was less subjectivity. The original idea was to look at small hatchbacks and large prestigious cars but it was soon realised that a fairer study was to include all cars and judge them large or small. Cars up to a new Golf or Focus were judged the top of the 'small' range. Cars like Mondeo and Vauxhall estates were judged at the bottom of the 'large' range. Clearly, some subjectivity was involved in this judgement.

It was found that about five minutes of observation was sufficient. The sample was an **opportunity sample**, as only those driving there at that time were part of the study.

◆ Ethical decisions

Observations in a public place are considered ethical because people might expect to be observed. However, drivers were in their cars, which might not be thought of as a public place. As only their gender and the size of the car they were driving was recorded, with no other data about them, it was thought that this fitted with ethical guidelines. However, there was no informed consent, no right to withdraw, no debrief (though possibly no deceit either) and the observer was competent to carry out the study. It was thought that driving on a main road through traffic lights in the middle of a fairly busy market town was enough of a public place to mean the study was ethical.

The observer made tally marks but on a very small note pad kept in the palm of her hand, and this was done after the car had passed, without other drivers noticing. For this reason the observer did not stand at one place but walked down the street as normal.

◆ Gathering the data

The actual data was collected at lunchtime (1.25 p.m.) on a Thursday. In all, the drivers of 51 cars were noted, so there were 51 participants. Many were judged to be 45 or over, with fewer young drivers of either gender.

◆ Results of the study

11 males and 18 females, were judged to be driving small cars. 16 males and 6 females, were judged to be driving large cars. The mean, median and mode, as well as the range, are not suitable for nominal data of this type and graphs are not really useful either, so a two-by-two table will suffice, as here. Numbers are tally marks for that category.

◆ Analysing the results

Interestingly, by chance, about the same number of males and females were seen (27 males and 24 females). Also, about the same number of small and large cars were observed (29 small and 22 large), again by chance. It suggests that, in the area where the observation took place, there is a balance in gender of drivers and size of car.

It looks as if there is a difference in gender and size of car, and in the direction predicted, because the two larger numbers are in the 'right' boxes. However, there were 11 males driving small cars, and this may mean the results are not significant. It was noticed that the males driving small cars seemed to be older (possibly over 60), which is something for further research.

The pilot observation checked:
- how long was needed
- how to make tally marks discreetly
- how to decide whether a car was 'small' or 'large' and which cars to eliminate.

	Male	Female	Totals
Car judged small	11	18	29
Car judged large	16	6	22
Totals	27	24	51

It is possible that the hypothesis is accepted (males are more likely to drive larger cars, with females driving smaller cars), with the exception of older males. This study will not show that difference, however, because age was not recorded.

◆ Carrying out a chi-squared test

The appropriate test for this study is a chi-squared test, as the hypothesis predicts a difference, it is an independent groups design and the level of measurement is nominal.

	Male	Female	Totals
Car judged small	A 11	B 18	29
Car judged large	C 16	D 6	22
Totals	27	24	51

The test involves calculating the expected values for the four boxes and then comparing the expected values with the observed values. The observed values are 11, 18, 16 and 6. The expected values are worked out for each cell by using the totals for each row and column. Expected value is the total of the row for that cell, multiplied by the total of the column for that cell, divided by the overall total (51).

The expected values for the cells A, B, C and D are:

> A – 29 times 27 divided by 51 = 15.35
> B – 29 times 24 divided by 51 = 11.29
> C – 22 times 27 divided by 51 = 11.64
> D – 22 times 24 divided by 51 = 10.35

This means that, all things being equal (and there is no difference in gender and size of car driven) the cells are 15, 11, 11 and 10, whereas they are in fact 11, 18, 16 and 6. These numbers are reasonably different. The test itself will show whether they are different enough.

The test involves, for each cell, taking E (expected value) from O (observed value) and squaring the result, then dividing that result by E. Having done that four times (once for each cell), add the four results to find the result for chi-squared. This is the value to look up in the critical value tables.

> A – (11 minus 15.35)^2 divided by 15.35 = 1.23
> B – (18 minus 11.29)^2 divided by 11.29 = 3.99
> C – (16 minus 11.64)^2 divided by 11.64 = 1.63
> D – (6 minus 10.35)^2 divided by 10.35 = 1.83
> TOTAL = 8.68

Chi-squared is 8.68 and this is the observed value to be compared with the critical value. The critical value for df=1 (which it does for a two-by-two table), p≤.05 and a one-tailed prediction is 2.71. As 8.68 is greater than that number, the result is significant and the null hypothesis can be rejected.

◆ Conclusions

A look at the table suggests there was a difference – more females (18) were driving small cars than men (11) and more males (16) were driving large cars than females (6). The expected values were quite a bit different from the observed values as well, which again suggests that the results were significant. The chi-squared test result was 8.68, which is considerably larger than the 2.71 needed for significance, so the null hypothesis is rejected and the study 'worked'.

Validity

The study was valid in that it was a naturalistic observation of real driving behaviour that was not affected by the observer. The cars were being driven either by males or females, which was what was measured. As a judgement was made about whether the cars were small or large, this may have led to some lack of validity – though a description of what was judged a small and large car is included to aid validity. Also it is not known whether drivers chose to drive that car or had no choice as it belonged to someone else. This affects the validity, as their choice would then not be due to operant conditioning or observational learning as is suggested.

Reliability

It would not be difficult to repeat the study, as there is enough detail. However, there were not many controls, which means that differences could be expected in the findings. This suggests a lack of reliability. On another day, or at another time, differences might occur. It would be useful to repeat the study a few times to test for reliability.

Generalisability

The sample was not chosen, but was an opportunity sample, so might be biased. The observation was at lunchtime on a weekday, so there may have been more people not working or retired in the sample, which makes it less generalisable to the whole population.

Credibility

The study is credible in its general findings as it is generally thought that women are less confident drivers as men and so may be pushed towards a smaller 'more manageable' car. However, insurers claim that women are safer drivers, which goes against this prediction – unless, of course, they are safer because they tend to drive smaller cars! It is hard to link the findings with learning theory but overall people would agree that more women drive smaller cars.

Overall, the study is credible in that a naturalistic observation is a good research method to choose and appears to give validity. It is less credible because the observation only lasted five minutes and was only done once, which suggests a lack of reliability.

Examiner's tip

You are likely to be asked about the validity, reliability, generalisability and credibility of your study. You do not need to come up with a definite answer but you need to present reasoned arguments about these issues to show that you understand what the terms mean and can apply them to your practical work.

Summary

The Learning Approach explains human behaviour as a series of acquired responses to environmental stimuli:

- Classical conditioning describes the process of learning through associating a stimulus with a reflexive action.
- Operant conditioning explains behaviour as a response to its consequences.
- Social learning is learning acquired through observing a role model and imitating the behaviour.

◆ Methodology

The Learning Approach predominantly uses the laboratory experiment as a means of investigating the mechanisms of learning. Observations are sometimes used to study the transmission of aggression of gendered behaviours. They may be over or covert, participant or non-particicpant, structured or naturalistic. You need to be able to define, evaluate and apply these terms. You also need to be able to describe and assess ethical guidelines as they relate to human participants.

Laboratory experiments are commonly used to study behaviour in controlled environments so that a causal link can be established between a stimulus and a response. They can involve human participants and animals, and you need to be able to describe the conditions of a laboratory experiment and assess its strengths and weaknesses.

When conducting your own observation as a practical for this approach, you need to use a chi-squared test to analyse the findings. You also need to have some understanding of inferential statistics.

When conducting your chi-squared test, you will use a table of critical values to compare your own calculated values and work out whether your results are significant. You do not have to perform a statistical test or remember formulae, but you do need to understand why they are used and how they were applied in your own practical.

◆ Content

You need to be able to describe the main features of classical conditioning, operant conditioning and social learning theory as explanations of human behaviour.

Classical and operant conditioning principles have been used to develop many therapies and treatments for maladaptive learning. You need to be able to describe and evaluate one behavioural therapy from either classical or operant conditioning for your studies:

- **Aversion therapy** is based on the principles of classical conditioning by associating the undesired behaviour with an unpleasant response.
- **Systematic desensitisation** is based on the principles of classical conditioning by associating a response with one that produces an opposite effect.

- **Token economy** is a treatment based on operant conditioning as tokens are given for desired behaviour, which can be exchanged for or rewards.

You also need to know how learning theory explains gender development, and be able to compare this explanation with that of the Psychodynamic and Biological Approaches.

◆ Studies

Key studies in the Learning Approach allow us to study a mechanism of learning through the use of animals or human participants. You need to be able to describe and evaluate Bandura, Ross and Ross's (1961) study of observational learning of aggression, plus one other.

◆ Key issues

You need to be able to describe and explain one key issue relevant to the Learning Approach by drawing on theories, ideas and studies you have learnt. You also need to prepare to use concepts, theories and studies you have learnt to explain a different issue that you may be presented with in the exam.

◆ Evidence of practice

You need to plan and conduct an observation on a topic relevant to the Learning Approach. Be prepared to comment on planning decisions that you have made and the data you collected. Make sure you can use appropriate psychological terminology relating to the experimental method and be able to justify your design decisions.

You also need to be able to present the data as tallies and to comment upon inferential statistics drawn from the chi-squared test. A large part of your experiment will be the discussion of findings in terms of objectivity, generalisability reliability, validity, and credibility.

Examzone _____ Practise

Section B

1. Describe the steps involved in operantly conditioning a dog to stay sat down while his owner walks away. (4 marks)

2. Outline what is meant by the terms 'extinction' and 'spontaneous recovery'. (3 marks)

3. Describe the method used in the study by Bandura, Ross and Ross (1961). (4 marks)

4. Evaluate the use of systematic desensitisation as a means of treating a phobia. (3marks)

5. Assess the strengths and limitations of classical conditioning as an explanation for learning. (4 marks)

Section C

6. In operant conditioning use may be made of reinforcement or punishment. Evaluate the use of reinforcers and punishers in changing behaviour. (6 marks)

7. Describe the Learning Approach explanation for gender development and evaluate this explanation in comparison to one other explanation. (12 marks: 6 AO1 6 AO2)

8. A study by Olds and Milner investigated pleasure centres in the brain. Rats had an electrode implanted that could deliver a small electrical pulse to an area of the brain called the hypothalamus. Rats rapidly learned to press a lever in a Skinner box in order to receive electrical stimulation to the brain. Rats would press the lever to the exclusion of all other activities, even eating and drinking, indeed to the point of exhaustion if allowed.

Use your knowledge of the Learning Approach to explain the findings of this study and evaluate it in terms of generalisability. (6 marks)

MCQ

Exam Advice

Questions on practicals

Questions relating to your practicals will not expect you to quote exact data, but will ask specific questions about the studies you did, e.g. identify a problem you encountered and how you dealt with it, or what your results showed and what conclusions you drew from them.

AS Psychology: what is being assessed?

The examinations to assess your performance in AS Psychology will measure three different skills. You can answer the questions accurately and gain good marks without knowing about these different skills. However, understanding them will mean you can target the answers more effectively. This will save you time and improve your chances of gaining high marks.

The examination questions do not identify which skill you need to use, so it is useful to be able to look at a question and recognise the skill required. Often it will be possible to recognise which skill is required by the presence of particular injunctions – words which tell you what to do. It is impossible to list all these words but some are listed below and should help you recognise and understand others you will come across.

The three skills are assessed using what are referred to as Assessment Objectives.

Assessment Objective 1 (AO1)
The first objective of assessment is to find out what knowledge you have. Typically you will be asked for factual information about theories and studies you have learned about. Two injunctions commonly used to request factual information are **outline** and **describe**. In general, describe requires more detail than outline. AO1 marks may also be available where you are asked to **identify** or **name** one or more theories, studies etc., in questions that also require you to apply higher skills in reasoning about those factual items.

Assessment Objective 2 (AO2)
The skill being assessed here is your ability to evaluate material. Evaluation is a more challenging skill and can be requested in a variety of ways. There are different kinds of evaluation and again paying attention to injunction words can help you use the right kind of skill for the question. The following list is not exhaustive but it identifies the main evaluation skills you are likely to encounter and briefly explains what is required for each term.

Assess: This goes beyond evaluation as you are also being asked to weigh the worth of the arguments you are making. Whereas in an evaluate question you may consider strengths and weaknesses, in an assess question you need to place a value on your arguments. For example, 'did Milgram's work contribute useful knowledge despite its ethical problems?'.

Compare: Here you are required to consider similarities and differences between two things. Remember you need to compare like with like and state both components to be sure of the mark.

Identifying the skill

Look for the injunction to get the skill correct. **Describe** or **Outline** usually indicate AO1 - knowledge. If you see any of the AO2 words: **Evaluate, Assess, Apply, Compare, Strength** or **Weakness**, then do as asked. Don't waste time describing as it doesn't get any marks!

Apply: this is a very practical aspect of psychology. The question will want you to use some knowledge you have and apply it to a real life scenario.

Evaluate: this allows you to include any or all of the other evaluation skills. In practice it will mainly be strengths and weaknesses.

Other key words to look out for, which will help you focus your answer, include the following.

Strengths: these are the good things about a study, theory or idea. Explain why it is a strength, e.g. because it can be generalised to other situations.

Weaknesses: these are the negative things about the study, theory or idea. Again explain why it is a weakness, e.g. because there was poor control over extraneous variables.

Assessment Objective 3 (AO3)

The skill being assessed here is your understanding of practical aspects of psychological research. Two areas of your understanding will be addressed.

How science works in the context of psychology:

these questions will ask about such things as ways of conducting research, controlling variables, hypotheses, ethical issues and so on.

Practicals:

these questions will assess the knowledge you developed from doing the practical tasks in the course, e.g. explaining what particular problems you found when trying to measure differences between two groups of people for the task related to the biological approach.

◆ What type of questions can I expect?

There are three types of question on the AS examination papers. There will be some multiple choice questions, some short answer questions and some questions that ask for longer, extended answers.

Multiple choice: most of these questions will ask you to select one correct answer out of four options. However there will be some questions that give more, or fewer, options, some may ask for two options to be selected, others might ask you to pair several things together. Most will be questions to assess AO1 or AO2 skills, though there may be an AO2 question from time to time.

Short answer: these will usually be worth between two and five marks. These questions only test one skill at a time, but overall they will assess all three skills.

Extended writing: There will be two or three longer questions on each paper. One of these questions will require a combination of skills, the others will be assessing just one skill.

Thinking scientifically

Psychology is a science so it is important to back up claims with evidence. Claims that cannot be supported are seen as weak and unscientific. Do a theory and findings from a study support each other? Have others found similar results? Can findings be applied to other groups or situations?

Old information - new contexts

Be prepared for questions that seem different to normal. Examiners try to find new ways of asking about what you have learned, so a question may ask you to use information in a new way. If you have practised this skill you will find it easier in the exam.

Managing time in the exam

After reading, thinking and planning time you have about one minute available for each mark. Stick to the amount you need to gain the marks. Lots of detail on something you know well is wasted effort if you get maximum marks half way through, and it will leave you short of time somewhere else.

Unit 1 at a glance

Exam: 1 hour 20 minutes. Worth 60 marks. Questions on anything from the Social and Cognitive Psychology sections of the specification. Typically you can expect 10-12 multiple choice questions, short answer questions on a wide range of material and two extended writing questions, one of which will be an essay.

Unit 2 at a glance

Exam: 1 hour 40 minutes. Worth 80 marks. Questions on material covered by the Psychodynamic, Biological and Learning Approaches. Multiple choice questions worth about 12-14 marks, a wide range of short answer questions, including methods questions, and two extended writing questions, one of which will be an essay.

Exam guidance

The assessment for AS psychology consists of two examinations, Unit 1 and Unit 2.

Unit 1

This examination is 1 hour 20 minutes long and is worth 60 marks. In Unit 1 you will be asked questions on the material covered by the Social and Cognitive Psychology sections of the specification. Marks will be split more or less equally between these topics. Some questions will relate to the "Methodology / How Science Works" sections of the specification and here the content described may not be tied to the subject content of these topics.

For example:
Two researchers were interested in studying people's attitudes towards the way newspapers treat celebrities. They agreed the best method to use was a survey. However, one wanted to collect quantitative data, while the other favoured qualitative data.

i.   Explain how the researchers might collect quantitative data for this study.   (2)
ii. Explain one advantage of using qualitative data.   (2)

Here, attitudes and how newspapers treat celebrities just provide a context, what you use to answer the question is knowledge about surveys, qualitative and quantitative data, all from the Methodology / How Science Works section of Social Psychology.

Unit 2

This examination lasts 1 hour 40 minutes and is marked out of 80. The Unit covers the Psychodynamic, Biological and Learning approaches. As with Unit 1, there will be similar numbers of marks awarded to each topic. One important feature of Unit 2 is the theme of gender development. The course asks you to compare the explanations of gender development offered by the three approaches and to be able to compare them. While it is not guaranteed that this type of question will be asked on every Unit 2 paper, it is an area that is likely to be featured quite often.

◆ Sections of the exam papers

Both Unit 1 and Unit 2 examinations will be divided into three sections, A, B and C. At the start of each section there will be an indication of how long the examiners think you need to spend on that section. Take notice of this information. It is there to help you.

Section A

Section A will consist of a series of multiple choice questions. Questions are most likely to assess AO1 and AO3 skills, however there may be an occasional AO2 question. Most of the questions will follow a format similar to the following example.

Researchers investigating how early childhood experiences affect us when we grow up wanted to use a survey to collect information. They created their sample by using all the adults living at number 3 in every street in a small town. Identify which type of sample this was.

☐ A Opportunity
☐ B Random
☒ C Systematic
☐ D Quota

Other formats may be used. So there may be a question where you are asked to put crosses against two items, or to map items in one column onto items in a second column, as here.

Identify which description best fits each of the three terms below by drawing a line between a term and its description.

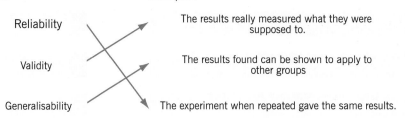

Term

Reliability

Validity

Generalisability

Description

The results really measured what they were supposed to.

The results found can be shown to apply to other groups

The experiment when repeated gave the same results.

Section B

Section B will be short answer questions. Each question will require one skill (AO1, AO2 or AO3) but all skills will be assessed within the section. There may be a short scenario followed by a series of questions designed to test your understanding of psychological research. Questions in this section will be worth up to five marks. In order to do well you need to read the question carefully and target the material accurately. This section will be worth about half of the marks available on the paper.

Section C

Section C is where longer, more detailed answers are required. This section will be worth about a third of the total marks on the paper. One of the questions will be marked using levels and will require you to combine both AO1 and AO2 skills. You need to think through and plan these answers before writing.

◆ Time management and level of detail

Good examination technique is matching the amount of material you include in your answer to the number of marks available, so you spend no longer than necessary writing, but don't miss marks either. A good indication of the time you should spend on a question is the number of marks available. For short answer questions (Section B) a guideline of writing for one minute per mark is a useful starting point. In a short answer question aim to make one more point than there are marks available. Remember that a well elaborated point or an example may gain an extra mark. For the extended writing in Section C make sure you develop points and balance your arguments to gain the higher marks.

Gender in Unit 2

For each approach you must be able to explain how it is believed gender appropriate behaviour emerges and provide evidence both for and against this view. You must also be able to compare the different explanations given by the approaches in terms of both similarities and differences.

Revision advice

 Succeed

◆ How to revise

Learning material for examinations should start the week you learn something for the first time in class! That might seem a bit drastic, but planning when you learn means you spend less time learning and the information stays in your head longer.

Step 1: Ideally within two days, and no longer than a week after learning a new topic go through your class notes. There are several different strategies that can be used, it may be typing up your notes, annotating, or using highlighter on notes you made. Whichever method you use, by going through the notes while the lesson is still fresh in your mind, you will find there are things you remember that are not in the notes, you may spot connections you didn't see at the time and you will also find you improve the organisation of the material. Going through the notes again consolidates your learning.

Step 2: Read and take notes from at least one other source, (e.g. book, website) on every topic, even if not needed for homework. File the notes with your class notes for future use.

Step 3: Start your main revision at least five weeks before the exam and preferably two months before. You may not spend any more hours revising if you start earlier but it will improve the amount of material you retain.

Revision techniques

The least effective way is just to read your notes. This is fine for the final 'top-up' before an exam, but it will not help you learn complex material effectively. Use a variety of techniques and work out which ones are best for you. Here are some suggestions.

- Take class notes and the ones made from other sources on the same area and amalgamate the notes.
- Use highlighters or coloured pens to mark different types of information and/or key points.
- Create spider diagrams or mind maps to help you link information together.
- Shorten detailed notes to a few key words. Use key words to cascade out the detail. Index cards are useful for this exercise and can be colour coded too.
- Do practice questions.
- Create a recording of the material you want to learn. As a second step, listen to a section then try and write notes about what you just listened to.
- For something that won't 'stick' (e.g. explanations of the IV and DV) create a mnemonic or put the information on a sheet of paper and stick it on the wall or somewhere else you will see it often.

Sleeping and Eating

Avoid revising very late. Your brain needs sleep to consolidate learning; if you work too late you won't be relaxed enough to sleep.

During revision your brain is making new memory connections. Eating sensibly helps create these connections; eat a balanced diet and proper meals, not snacks.

Spaced learning

Evidence from psychological research shows that if material is learned at spaced intervals instead of all at once it will be learned more thoroughly and be more resistant to forgetting. Schedule your revision so that you can space it out over a longer period.

◆ What to revise

Matching the amount of material you learn with the amount you will need in the exam is important. You need to make sure you know enough material to answer the questions set, without going over the top. Remember, questions can be asked on everything in the specification, so it is unwise to leave something out, "because it was asked last time". The Edexcel specification is very detailed, this is to help make it clearer what you need to learn. Ensure you have a copy of the specification to hand when you are revising so you can map the material onto it.

Definition of the approach: Be able to make four points that define the approach, be able to relate the material to things you have learned and the way that the approach is used (2-3 marks each). Give a two to three mark definition of every term listed. Remember: examples can help too.

Methodology/How Science works and Methods: Explain clearly what each term means, show how the term relates to the practical aspects of psychology, with examples, and evaluate appropriately. E.g. explain how a research method may be used, with an example, give advantages, disadvantages, strengths and weaknesses. Typically, aim for enough to gain four to five marks for descriptions and the same for evaluations.

Content: For most items you should be able to describe for up to six marks, and evaluate for a similar amount. There are a few places where slightly less is enough. Where the specification uses define or briefly, three marks' worth of material is probably enough.

Studies in detail: For all studies, be able to describe the method for five marks, the findings (results plus conclusions) for five marks, as well as accurately identifying it and giving the aim.

Key issue: Describe the key issue you studied for up to five marks and apply at least two different concepts/theories from the relevant approach to explain it for eight marks. Be able to apply these concept/theories to an issue given in the exam.

Practical: Describe what you did in your practicals, show awareness of problems you encountered, what your results showed, what you learned from conducting the practical and what conclusions could be drawn from the experience (five marks each).

Take a break

Remember, your mind can only remain focused on something for quite a short time. Give yourself regular short breaks during revision to aid your concentration. Have a set of little rewards to give yourself to maintain motivation. Maintain discipline! Don't let a five-minute break creep up to 10.

Managing time during revision

Identify when you are going to revise and divide up the time to cover all subjects and topics in rotation. Identify time off for relaxing and socialising too. If it's hard to keep to your revision timetable put a copy in the kitchen so the rest of the family know when you should be revising.

Glossary

ABC model of operant conditioning: a model that explains learning as being shaped by the consequences of a behaviour; if a behaviour is punished, repetition is less likely than if the consequence is reward.

Acoustic code: information held in memory according to its sound. Acronym: a word created from the first letter of each word in a phrase.

Adoption studies: a study of people who have been adopted that compares the adopted person's behaviour traits to that of their biological and/or adopted families to test the effects of nature and/or nurture on human behaviour.

Agency Theory: theory proposed by Stanley Milgram that explains obedience in terms of the person acting as a component of a system as opposed to of their own free will.

Agentic state: a mental condition proposed by Milgram, in which he suggested independence and autonomy and, most importantly, conscience, are suppressed as the individual acts as an agent for someone else.

Alpha bias: a form of gender bias where gender differences are emphasised often to the detriment of females.

Alternative hypothesis: a hypothesis that is not the null, i.e. it suggests a definite difference will be found in the data

Anal expulsive character: the adult characteristic formed by fixation at the anal stage if the child is allowed to be messy during toilet training, which leads to an adult who is messy, and disorganised.

Anal retentive character: the adult characteristic formed by fixation at the anal stage if parents are over-indulgent about the child refusing to go during toilet training. This can lead to a tidy, organised adult.

Anal stage: the second of Freud's psychosexual stages, where pleasure is centred on the anus. Focus is on toilet training and the stage ends with successful toilet training.

Analysand: the patient undergoing psychoanalysis.

Anecdotal evidence: evidence that has been gained without scientific proof.

Androgen insensitivity syndrome: when a genetic 'male' with XY chromosomes is not exposed to male sex hormones and so develops female sex organs.

Androgenital syndrome: when a genetic 'female' with XX chromosomes is exposed to male sex hormones during development, causing the foetus to develop with male sex organs.

Antecedent: a *stimulus* (lights, noises) that triggers behaviour. Articulatory suppression task: a task that prevents rehearsal.

Association: the pairing of two situations/experiences that typically results in the same behaviour being produced from either.

Assumptions: what a theory holds as being a basic underpinning truth.

Attention filter: we cannot process all the information that bombards our senses, so an attention filter holds this information for a brief period whilst we decide what to give attention to.

Attitude: a belief held by a person, measurable by the survey method.

Authority figure: a person who represents power or status in some way.

Autism: a developmental disorder that is characterised by an inability to interact and build relationships with other people.

Autonomous state: a mental condition proposed by Milgram, in which the person is acting and thinking as an autonomous, independent individual, and in which individual conscience is fully active.

Aversion therapy: a treatment that involves associating an undesirable behaviour with a negative stimulus.

Beta bias: a form of gender bias where it is assumed there are no differences between the genders.

Behaviour: a *response* that could be observed and measured as a result of the antecedent.

Behaviourism: an approach that believed only observable and measurable behaviour should be studied.

Behaviour shaping: the process of shaping behaviour that does not occur naturally, by rewarding similar behaviours.

Brain lateralisation: the extent to which brain functions are controlled by each hemisphere of the brain.

Case history: the detail of the case that is the subject of a study.

Case study: a research method which uses other research methods to study one unique individual or small group to give in-depth, detailed and rich information.

Categorisation: the first stage in the process of social identification, which involves grouping other people into social categories or sets.

Castration fear: part of Freud's ideas about the Oedipus complex where, between the ages of 3 to 5, boys desire their mother's attention and sexual feelings are involved. They want to take the place of their father, and so fear him, and fear castration.

Catharsis: the term for releasing energy that is being used to keep unacceptable thoughts and wishes unconscious. When those thoughts are revealed to the patient, they experience catharsis and are free to move on from those repressed thoughts.

Cause and effect relationship: a link made between the independent variable and the dependent variable.

Central nervous system: the general name we give to the structures in the body that make up the brain and the spinal cord.

Classical conditioning: learning to associate two stimuli in the same way so that the same response is displayed to both.

Closed questions: questions that are limited in the way they can be answered, e.g. yes/no or by picking a number to represent your view.

Cognition: mental processes, such as thinking, language, memory, perception and problem solving.

Cognitive interview: a type of police interview that uses special techniques to encourage witnesses to recall accurately.

Comparison: the final stage in the process of social identification, involving the (usually favourable) comparison of the in-group with the out-group.

Competent: the capacity to deal professionally with issues that arise during the course of a research programme.

Concurrent validity: a way of establishing validity that compares evidence from several studies testing the same thing to see if they agree, thus making the results more valid.

Conditioned response: a learnt behaviour that is shown in response to a learnt stimulus, e.g. fear of dogs is a response that was learnt when one bit you.

Conditioned stimulus: a stimulus that has been associated with an unconditioned stimulus so that it now produces the same response, e.g. the colour yellow makes you feel ill because the taste of school custard once made you ill.

Conditioning: learning that involves a relatively permanent change in behaviour due to environmental conditions.

Confounding variable: a variable that affects the findings of a study directly, so much so that you are no longer measuring what was intended.

Conscious mind: according to Freud, that part of the mind that we know about and can access easily.

Construct validity: the extent to which you have operationalised your variables to investigate the theoretical idea: are you actually measuring what you intended to?

Counterbalancing: when participants systematically experience the experimental conditions in a different order, e.g. participant 1 experiences condition A then B, whilst participant 2 experiences condition B then A

Contextual cue: a cue from the environment or context.

Continuum: not distinctly different processes, but rather one process that operates at many levels.

Control group: a group of participants that does not experience the experimental situation but acts as a baseline against which to judge any change.

Correlation designs: where one participant provides data for two measures which are then tested to see if they show a relationship. There are two variables, but not an IV or a DV – both variables are measured and both are of interest.

Covert: relating to an observation in which those taking part are not aware that they are being observed.

Critical value: a statistical cut-off point. It is a number presented on a table of critical values that determines whether the result is significant enough for the null hypothesis not to be accepted.

Cross-cultural reference: the testing of the same hypothesis in different cultures to see if the effect found is culture-specific.

Cross-sectional studies: where two or more conditions from the same time are studied, to make comparisons.

Cue: something that is present during the learning phase which, reinstated when recalling, could improve memory as it acts as a trigger for the original memory.

Debrief: the process of advising the participant what the true aims and nature of the study were and gaining their insights about the research process.

Deception: deliberately misleading or not informing the participant in research about the nature and aims of the research or some aspect of it.

Defence mechanisms: the term for various ways that unconscious wishes and desires are kept hidden, such as by means of repression, denial, displacement, projection and regression.

Dependent variable: the measured variable.

Descriptive statistics: summary of data into meaningful comparisons, e.g. by using measures of central tendency and dispersion to see whether there is a difference amongst the data sets.

Directional hypothesis: a prediction of the study findings that indicates the direction of the results.

Dormant: lying in wait, inactive until triggered.

Dream and symbol analysis: a research method used by Freud that involves analysing the manifest (described) content of the dream to uncover the latent (unconscious) content, which is hidden by symbols that have to be interpreted.

Dual task technique: performing two tasks simultaneously.

Ecological validity: a way of assessing how valid a measure or test is, that is concerned with whether the measure or test is really like its counterpart in the real world.

Ego: for Freud, the second part of the personality to develop. The ego is rational, psychological and seeks to maintain balance between the demands of the id and the control of the superego.

Ego ideal: according to Freud, a person's idea of what they should be like and what they ought to do. It is part of the superego.

Elaborative rehearsal: giving information meaning or relating it to something personal.

Electra complex: the way in which a girl identifies with her mother and learns her gender role. The girl has penis envy and identifies with her mother to possess her father.

Encoding: the process of placing an experience into a form that can be used and stored by the memory system.

Engram: a memory trace that causes a physical change to the neural architecture of the brain.

Ethical guidelines: a set of principles for the conduct of research designed to protect the rights and dignity of the participants, administered by the governing body for psychology in the country where the research is taking place.

Ethics: ideas in a society about what is right and wrong. People act ethically when they do what is right and avoid doing what is wrong according to social and cultural norms. In psychology, ethics involve treating participants – both animal and human– according to social views about what is right.

Experimental hypothesis: a prediction of what you expect to find from conducting an experiment.

Experimental validity: the extent to which the research process demonstrates a consistent and realistic attempt to test the hypothesis.

Explicit memory: the conscious recollection of information.

Extinction: the suppression of a conditioned response.

Extraneous variable: a variable that may have affected the dependent variable but that was not the independent variable.

Eyewitness testimony: The statement given by a witness to an event/crime.

Field study: a piece of research that takes place in the setting where the behaviour being studied would naturally occur.

First order conditioning: a new association takes place between a conditioned stimulus and a new stimulus, that eventually results in the same response being given to both.

Fixation: Freud's term for the libido being locked into a stage because the child was frustrated or over-indulged at that stage.

Fixed ratio schedule: when a reinforcer is given after a certain number of behaviours are shown.

Flashbulb memory: a vivid memory often associated with an emotional event.

Free association: a research method used by Freud which involves the patient allowing a stream of consciousness so that the analyst can analyse the connections, to uncover unconscious thoughts.

Fully-informed consent: an ethical issue that involves the participant in research being given all the relevant information about the aims and nature of the study and the procedures involved before they agree to take part.

Functional scans: a brain scan that allows us to see which parts of the brain are working during different activities.

Generalisability: when findings from a study can be applied to other situations, in order to build a scientific body of knowledge.

Generalisation: the transfer of knowledge gained in one situation (e.g. during a specific research setting) to another (e.g. real life).

Genes: a unit of heredity that contains DNA carrying information from one generation to the next. Each gene influences development by triggering the production of enzymes and proteins that are involved in the production of certain cells.

Genital stage: the fifth of Freuds' psychosexual stages, that occurs with puberty. If the libido (sexual energy) is left behind in previous stages, then the person has not much energy for opposite sex friendships and relationships, which ought to be developing at this stage.

Gonads: the sex organs of an individual.

Hierarchy of fears: a list of fears ranging from least to most feared objects or situations.

Higher order conditioning: when new associations take place that build upon simple learning through classical conditioning.

Hippocampus: a structure of the brain thought to be responsible for the transfer of information between short- and long-term memory.

Hormones: chemicals that are released into the bloodstream and change the functions of the body in some way.

Hypothalamus: the body's regulator – this part of the brain controls many internal systems of the body.

Hypothesis: a specific testable statement or prediction about the outcome of a test.

Id: for Freud, the first of three parts of the personality to develop. The id is demanding, biological because instinctive, and acts on the pleasure principle.

Identification: the second stage in the social identity process. The individual psychologically identifies with their in-group, adopting their group norms and values.

Independent measures: an experimental design whereby each group involved contains different people. For every condition of the experiment, a different group of participants will be used.

Independent variable: the manipulated variable of an investigation.

Inferential statistics: are statistical tests that can show how strong a difference or relationship between variables is, e.g. Spearman's, Mann-Whitney and chi-squared.

Information processing model: a model used to understand the flow of information through the cognitive system, from input to process then to output.

In-group: a group that you believe yourself to be a member of.

Interval/ratio data: a level of measurement, the highest level, which means that numbers have equal intervals between them and can be treated mathematically.

Interview: a data-gathering technique involving asking questions directly of participants. It can be unstructured, semi-structured or structured, and is usually conducted face to face.

Implicit memory: memories that we do not have to consciously recall.

Incidental: recall that is not anticipated.

Intentional: recall that is anticipated.

IQ: Intelligence Quotient – the generally accepted measure of human intelligence.

Laboratory experiment: an experiment conducted in a controlled environment.

Latency period: the time after the phallic stage and before puberty when desires are repressed and school, sport and same sex friendships are the focus.

Latent content: the content of a dream that is hidden within symbols in the manifest content. An analysis of the symbols will reveal the latent content and thus reveal hidden wishes and desires in the unconscious.

Law of effect: the principle that we learn by the consequence of our actions. A positive outcome will encourage us to repeat the behaviour, whilst a negative outcome will stop us repeating the behaviour.

Lesion studies: a study, usually conducted on animals, involving the deliberate damage of an area of the brain to test the effect this has on behaviour.

Libido: sexual energy, which occurs through stages. If fixation occurs at a stage, then libido can be locked there causing the adult to seek that sort of satisfaction.

Likert scale: a way of gathering quantitative data that introduces some flexibility by giving the participant options that represent their level of agreement with a statement.

Longitudinal studies: are studies where the same participants are studied over a period of time, usually to look for developmental trends.

Long-term memory: memories that are held for a long time. Manifest content: the content of a dream that is clear and described by the dreamer.

Matched pairs design: an independent measures design where the experimental groups are matched on important characteristics, e.g. background, age.

Mean recall: the mean average number of words recalled. The mean is calculated by adding all the scores together and multiplying the sum by the number of scores.

Memory: a cognitive function used to retain information and recall it when needed.

Meta-analysis: when a researcher collates all previously conducted studies on the same topic and investigates the similarity or differences in findings between the studies.

Method: in this context it is the technique used to gather data, e.g. a survey.

Minimal group: a group set up for the purpose of research that has no meaningful basis for membership.

Modality free: not restricted to one type of information (e.g. visual) but can deal with all sensory experience.

Modelling: a way of learning by imitating the behaviours of others.

Moral strain: the consequences of going against your own conscience and doing something you know to be wrong.

MRI scan: Magnetic Resonance Imaging – a type of structural brain scan that uses a magnetic field to show a picture of the brain inside the skull.

Naïve participant: one who seems to be a participant in research but is in fact part of the research script and is uninformed about what is happening.

Natural experiment: an experiment where the IV occurs naturally and is not manipulated.

Naturalistic observation: a study that takes place in the natural setting of the participants.

Nature-nurture debate: the debate over what has most influence over our behaviour – our genes and our biology, or our environment and experiences.

Negative correlation: a relationship between two variables where, as one score rises, the other falls.

Negative reinforcement: an unpleasant consequence to not performing a behaviour, so we repeat the behaviour to avoid it.

Neuron: a cell in the nervous system that receives or passes on information through electrical impulses.

Neuroses: mental health problems, including phobias, obsessions and hysteria, where the individual realises there is a problem and is able to focus on it and take steps to fix it.

Neurotransmitter: a chemical involved in passing information from one neuron to another in synaptic transmission.

Neutral stimulus: any environmental stimulus that does not naturally produce a behavioural response, e.g. a computer does not naturally produce a fear response.

Nominal data: a level of measurement, the lowest level, where numbers are just numbers in categories not scores in themselves, e.g. there are 8 cold days and 7 hot days.

Non-participant observation: when the observer is not a participant in the situation.

Non-directional hypothesis: a prediction of the study findings that does not indicate the exact direction of the results.

Null hypothesis: a prediction used in research that states no effect (other than that which might happen by chance) will be found.

Obedience: a type of social influence where an individual follows the rules or orders given by an authority figure.

Objective: something that is externally verifiable and observable by others.

Observation: social learning takes place through observation – watching and observing the behaviour of others. Also a widely-used research method.

Observational learning: learning from watching other people.

Observed value: the value given by a statistical test, such as rho for Spearman's. It is compared with the relevant critical value to see if a null hypothesis should be retained or not.

Oedipus complex: part of Freud's ideas about child development, where the boy fears his father whilst also feeling guilty about it. He identifies with his father, becoming his father, so that he can have the desired relationship with his mother and not feel guilty about it.

One-tailed hypothesis: the same as a directional hypothesis, this is a prediction of the study findings that indicates a direction of the results.

One-trial learning: an evolutionary advantage or survival mechanism to ensure quick learning takes place.

Open questions: questions that allow the respondent to answer in any way they choose.

Operant conditioning: learning through the consequence of actions.

Operational definition: when a variable is defined in its most detailed form.

Operationalise: defining the elements of the research in order to make them testable.

Opportunity: a sampling method using the people who happen to be available at the time and place when the study is conducted.

Oral character: the adult characteristic formed by fixation at the oral stage. If frustrated with regard to pleasure to the mouth the adult can be envious, pessimistic and sarcastic. If over-indulged the adult can be optimistic, admiring of others and gullible.

Oral stage: the first of Freud's psychosexual stages, where pleasure is centred on the mouth. The stage ends with weaning.

Ordinal data: a level of measurement, the middle level, where numbers are rankings rather than scores in themselves, e.g. a rank order for attractiveness on a scale of 1 to 5.

Out-group: a group that has something in common with one of your in-groups, but which you are not a member of.

Overt: relating to an observation in which those taking part are aware that they are being observed, though they may not know why in great detail.

Participants: people who take part in research studies and allow their responses to be measured (previously known as subjects).

Participant observation: when the observer is a participant in the situation as well as being the observer.

Pavlovian conditioning: the same as classical conditioning – learning by associating a neutral stimulus with an unconditioned stimulus to effectively produce an unconditioned response after repeated associations.

Penis envy: a concept of Freud's where he claims that in the phallic stage girls realise that they don't have a penis. Freud thought that this was an important feature of girls learning their gender identity and is part of the reason for girls identifying with their mother as a reaction against feelings for their father.

PET scan: Positron Emission Tomography – a type of functional brain scan that shows an image of a working brain.

Phallic stage: the third of Freud's psychosexual stages, where pleasure is focused on the genital areas. The child goes through the Oedipus or Electra complex, experiences castration fear or penis envy, and resolves the conflict by identifying with the same sex parent, so they 'learn' their gender.

Phobia: a fear that is strong enough to disrupt a person's life, so that they cannot do things they need or want to do.

Pilot study: a test of the research materials and process on a few people to iron out any faults before it is applied to the sample for real.

Pituitary gland: a small gland within the body that produces the sex hormones and releases them into the body.

Placebo: a substance given that is said to be the active material but is simply an inactive agent, e.g. water.

Population validity: the extent to which a sample represents the target population – high validity means that it is a true reflection.

Positive correlation: is a relationship between two variables where, as one score rises, the other rises too.

Positive reinforcement: a pleasant outcome that encourages repetition of a behaviour.

Post-event information: information that is introduced after an incident that becomes incorporated into the original memory as though it had always happened.

Preconscious mind: according to Freud, part of the mind that is accessible though not at that moment – it contains what we can know about it, but is not currently conscious.

Prejudice: a fixed, pre-set attitude, usually negative and usually applied to members of a particular social category.

Primacy effect: words recalled at the beginning of a list as they are transferred into long-term memory.

Primary reinforcer: a reinforcer that satisfies a basic need.

Proactive interference: a difficulty in remembering new information because it is affected by old memories.

Probability: how likely it is that something will happen – a statistical measure of the likelihood that something is true or that something will happen.

Procedural memory: memory for skills, such as riding a bicycle.

Psychoanalysis: Freud's therapy, where the analyst listens to the analysand, such as about their dreams or using free association, to uncover unconscious wishes and desires, reveal them, and thereby cure the patient.

Psychoses: mental health problems, such as schizophrenia, where the individual is not able to help themselves because they are not aware they have a problem or at least do not have the awareness to change.

Qualitative data: data consisting of words, text, ideas that are not reducible to numbers or quantities.

Quantitative data: data consisting of amounts measured by numbers (numerical data).

Quasi experiment: an experiment whereby the independent variable differs between groups naturally and cannot be controlled by the experimenter. Participants can only be part of one group or another and random allocation to groups is not possible.

Questionnaire: a survey method consisting of a series of questions for participants to answer, usually written, often by post.

Quota opportunity sample: an opportunity sample involves using participants who happen to be available when the research is taking place. In a quota opportunity sample, the participants who are available must fit certain criteria, e.g. being in a certain age category.

Random allocation: participants randomly placed into a learning condition, usually achieved by computer generation or picking a name from a hat.

Random assignment: where every participant has an equal chance of being in any of the treatment conditions. It avoids bias by having too many of one type of participant in one condition.

Rating scales: when a participant decides on a rating to give to a question, e.g. on a scale of 0 to 5 or on a scale between 'strongly agree' and 'strongly disagree'.

Realistic conflict theory: states that hostility and prejudice between groups stems from competition for scarce resources, based either on the history of the groups' relationships or on the current situation

Recency effect: the most recent words at the end of a list, recalled because they are new to short-term memory.

Reciprocal inhibition: two emotional or physical states cannot coexist.

Reinforcement: the consequences of our behaviour.

Reliability: the consistency of a method as it is applied to the participants, measurable by the ability to replicate the study and also by the consistency of the results found.

Repeated measures design: where the same participants undergo all conditions of the study.

Repression: a defence mechanism, according to Freud, where a person does not remember something and cannot access particular memories because they are in the unconscious.

Reliable data: data found again when a study is done again. Only reliable data can give scientific findings.

Replication: the ability to recreate accurately the procedure of a study on different samples of the same population in order to establish the reliability of the results.

Research question: the idea behind a specific research study. Usually based on a theory or observation of a phenomenon, it is a question that forms the basis of a test.

Retention: the capacity to remember what has been observed.

Retrieval: the process of recalling a stored memory.

Retroactive interference: a difficulty in remembering old information because new information that is similar has been learnt.

Right to withdraw: participant's the right to leave a research study at any stage and to take their data with them.

Sample: a selection from the target population chosen to represent it by participating in research.

Sampling technique: a method for selecting a sample of participants from the target population in order to take part in research.

Schema: a packet of knowledge used to understand the world around us and new experiences.

Schizophrenia: a mental illness that causes people to lose touch with reality.

Scientific method: any method used by psychologists that involves objective, systematic procedures.

Secondary reinforcer: a reinforcer that alone does not satisfy a basic need but can be exchanged for one that does.

Second order conditioning: building on first order conditioning, a new stimulus is associated with first order stimulus to result in the conditioned response.

Self-report data: data compiled by a participant, usually through written questionnaires.

Semantic code: storing the meaning of an item in memory.

Semi-structured interview: a one-to-one conversation with a set purpose where the questions are broadly set out at the beginning but which has the capacity to develop flexibly as the interview progresses.

Sensory memory: initial storage system to hold incoming sensory information.

Short-term memory: a temporary and limited storage system for sensory information.

Significance: a statistical measure of how likely it is that the results of a study are due to chance factors.

Situationist: the view that much of our behaviour is determined by the constraints of the situation in which the behaviour is displayed. This is opposite to the view that most of our behaviour stems from deep-seated personality characteristics.

Slips of the tongue: a research method used by Freud that involves analysing mistakes to uncover unconscious thoughts and desires.

Social categorisation: the act of grouping people according to some category.

Social comparison: the act of comparing social groups with each other.

Social identification: the act of personally accepting that you belong to a particular group by accepting their norms.

Social identity theory: a proposal that human beings categorise themselves and others into in-groups and out-groups. In order to maintain a positive social identity, unfavourable comparisons are made between the two and prejudice can develop.

Social learning: learning by watching and imitating others.

Spontaneous recovery: the revival of a dormant conditioned response.

Standardised procedure: a set of instructions used in a research study so that all participants are given the same orders.

State cues: a physical, mental or emotional state that can be used to trigger a memory when last in that same state.

Stereotypes: classifying members of a social group as if they were all the same, and treating individuals belonging to that group as if no other characteristics were important. Often underlie prejudices.

Stimulus generalisation: a conditioned response to a stimulus may be triggered by a stimulus that closely resembles the conditioned stimulus.

Stimulus material: any object or situation that triggers a response or can be mentally processed.

Structural: the physical features of an object or word.

Structured interview: a one-to-one conversation in which the questions are laid out in advance and are dealt with in a set order.

Structured observation: in which all data is collected by observation but the situation is not natural; it is set up or structured.

Study: a piece of research where data is gathered by a researcher.

Subjective: something that is not directly public or observable (inner experience), cannot be directly verified by others, and involves inference that may be unique to the inferrer.

Subjective interpretation: when a researcher imposes their views on data. In case studies in particular, it is often necessary to select the information to be included, so subjective interpretation is likely.

Successive approximations: any behaviour that closely resembles the target behaviour.

Superego: for Freud, the third and last part of the personality to develop. The superego is moral and social because it brings control of parents and society which the ego has to take into account.

Survey: a technique of collecting opinions from large numbers of people, generally involving the use of questionnaires.

Synapse: a junction between two neurons where information can be passed from one to the other.

Systematic desensitisation: the gradual association of an undesirable behaviour with relaxation. Often used on phobics.

Target population: the people that you wish to apply the findings of your research to.

Thematic analysis: a quantitative analytical technique requiring the researcher to process the data for recurring ideas and use these as a framework to explain the meaning of the data and relate it to the research question.

Theory: an idea or set of ideas that attempts to explain some issue or phenomenon, testable by research studies.

Time sampling: making a tally mark at regular intervals to make the observation and collection of data fair.

Tip of the tongue phenomenon: when we know something but cannot recall it.

Token economy: a treatment that involves giving secondary reinforcement for desirable behaviour, that can be saved and exchanged for primary reinforcement.

Transference: the term used when an analysand transfers feelings onto an analyst, such as love or hate, as part of the psychoanalytic treatment. This is expected and part of their recognition their unconscious fears and desires.

Triangulation: taking data gathered from different research methods and pooling it to generate themes.

Trigram: a group or sequence of three letters.

Two-tailed hypothesis: the same as a non-directional hypothesis, this is a prediction of the study findings that does not indicate the exact direction of the results.

Twin studies: research involving the study of twins to see if they share any of the same characteristics. By studying twins who were raised by different families it is possible to see if traits are controlled by genes or the environment someone is raised in.

Unconditioned response: any response that occurs naturally without learning.

Unconditioned stimulus: any stimulus that produces a natural, unlearnt behavioural response.

Unconscious: the area of the mind, according to Freud, that we cannot access, but that guides us strongly.

Unstructured interview: a one-to-one conversation where there may be a broad agenda but the questions are loose and very flexible.

Valid data: data that represents the real world and in that way is 'true'.

Validity: measuring what you claim to measure, and having findings about real-life situations and behaviours.

Vicarious reinforcement: learning through the consequence of another person's behaviour.

Visual code: retaining a picture image in the memory system.

Index

ABC model of operant conditioning 136
Abernethy 52, 55
Ablatio Penis: normal male infant sex-reassigned as a girl (Money, 1975) 110–112
Abu Ghraib prison 26–27, 36
Adler 70
Administrative Obedience: Carrying Out Orders to Use Psychological-Administrative Violence (Meeus & Raaijmakers, 1985) 16
    comparison with Milgram 16
adoption studies 100–101, 124
advertising, cars 148
    influence on behaviour 147
Age and Levels of Processing (Ramponi et al., 2004) 57
Agency Theory 6, 12, 17–18, 21, 27, 29, 36
    evaluation of 17
agentic state 6, 17
Ainsworth, Mary 45
alternative hypothesis 8
anal stage 70, 71, 81, 87
animals, use of in research 102–103, 108
anorexia, influence of role models on 146–147
AS Psychology 154–159
    assessment objectives 154–155
    exam guidance 156–157
    practicals 155
    questions 155
    revision 158–159
Asch 7
association 127
Atkinson and Shiffrin 48, 68
autism 114–115
autonomous state 6, 17
aversion therapy 138, 152
Axline 88, 97
Bachrach 88, 97
Baddeley and Hitch 48, 68
Bandura, Ross and Ross (1961) 130, 137, 142–143, 147
Baron-Cohen et al. (2005) 114
Bartlett, Frederick 49, 58, 68
BBC prison study, the 24–25
behaviour-shaping 137
behavioural study of obedience to malevolent authority (Milgram) 12–17, 130
    aim 12
    conclusions 13
    ecological validity 14
    ethics 15
    evaluation 14–15

    method 13
    reliability 15
    results 13
    variations 14
behaviourism 127
Bellis et al. (2001) 112
Biological Approach 98–125
    advances in 99
    definition 98–99
brain lateralisation 98, 106–107, 124
brain scanning techniques 102
Branch Davidian 29
Branthwaite and Jones 23
Brewer and Rothbart 23
Brown and Kulik 60
Brown and McNeill 50
Bussey and Perry (1982) 140
Calley, Lt. William 28
case histories 72
case study research method 72–75
    issues 73–75
    strengths and weaknesses 73
castration fear 82, 87
central executive 48
central nervous system 98, 99
    and human behaviour 104
Charlton 40
chi-squared test 132, 133, 150, 152
classical conditioning 126, 127, 134–135
Clifford and Hollin 58
closed question 8
cocaine-reinforced behaviour in rats: effects of reinforcement magnitude and fixed-ratio size (Pickens and Thompson, 1968) 144
cognition 38
Cognitive Approach 38–69
    definition 38–39
cognitive interview 60–61
Collins and Loftus 49, 68
Common In-group Identity Model 19
concordance rates 100
conditioned emotional responses (Watson and Raynor, 1920) 145
conditioned response (CR) 134, 135
conditioned stimulus (CS) 134
confounding variable 43
conscious 70, 80
consequence 127
construct validity 45
context cue 63
context-dependent forgetting 50–51
Context-dependent Memory Experiment (Godden and Baddeley, 1975) 54–55
Cook (1988) 137
correlational designs 75–78, 92–94

    strengths and weaknesses 77–78
covert observation 128, 129
Craik and Lockhart 46–47, 68
Craik and Tulving 38, 46–47, 56–57, 69
Cramer 89, 92–94, 97
    and Skidd (1992) 140
critical value tables 133
cross-sectional studies 79
Cue-dependent Theory of Forgetting 38, 50, 62–67
    evaluation 52
cult behaviour 29
Dann and Doise 23
Darby, Joe 27
data, gathering 9
    qualitative 8
    quantitative 8
defence mechanisms 70, 80, 81
demand characteristics 44
denial 70, 80, 81
dependent variable (DV) 42, 102
designing surveys 9
Devlin Report 59
Dibs: personality development in play therapy (Axline, 1964) 88
directional hypothesis 41, 62, 148
discrimination 18
displacement 53, 80, 81
dream analysis 72, 90
Duka 51
Duration of Short-term Memory (Peterson and Peterson, 1959) 56
Ebbinghaus 56
ecological validity 44, 45
effectiveness of psychoanalytic therapies (Bachrach et al., 1991) 88–89
ego 70, 80
Eichmann, Lt. Col. Adolph 12, 17
elaborative rehearsal 46
Electra complex 75, 83
encoding 39
    specificity principle 50
ethical issues 6, 7, 10–11, 15, 30, 64, 74, 116, 103, 116, 130, 149
experimental control 43
experimental hypothesis 41, 63, 119
Experimental Study in Nurse-Physician Relationships (Hofling et al., 1966) 20–21, 45
experimenter effects 44
explicit memory 47
extraneous variables 43
evaluating findings 35
    survey methods 11
eyewitness testimony 58
    reliability of 58–59
false memory 91

fear as conditioned response 135
female violence 147
field experiment 40
findings, evaluating validity of 35
    presentation of 66
Fisher, Geiselman and Amador 60
fixation 71
flashbulb memory 60
Foetal Alcohol Syndrome (FAS) 117
football crowd violence 28
forensic evidence 58
forgetting 38
    experiments 62–67
    theories of 50–53
free association 72
Freud, Sigmund 70–97
    case studies, credibility 75
        Little Hans 86–87
        strengths and weaknesses 73
        use of 72
    gender development, explanation of
        82–83
    personality, theory of 80–81
    psychosexual development, theory of
        70, 80, 81–85, 109
        strengths 83–84
        weaknesses 84
    theories 71
        role of unconscious in 80
Gaertner 19
Geiselman 61
gender development and behaviour 70,
    80, 82–83, 110–112, 140–141
        biological influences on 105,
        108–109
genes 98, 99, 124
    and human behaviour 105
genital stage 70, 82
Godden and Baddeley 51, 52, 54–55,
    69
Goodlett, Marcussen and West (1990)
    117
Gottesman and Shields (1966) 113
Grant 55
Grant and Bredahl 51
Hebb, D. O. 98–99
Herz 51
higher-order conditioning 135
Hofling 20–21, 35, 37, 45
hormones 98, 106, 124
    problems with 109
Hyde and Jenkins 47
hypothesis 8, 41–42
    questions to test 32
    research, developing 31
id 70, 80
identification 75
identity, personality and defence
mechanisms (Cramer, 1997) 89
imaginal processing 57
implicit memory 47

in-group 6
independent groups design 132
independent measures design 42
independent variable (IV) 42, 102
inferential testing 122, 132–133
information processing 38, 39, 46–47
interference 53
intergroup conflict and co-operation: the
Robber's Cave experiment (Sherif et al.,
    1961) 24
interval/ratio data 132
interview, types of 9
Jung 70
Karniol and Aida (1997) 140
Kebbell and Wagstaff 61
Koresh, David 29
laboratory experiments 40, 131, 152
Lang 51
Langlois and Downs (1980) 140
latency 70, 82
law of effect 127
Learning Approach 126–153
    definition 126
    explanation of gender development
        140–141
lesion studies 99, 124
levels of processing 47, 68
Levels of Processing Experiment
    (Craik and Tulving, 1975) 56–57
Levels of Processing Model of Memory
    (Craik and Lockhart, 1962) 38,
    46–47, 68
Levels of Processing Theory 46, 56
Likert-type scale 9, 32
Little Albert 130, 135, 145
Little Hans 86–87, 91, 97
Locksley, Ortiz and Hepburn 23
Loftus, Elizabeth 45, 58
long-term storage 39, 48
longitudinal studies 78–79
maintenance rehearsal 46
male brain function 115
    structure 114–115
Mann-Whitney test 118, 122, 133
Masson 75
matched pairs design 42, 132
McGeoch and McDonald 53
Memon 61
memory 38, 39, 47
    experiments 54–57, 62–67
    flashbulb 60
    reliability of 58–59
    theories of 46–49
Meeus and Raaijmakers study 16
    comparison with Milgram 16
Miles and Hardman 51
Milgram, Stanley 6, 12–17, 27, 29, 35,
36, 128, 130
Minimal Groups Study 19, 22–23
Money, Dr John 110–112, 125
moral strain 6, 17

morality principle 80
Morris 47, 57
MRI (Magnetic Resonance Imaging) scans
    102, 112, 124
Multi-store Model of Memory
    (Atkinson and Shiffrin, 1968, 1971)
    47, 48, 68
My Lai massacre 28–29
natural experiment 40
naturalistic observation 129
nature-nurture debate 100, 105, 126
negative correlation 76
negative reinforcement 136
Neisser 60
neuron 98
neurotransmitter 98
neutral stimulus (NS) 134
nominal data 132
non-directional hypothesis 41, 62
non-participant observation 128, 129
null hypothesis 8, 41–42, 63
obedience 12
    during conflict 28
    studies 12–21, 26–27, 28
    theories 6
objectivity 44
observation 127, 128–129
    evaluation of as a research method
    129
Oedipus complex 70, 71, 75, 80,
    82–83, 87
one-tailed hypothesis 41, 62, 119
one-trial learning 135
open question 8
operant conditioning 126, 127, 136–137
operationalisation 42
    of variables 35
opportunity sampling 10
oral stage 70, 71, 81
order effects 42–43
ordinal data 132
out-group 6
overt observation 128, 129
participant design 42, 1323
    observation 128, 129
    variable 43
Paul and Lentz (1977) 139
Pavlov, Ivan 134–135
Pavlov's theory 134–135
Pavlovian conditioning 134
penis envy 83
PET (Positron Emission Topography)
    scans 102, 112–113, 124
Peterson and Peterson 56, 69
phallic stage 70, 71, 82
phonetic processing 46, 57
phonological loop 48
Pickel 59
Pickens and Thompson, 1968 144
Piliavin 40
placebo 51

positive correlation   76
positive reinforcement   136
post-event information   58
preconscious   70, 80
prejudice   6, 18
pregnancy, drug use during   116–117
primary acoustic store   48
primary reinforcer   136
projection   70, 80, 81
pseudo-hermaphrodites   108
psychoanalysis, use of with abnormal and
normal clients   91
Psychodynamic Approach   70–97
    definition   70
psychosexual stages   80, 81–82
punishment   136
puzzle box   127
qualitative data   8, 72, 128
    analysing   74
    evaluating   73–74
    subjective interpretation   35
quantitative data   8, 128, 148
qualitative research   34
quantitative research   33–34
quasi-experiment   118
question, closed   8
    design of to test hypothesis   31
    open   8
    operationalising   31
    research, developing   30
questionnaires   9
    use of to carry out a survey   30–35
Quillian, Ross   49
Rainer et al. (1997)   112–113
Ramponi   57, 69
random sampling   10
receptor   98
reciprocal inhibition   139
reconstructive memory   49
Reconstructive Theory of Memory
    (Bartlett, 1932)   68
regression   70, 81
rehearsal   46
Reicher and Haslam   24–25
Reimer, David   108, 109, 110–112, 116,
    125, 141
Reiner and Gaerhart   116
reinforcers   136–137
reliability   11, 44–45
repeated measures design   42, 132
representativeness   9
repression   70, 80, 81, 87, 91
research hypothesis, developing   31
rethinking the psychology of tyranny: the
    BBC prison study (Reicher and Haslam,
    2006)   24–25
retrieval   38

right to withdraw   10
Robber's Cave experiment, the   24
role models   137
    influence on anorexia   146–147
    influence on female violence   147
sample   9
sampling methods   6, 8, 10, 79
Schab   51
schizophrenia   113
secondary reinforcer   136
self-report date   8, 92–94
self-selecting   10
semantic processing   46, 57
semi-structured interview   9
sensory storage   39, 48
sexual orientation and early childhood
    experiences   91
Sherif et al   24, 27
short-term storage   39, 48
situational variable   43
situationist   12
Skinner, B. F.   127, 136, 144
    box   127, 136
slips of the tongue   72, 73
Smith   51
Smith and Elsworth   59
Smith and Vela   52
Social Approach   6–37
    methodology   36
social categorisation   6, 18, 22–23
    comparison   6, 19
    identification   6, 18
Social Categorisation and Intergroup
Behaviour (Tajfel et al., 1971)   22–23
    aim   22
    conclusion   23
    evaluation   23
Social Identity Theory (Tajfel, 1970)   6,
12, 18–19, 29, 34, 37
    evaluation   19
social learning   109, 126, 127
    theory   137
social psychology   6
    definition   6
    ethics   7
    history   6–7
spatial ability, experiment to test whether
males have better than females   118–123
spontaneous recovery   135
Spearman's Rank Correlation Coefficient
    (Spearman's rho)   77, 92, 94, 133
Spreading Activation Model of Semantic
    Memory (Collins and Loftus, 1975)
    49, 68
state cue   63
state-dependent forgetting   51
stimulus and response   126, 127

generalisation   135
    material   63
storage   38, 39
stratified sampling   10
structural processing   46, 57
structured interview   9
structured observation   128, 129
study of processing (Craik and Tulving,
    1975)
subjectivity   11
superego   70, 80
superstition in the pigeon (Skinner, 1948)
    144
survey   8
    designing   9
    methods, evaluating   11
    planning   30–31
symbol analysis   72
synapse   98
systematic desensitisation   139, 152
Tajfel   6, 12, 18, 19, 22–23, 27, 37
Talarico and Rubin   60
tallying   128, 129, 148
target population   10
television, effects of   40
Thalidomide   116–117
Thorndike   127
tip of the tongue phenomenon   50
token economy   139, 153
trace decay   52
transference   75
transgender operations, ethics of   116
transmission of aggression through
    imitation of aggressive models
    (Bandura, Ross and Ross, 1961)
    142–143
triangulation   72
Triplett, Norman   6, 7
Tulving   50
twin studies   100, 110–112, 113, 124
    evaluation   101
two-tailed hypothesis   41, 62
unconditioned stimulus (US)   134
unconscious   70, 80, 87
unstructured interview   9
validity   11, 45
variables   40, 42
vicarious reinforcement   127, 137
visuo-spatial scratchpad   48
volunteer   10
Watson and Raynor (1920)   135, 145
Went, Daphne   108
Winograd and Killinger   60
Working Model of Memory (Baddeley and
    Hitch, 1974)   48, 68